Welfare Goes Global

Welfare Goes Global

Making Progress and Catching Up

RICHARD ROSE

OXFORD
UNIVERSITY PRESS

OXFORD
UNIVERSITY PRESS

Great Clarendon Street, Oxford, OX2 6DP,
United Kingdom

Oxford University Press is a department of the University of Oxford.
It furthers the University's objective of excellence in research, scholarship,
and education by publishing worldwide. Oxford is a registered trade mark of
Oxford University Press in the UK and in certain other countries

© Richard Rose 2024

The moral rights of the author have been asserted

All rights reserved. No part of this publication may be reproduced, stored in
a retrieval system, or transmitted, in any form or by any means, without the
prior permission in writing of Oxford University Press, or as expressly permitted
by law, by licence or under terms agreed with the appropriate reprographics
rights organization. Enquiries concerning reproduction outside the scope of the
above should be sent to the Rights Department, Oxford University Press, at the
address above

You must not circulate this work in any other form
and you must impose this same condition on any acquirer

Published in the United States of America by Oxford University Press
198 Madison Avenue, New York, NY 10016, United States of America

British Library Cataloguing in Publication Data

Data available

Library of Congress Control Number: 2023948113

ISBN 9780198908463

DOI: 10.1093/oso/9780198908463.001.0001

Printed and bound by
CPI Group (UK) Ltd, Croydon, CR0 4YY

Links to third party websites are provided by Oxford in good faith and
for information only. Oxford disclaims any responsibility for the materials
contained in any third party website referenced in this work.

Contents

List of Figures	vii
List of Tables	ix
Introduction: Welfare Important Everywhere	1

I WELFARE ACROSS TIME AND SPACE

1. Making Progress Globally	13
1.1 The welfare of individuals	15
1.2 Making progress nationally	19
1.3 Globalization is about catching up	22
1.4 The Global Welfare Database	25
2. The Welfare Mix	33
2.1 Modelling the welfare mix	35
2.2 Evolution of the welfare mix	37
2.3 Politics shapes the welfare mix	42
2.4 Aspirations global but resources national	44
3. Welfare about More than Money	49
3.1 Money as an input to the welfare mix	51
3.2 Soft spots in hard numbers	55
3.3 Unofficial economies add to the welfare mix	59
3.4 What social indicators add	64
4. The Development of Welfare	69
4.1 Multiple resources for development	71
4.2 A Global Index of Development	76
4.3 Accounting for global differences in welfare	79

II BASIC FORMS OF WELFARE

5. Health: Living Longer and Avoiding Death	87
5.1 Life expectancy increasing	88
5.2 Infant mortality decreasing	94
5.3 Lifestyles and avoidable deaths	97
5.4 The globalization of health	103

6. Education: Quantity and Quality — 107
    6.1 Literacy goes global — 109
    6.2 More education — 113
    6.3 More learning — 117
    6.4 The globalization of education — 122

7. Work for Women — 127
    7.1 Employment and gender — 128
    7.2 Accounting for gender inequality — 135
    7.3 Rethinking what work is — 138
    7.4 Uneven globalization of gender equality — 141

III THE GLOBALIZATION OF COUNTRIES AND PEOPLE

8. Countries Going Global — 147
    8.1 Many countries making progress — 148
    8.2 Some countries catching up — 150
    8.3 Accounting for national differences — 157
    8.4 Outlier countries — 159

9. People Going Global — 165
    9.1 World population skewed — 166
    9.2 Welfare of the world's population — 169
    9.3 How population growth impacts global welfare — 173
    9.4 Where most people without welfare live — 175

10. Unfinished Business — 181
    10.1 Catching up sooner or later — 183
    10.2 Most but not all people at global standards by 2050 — 189
    10.3 Redefining welfare goals — 191
    10.4 Global challenges to global welfare — 194

Appendix: The Global Welfare Database — 199

Index — 207

The Global Welfare database is available for download from www.oup.co.uk/companion/WelfareGoesGlobal for further analysis and teaching purposes.

List of Figures

1.1.	A model of individual welfare in society	16
1.2.	Majorities use welfare services annually	17
2.1.	Purposes of public expenditure by European states	41
3.1.	Shadow economy contracts with development	61
3.2.	Gross domestic product and literacy contrasted	65
4.1.	Development varies within and between continents	78
4.2.	A social resources model of national welfare	80
5.1.	Life expectancy of women	90
5.2.	Female/male inequality in life expectancy	92
5.3.	Catching up with a fixed target: zero infant mortality	95
5.4.	Deaths from road accidents	102
6.1.	Adult literacy across continents	110
6.2.	Countries differ in mathematical skills	118
6.3.	Countries with most English speakers	121
7.1.	Female and male participation in employment	131
7.2.	Gender inequality in employment	137
7.3.	Women spend more time in unpaid work than men	139
8.1.	Countries progressing in all forms of welfare	149
8.2.	More countries catching up with global standards	154
8.3.	Times countries at global standards	156
8.4.	Estimated and actual female life expectancy	160
9.1.	Population at global welfare standards	170
9.2.	Most people with welfare live in developing countries	172
9.3.	Impact of population growth differs by welfare measure	174
10.1.	Countries at global standard of welfare, 2050	186

List of Tables

1.1.	Countries in the Global Welfare Database	28
2.1.	Public and private expenditure on health	37
3.1.	Paid and unpaid work	63
4.1.	Continental differences in resources	71
4.2.	Development Index: principal component analysis	77
5.1.	Development lengthens lives of women and men	93
5.2.	Development reduces infant mortality	97
5.3.	Development increases female smoking but not male	99
5.4.	Development reduces fatal road accidents	103
5.5.	High degree of globalization in health	105
6.1.	Influences on achieving adult literacy	112
6.2.	Influences on enrolment in secondary school	115
6.3.	Two models of influences on PISA mathematics scores	119
6.4.	Globalization of education	122
6.5.	Generational turnover creates progress everywhere	124
7.1.	Contrasting influences on female and male employment	133
7.2.	Muslim differences influence female employment	135
7.3.	Influences on gender equality	137
7.4.	Africa leads in women's employment	143
8.1.	Developing countries progressing faster	152
8.2.	Influences differ with forms of welfare	158
8.3.	Biggest outliers in welfare achievement	162
9.1.	World's most populous countries	167
9.2.	Global distribution of people without welfare	176
10.1.	Distance from global welfare standards	184
10.2.	Population growth to 2050 by continent	189
10.3.	World population at and below global standards, 2050	190
A.1.	Key measures of welfare by country and continent	200

Introduction

Welfare Important Everywhere

People on every continent want good health, education, and employment; the Universal Declaration of Human Rights of the United Nations describes these conditions as inalienable human rights. Progress over many decades has resulted in billions of people today enjoying a standard of welfare that was unthinkable to their grandparents. Progress is even more important to the billions of people who have yet to attain the welfare of global standard-setters. That is why this book takes a global view of the welfare of the world's eight billion people.

Ordinary people do not monitor progress in welfare by turning to government statistics or following political debate: they can see it happening in their own lives and families. The average Indian girl born in 2019 can expect to live seventy-two years. While this is eleven years less than her British counterpart, it is twelve years more than the life expectancy of her mother and thirty-two years more than that of her grandmother. A similar transformation has occurred in education. In highly developed countries everyone takes literacy for granted, but this is not the case in the households of dozens of developing countries. The average Indian youth can expect to have at least a secondary school education; only half of their mothers are literate, and a majority of grandparents are illiterate.

Where people live greatly influences their welfare. Studies of differences in welfare between American states and European countries ignore the much greater differences in welfare between developing countries on every continent and countries that set global welfare standards. What is considered a low standard of welfare in a Scandinavian country will appear enviously high in poor countries. In an era of global migration, this is immediately evident within families. The average ethnic Mexican living in the United States will live years longer than aunts and uncles in Mexico, and young Mexican-Americans will have double the chance of enrolling in tertiary education than their Mexican cousins.

Developed countries usually set global standards for welfare. However, in total the highly developed countries of Anglo-America, Europe, and the Pacific Rim from Australia to Korea have less than one-sixth of the world's population,

Welfare Goes Global. Richard Rose, Oxford University Press. © Richard Rose (2024).
DOI: 10.1093/oso/9780198908463.003.0001

and the median developed country has barely one-tenth of 1 per cent of that population. By contrast, India and China each have a population that is substantially larger than the total population of all highly developed countries. In the statistical sense, the welfare of the population of India and China is closer to being normal than that of Scandinavian countries that are often used to set the norm for evaluating welfare.

The aim of this book is to answer big questions. How many of the world's eight billion people are at the global standard of health, education, and employment today? In an era of globalization, how much progress is evident among the billions of people who are not at high standards of welfare? How much do standards of welfare differ between countries within continents and between continents—and are the differences between countries narrowing or growing wider? To what extent is there agreement about normative goals of welfare in countries that differ in culture and religion?

In this book globalization refers to the extent to which people are progressing toward a healthy life, an education fit for the twenty-first century, and equal treatment of women as well as men in employment. Globalization is a bottom-up process that must occur within societies. Babies are not delivered by the World Health Organization in Geneva but within the mother's home or in a local maternity facility, and children become literate by going to a local primary school. The great majority of adults work in local labour markets or move within their country in search of work.

Going global in welfare is different from economic globalization, which is about trade between countries in goods and services and the movement of capital across continents. The globalization of welfare is only indirectly influenced by economic globalization. While the war in Ukraine encourages governments to consider economic deglobalization as a means of increasing national security, it also emphasizes the need for governments in developing countries to raise the welfare of their citizens to increase their ability to protect their national security.

A country's welfare reflects the combined resources of all the institutions that make up its welfare mix: the household, the market, and the state. The weaker the state, the more households and markets influence popular welfare. The government's contribution to this mix varies greatly with a country's resources. In a large majority of countries, the state's resources for promoting welfare are much less than those of post-industrial societies. Few of the activities of multinational corporations and institutions engaged in global finance are visible to those attending schools and health clinics in rural areas of Africa,

Asia, and Latin America. When a world recession occurs, people may see their income from employment fall, but this does not make them illiterate.

Describing welfare as going global emphasizes that it is a dynamic process in which the welfare of developing countries is progressing; it is definitely not a claim that a high standard of welfare has been reached everywhere. While life expectancy on every continent has been increasing from one generation to the next, there is still a big gap between the average female life expectancy of sixty-four years in sub-Saharan Africa and eighty-three years in Europe. The significance of differences in globalization increases when account is taken of differences in national populations. An increase of one year in the life of the average Chinese affects 175 times more people than a similar increase in the life expectancy of a citizen of the average European country.

Rates of progress differ between forms of welfare. Progress in life expectancy reflects an accumulation of influences over more than half a century, while infant mortality shows contemporary success in applying a known technology to a social ill. National literacy is a legacy of the education available when many of today's adults were children half a century ago, while the years that today's youths spend in school reflect the current reach of an educational system. The number of women included in statistics of employment is affected not only by national economic conditions but also by how many women are not counted because they work in the shadow economy or work unpaid within their household.

Making progress does not ensure that a society is catching up with global standards. This is most likely to happen if there is a fixed welfare goal—for example, achieving complete adult literacy. Because average literacy in highly developed countries is almost 99 per cent, this leaves global standard-setters with little scope for further progress. By contrast, where literacy is not up to this standard, there remains scope for catching up. In Latin America 20 per cent of the adult population is not literate, and in sub-Saharan Africa 36 per cent are illiterate.

A country can be making progress yet not catch up if leading countries are also making progress toward open-ended goals such as living longer. For the gap to be closed, the annual rate of progress of a developing country must be significantly greater than that of the countries it is targeting. It is even possible for a country to be making progress and simultaneously falling behind leading countries. This has been happening to the life expectancy of Americans. In the year 2000 female life expectancy was seventy-seven years in the United States, three years behind Switzerland. By 2019 American life expectancy had risen to eighty-two years; however, instead of catching up, it had fallen four years behind Switzerland.

This book systematically compares health, education, and female employment in 127 countries that collectively have 95 per cent of the world's population. Comparisons make use of data compiled by international organizations such as the United Nations and the World Bank. For clarity, most tables report national results in continental groups; because of their massive populations, India and China are each treated as a continent.

Since major forms of welfare tend to change slowly, the book deals with the cumulative effect of changes over three decades since 1991. It thus avoids drawing conclusions from events that can have a short-term impact, such as an economic recession that is usually followed by an economic recovery. In many countries, life expectancy rose in one year of the pandemic as well as contracting in another. Ending the statistical analysis at 2019 provides a baseline for assessing how much or how little effect the COVID-19 pandemic will have once evidence of its long-term effect is available in a decade hence.

The first three chapters focus on the meaning of welfare across time and space. The first chapter sets out a model of major influences on the welfare of individuals. Whatever a society's welfare, it can make substantial progress by compounding a small annual rate of change for decades. However, globalization is about more than making progress. It is also about catching up with countries that set global standards of health, education, and employment. To determine the extent to which this is happening requires evidence. The book's Global Welfare Database consists of objective measures of welfare such as life expectancy, literacy, and employment collated from a multiplicity of international organizations. The data is much more precise and verifiable than subjective measures of wellbeing such as happiness or life satisfaction.

There is nothing inherently 'statist' in welfare. For millennia before the creation of the modern welfare state, the household was the chief source of an individual's education, care in ill health, and work. The household remains a significant source of welfare today, especially in low-income countries in which the state has few resources. Chapter 2 explains how the welfare of people is the outcome of a mix consisting of inputs from the state, the market, and households. The education of children reflects what they learn within their family as well as at school. Work is not confined to paid employment, since housework is time-consuming even though it is unpaid. Globalization not only reflects an increase in total welfare within societies but also changes the significance for individual welfare of institutions in the welfare mix.

Economic theories of welfare are reductionist: they assume that to understand the globalization of welfare we only need measures of the officially recorded gross domestic product and incomes recorded in ways that can be monitored by tax collectors. However, Chapter 3 shows that welfare is about more than money. Especially in developing countries, people do not rely exclusively on their officially recorded income. They can earn cash in the shadow economy, and unpaid work in the household makes a disproportionate contribution to the household's welfare. In cross-national comparisons, the value of money is problematic because of big differences in the cost of living. The surest way to assess welfare is to use social indicators about such topics as births and deaths; by comparison, economic indicators are soft numbers.

Differences in national welfare are often attributed to countries being at lower levels of economic development. However, development is a multifaceted phenomenon and its varied components can be at very different levels. An oil kingdom can have a very large gross domestic product but also a very corrupt system of government. Chapter 4 identifies elements of development that affect an individual's welfare. These include urban centres with good schools and hospitals; public services delivered without bribery; and the freedom to do and say what you want that comes with living in a democracy. These elements form a single Index of Development. The Index is used, along with indicators of historical and cultural measures, to account for differences between countries in their health, education, and employment.

Part II compares the global distribution of health, education, and work; each directly affects the life of people wherever they may live. Each form of welfare differs in how it is measured and the extent to which it is influenced by the state, the market, and the household. There is global data to determine high global standards, how much countries not at these standards have progressed in the past three decades, and which countries are catching up with global standards and which are not.

Complementary measures of health are examined in Chapter 5. Life expectancy has been increasing in both highly developed and less developed countries from one decade to the next. Because life expectancy is an open-ended goal, developing countries that are making progress cannot be sure of catching up with global leaders that are also making progress. By contrast, there is a fixed goal for infant mortality. Countries on every continent are not only making progress in reducing infant mortality but also beginning to catch up with countries that have virtually eliminated infant mortality. The significance of adult lifestyle choices that risk avoidable mortality is shown by examining cross-national differences in smoking and deaths from road accidents.

Education divides people within as well as between countries. In the least developed countries, achieving the complete literacy of the population is a work in progress, because there is a legacy of older generations having grown up without any formal education. Chapter 6 documents the extent to which youths everywhere are now literate because they get primary schooling. Most countries also offer two stages of secondary education, compulsory and voluntary, before young people seek employment or continue into tertiary education. The quality of education is indicated by what young people learn while attending school. The results of international mathematics tests show major differences in the achievement of Asian and Western youths.

Work takes three different forms. Employment in the officially recorded economy is particularly important when welfare benefits are linked to paying taxes deducted from wages. Work in the shadow economy produces a cash-in-hand income but no tax revenue for government. Unpaid work in the household is particularly relevant to provide care for children and the elderly. Chapter 7 sets out the extent to which most people employed in the official economy are men, and most unpaid household work is done by women. The proportion of women and men recorded as employed in the official economy tends to be highest in less developed countries where wages are lowest and agricultural work plentiful. The exception is the Middle East, India, and select developing countries where cultural norms discourage women from working outside their home and produce the highest level of gender inequality.

Part III addresses the globalization of welfare in countries and in the world's population as the result of varying national rates of progress. Chapter 8 shows major differences between countries in their extent of globalization. The great majority are partly rather than completely globalized. Three-quarters of countries are at a high global standard for at least one measure of welfare, but only two are at the global standard for all six measures. Three significant influences account for unbalanced welfare: the resources combined in the Index of Development; the legacy of a communist regime; and conflicting cultural values about the role of women in society. The statistical analysis also identifies countries that are exceptions to the overall global pattern. China has a much higher level of welfare than would be expected given its resources, while welfare in India is much lower than its resources could provide.

People, not countries, are the basic unit for assessing welfare, and the distribution of the world's population is greatly skewed. Half the world's population lives in just seven countries. Thus, progress in welfare in China and India can affect twenty times more people than in Britain and four times as many people as in the United States. Chapter 9 shows that while a minority of countries is at global standards on each measure of welfare, a substantial majority of the world's population is at global standards on four measures. On average across six measures of welfare, highly developed and Latin American countries contribute more than their share of the world's population to the globalization of welfare, while India and African countries contribute a disproportionately large share of the global total of people who lack welfare.

Forecasting future welfare by projecting past rates of national progress shows that billions more people will catch up with today's global standards of health and education by 2050 or sooner. The globalization of employment is less certain because development enables more people to spend more years in education and retirement. There is also the possibility that cultural inhibitions about women working outside the home may be relaxed where they are now influential. Countries that have already achieved global standards are adopting new goals. Health is now viewed in terms of extending the quality as well as the quantity of years of life. Where infant mortality has reached its practical limit, there is now a focus on the right of women to choose whether or not to bear a child. In education, there is a continuing tension between teaching skills that are useful for employment and learning that contributes to understanding major experiences during one's life.

The book concludes by considering global problems that affect the collective welfare of the world's population, such as climate change and the threat of another global pandemic. These problems are what economists describe as global goods, since neither individuals nor national governments can provide them on their own. To produce these goods requires international cooperation for success. While institutions such as the United Nations and the World Health Organization cry out against these wicked problems, they lack the power to compel big national governments to cooperate.

Given the manifold forms that welfare takes, more could be said about many topics discussed in this book. However, expanding the discussion would obscure the big issue that it addresses: how many people in the world today enjoy high standards of welfare and how much progress is being made by those who do not. The answers for the most part are positive, in contrast to gloomy forecasts that proliferate in the media. This contrast is due to this book's conclusion being based on the analysis of a vast volume of evidence about the condition of the world's people over three decades. By contrast, media forecasts of gloom and doom tend to be generalized from the worst things happening somewhere in the world at the moment.

The welfare of the world's peoples is relevant to a much larger audience than social scientists specializing in a single field of European or American welfare and is especially relevant to people living in developing countries. So readers can see for themselves the degree to which the world is going global in different fields, much statistical evidence is presented in readily understood descriptive figures that highlight differences between and within continents. This is a prelude to testing explanations of cross-national differences in welfare using regression analysis. For a large audience the most important evidence of progress is not provided by asterisks showing statistical significance. It takes the form of interocular significance: evidence that hits you between the eyes.

Research on the growth of government led me to study welfare because spending on education and health care have been prime causes of government growth (Rose, 1985). Because the Japanese have a high level of welfare but not a big state, in *The Welfare State East and West* I developed the initial model of the welfare mix and applied it to Britain as well as Japan (Rose and Shiratori, 1986). After the fall of the Berlin Wall, I used the model to compare how welfare had developed between 1949 and 1989 in communist societies compared to societies that were highly developed and free (Rose, 1994). Sample surveys conducted in seventeen post-communist societies showed how people were using unofficial as well as officially recognized resources to cope with the effect on their welfare of the transformation of their society (Rose, 2009). Paying attention to what welfare state models ignored made the World Bank and UN agencies commission me to write reports on Africa, Latin America, and Asia, as well as ex-communist countries. Concurrently, I became a *pro bono* consultant to Transparency International's Global Corruption Barometer survey, which accepted my recommendation to collect survey data about the public's use of welfare services in 125 countries (Rose and Peiffer, 2019).

In researching and giving seminars in forty-five countries on six continents, I have had help from many sources. Chief among them are the late Heinz Kienzl, founder of the Paul Lazarsfeld Gesellschaft Vienna and former general director of the Austrian National Bank; the British Economic and Social Research Council; and associations for more than four decades with the Wissenschaftszentrum Berlin and the European University Institute Florence. I have benefited intellectually from discussions with Jim Buchanan, Douglass North, Lynn Ostrom, and Herb Simon, Nobel laureates in economics who have thought afresh about welfare outside the bounds of conventional economics. Sandra Horvath of the Humboldt University Berlin has been extremely competent in putting together a database that in printed form would cover hundreds of pages, and Karen Anderson has been a superb copy editor.

Helpful comments on the manuscript in progress have been received from Kenneth Newton, Donley Studlar, and Frank Vibert.

References

Rose, Richard, 1985. *Understanding Big Government.* London: Sage Publications.

Rose, Richard, 1994. 'Comparing Welfare across Time and Space', *Eurosocial Report*, 49. Vienna: European Centre for Social Welfare Policy.

Rose, Richard, 2009. *Understanding Post-Communist Transformation: A Bottom Up Approach.* London: Routledge.

Rose, Richard, and Peiffer, Caryn, 2019. *Bad Governance and Corruption.* London: Palgrave Macmillan.

Rose, Richard, and Shiratori, Rei, eds., 1986. *The Welfare State East and West.* New York: Oxford University Press.

PART I
WELFARE ACROSS TIME AND SPACE

1
Making Progress Globally

Evaluating national achievements without cross-national comparison can easily lead to false conclusions. For example, Britons have regarded the National Health Service as successful because the population's health has increased substantially since it was introduced in 1948. However, comparison across space implies a different evaluation. Three decades ago, life expectancy in countries such as Ireland and Korea was lower than in Britain. Now it is higher in both countries, and British life expectancy ranks in the bottom third of European countries.

Even though the institutions that influence an individual's welfare are specific to a single country or household, they are not unique. The scientific basis for maintaining good health or treating problems of ill health is not determined by the colours of a country's flag. The answers to questions set in arithmetic tests do not depend on the language in which questions are asked but in the logic of formulas that transcend linguistic differences. The pay and conditions of employment do vary between countries, but within-country differences in pay between bankers and unskilled workers can be bigger than differences in average incomes between developed and low-income countries.

Politicians can selectively draw comparisons between countries to bolster their partisan views. Many American politicians defend the country's health care system by claiming it is superior to the 'socialist' system of the United Kingdom. This assertion is undermined by empirical evidence: life expectancy is higher in Britain than in the United States. Moreover, the gap between the two countries has been rising over the decades. Even though American life expectancy continues to rise, it is doing so at a slower rate than the average 'socialist' system in Europe. Since most citizens lack accurate knowledge of welfare in other countries, this enables politicians to get away with making specious comparisons.

To understand global progress in welfare requires learning whether and how much change is occurring over decades. Even though most forms of welfare change slowly, as long as progress is steady, compounding a small annual

Welfare Goes Global. Richard Rose, Oxford University Press. © Richard Rose (2024).
DOI: 10.1093/oso/9780198908463.003.0002

increase for a decade or longer can have a significant impact. As Aristotle wrote, it is a sophist fallacy to think that just because a little is a little, a lot of littles do not add up to something big; they do. Progress occurs through the interaction of individuals within their households, with institutions of the market and with social policies of the state. Since progress often depends on trial-and-error learning, the longer the time span, the greater the likelihood of welfare standards rising nationally. In the past three decades, there has been an increase in the health and education of the population of most countries on every continent, whether their starting point was initially high or low (see Figure 8.1).

In this book the global standard of welfare is set by the continent in which the mean country is highest of the seven geographical groupings. Setting standards separately for health, education, and employment leaves open whether countries high in economic development set global standards for all forms of welfare. The extent to which countries and continents fall short of a global standard is a matter of degree. In Africa, where literacy is lowest, 64 per cent of adults in the median country are literate. Setting the global standard as the median for the top group avoids the fault of league tables that make a single country the global standard-setter. It also allows for inequalities, since half the countries in the leading continent will be below the median standard-setter and half will be above.

Catching up with a leading country requires making progress at a faster rate than countries with higher standards of welfare. For example, in 1991 female life expectancy in Pakistan was more than a year higher than in India. In the following three decades, life expectancy rose in both countries, but not at the same rate. In India the increase in life expectancy was one-quarter of 1 per cent higher than in Pakistan. The effect of compounding this small difference is that by 2019 the life expectancy of women in India had risen to become three years higher than in Pakistan.

Because the word 'welfare' is used in many different ways, the next section sets out this book's approach to the meaning of welfare to individuals. The two sections that follow explain how progress in welfare can occur nationally and what is required for national populations to catch up with global standards for health, education, and female employment when targets are fixed or open-ended. The chapter concludes with a description of the sources of data that make up the book's Global Welfare Database and describes the countries and continents that it covers.

1.1 The welfare of individuals

There is a broad international consensus about the desirability of health, education, and work. A long life is better than a short life, and infant mortality is bad. Literacy is preferable to illiteracy, and young people should have more education than their grandparents. Although there is global agreement about the importance of work, there are cross-cultural differences about whether women should work only within their household and men work for a wage, or whether women should have the same right to work and be paid for their work as men.

Health, education, and work are important in themselves and because they increase the capability of individuals to make important choices that influence their lives. As Amartya Sen (2001) emphasizes, it is insufficient for people to have the notional freedom to make choices if they have bad health and lack the education and income to make their choices effective. Although Sen is a world-famous economist, he rejects the reductionist economic assumption that a given income is sufficient for people to enjoy their lives.

Conflicting political views about how to achieve progress in welfare are voiced in both democracies and autocracies. Most autocracies claim to promote the welfare of their people but are free of accountability to their subjects if they concentrate on promoting the welfare of their rulers. Among democratic politicians, US President Ronald Reagan argued that the government created more problems than it resolved, and British Prime Minister Margaret Thatcher proclaimed, 'There is no such thing as society'. However, individuals cannot provide for themselves many major public institutions that deliver welfare, such as hospitals and universities. Communitarian philosophers emphasize the collective responsibility of society for individual welfare, and Scandinavian social democratic governments have created welfare states based on this philosophy (Etzioni, 1996; Sandel, 1998).

A model of individual welfare

Individuals have a significant influence on all forms of their welfare. They influence their personal health by the food they choose to eat or avoid, the exercise they do or do not do, and whether they smoke and drink alcohol to excess. In order to get good examination results and educational qualifications, individuals must apply themselves to learning required skills and knowledge. A youth's ability to get a job and remain in employment depends on how they perform at work as well as on the state of the national economy.

Individuals do not acquire their welfare in isolation; it is the outcome of interaction with their household and institutions of the market and the state (Figure 1.1). The state requires that youths must attend school for a number of years free of charge, while parents influence their children's willingness to study. The market is the primary source of employment, and an individual's education influences whether and how they are employed. The state collects taxes on individuals to pay for the health, education, and employment services that it provides. Not-for-profit civil society institutions are not independent institutions because they rely on cash flows from the state, the market, and often individuals. Collectively, the household, the market, and the state set parameters within which individuals get their welfare.

Today the globalization of welfare has reached the point at which a majority of households on every continent have access to one or more forms of welfare during the year (Figure 1.2). Contact with public services differs much less between countries and continents than the big cross-national differences in the achievement of welfare. On all continents more than half of households have contacted a doctor or health worker at least once in the past year. The proportion doing so in sub-Saharan Africa, 62 per cent, is just as high as in Western Europe. This does not mean that the treatment that people receive in less developed countries is equal to health care in highly developed countries. It is more likely to reflect the fact that poorer health, as indicated by a much higher rate of infant mortality and lower life expectancy, causes more Africans to need and seek treatment for their ills (Chapter 5).

The proportion of households accessing education services in African countries is two-thirds higher than in Western Europe and twice that in ex-communist countries. This is because contact depends on the number of

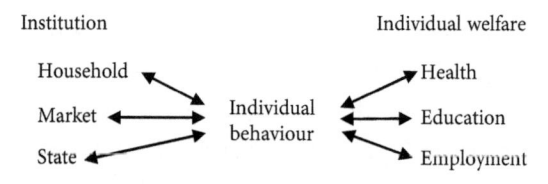

Figure 1.1 A model of individual welfare in society

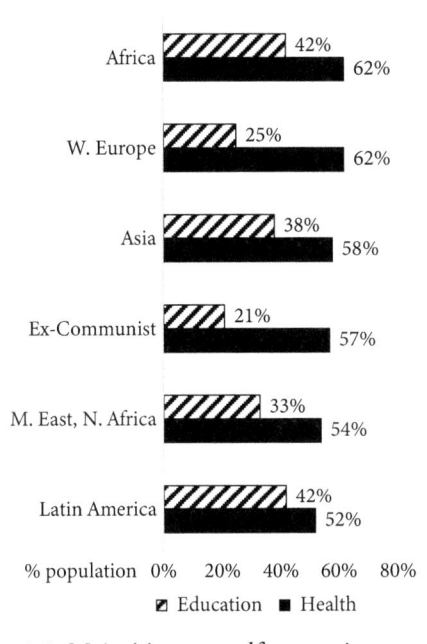

Figure 1.2 Majorities use welfare services annually

Source: Transparency International Global Corruption Barometer surveys in Rose and Peiffer, (2019), pp 69-70.

Bar chart data (Education / Health):
- Africa: 42% / 62%
- W. Europe: 25% / 62%
- Asia: 38% / 58%
- Ex-Communist: 21% / 57%
- M. East, N. Africa: 33% / 54%
- Latin America: 42% / 52%

children in a household as well as on how many years of free compulsory education the state provides. Family size in less developed countries of Africa and Asia is more than double that in Western Europe and ex-communist countries. Thus, even though African youths have fewer years of schooling, more African households are likely to have at least one child in primary school, making class sizes very large (see Chapter 6).

Work in one form or another is part of the everyday routine of almost every household, but being employed in the officially defined labour force varies within as well as between households. For the purpose of comparison between countries, international statistics define national employment as the percentage of the population aged 15 to 65 that is in officially recognized jobs. On this definition, the proportion of women in employment varies across continents. It averages 32 per cent in the Middle East and North Africa region and 62 per cent in Africa, where low household incomes mobilize a high proportion of women into the labour force. This results in gender equality, the ratio of women to men in employment being higher in Africa than in highly developed countries, where 15-year-olds are more likely to be in school and may retire with a pension before they are 65 (see Chapter 7).

The importance of different types of welfare varies during an individual's life cycle. Education is of primary importance in childhood and youth. This is true not only where secondary education is free and compulsory but even more so where it is in short supply and parents must struggle to get schooling for their children. For adults a job is important not only for the money it provides but also because it gives individuals social status and interaction with people at work. Health is distinctive in being important at all stages of life from early childhood to old age.

Distinctive forms of welfare

The idea of welfare is a high-order abstraction providing an umbrella that covers a heterogeneous variety of conditions that influence the wellbeing of individuals but differ from each other in many respects. In this book three different fields of welfare are assessed—health, education, and female employment—in order to determine whether what drives progress is the same or different across each of these fields. Education is of major importance in childhood and in determining the life chances of adults. Paid employment is of primary importance to men for most of their adult life, and for women it is important to have a fair choice between the number of years they are in paid employment and the years spent in working unpaid within their household. The extent of globalization is examined separately for each form of welfare. Comparing progress across different fields provides a robust test of the extent to which a country's progress is uniform or differs from one field to the other. To make comparisons between the open-ended goal of life expectancy and fixed goals such as achieving 100 per cent national literacy, the global standard is fixed at the highest achievement of any continent at the start of our period for measuring progress.

The efforts of social scientists and economists to reduce different characteristics of an individual's welfare to a single measure, whether it is happiness or gross domestic product per capita, face a structural obstacle. Even though health, education, and employment can each be measured quantitatively, they cannot be added up. Statistics about expected years of life, different levels of education, and the ratio of women to men in the labour force are incommensurable. Reducing welfare to a single indicator, whatever its appeal, obscures more than it illuminates.

Many forms of welfare that are the subject of study in highly developed countries are not suitable for comparison across a global range of more diverse countries. Social security and pension programmes are the biggest entries in the government budgets of highly developed countries. However, such pensions are very limited or non-existent in most developing countries because government lacks the resources to fund them. When people need money, they often fall back on their family and friends for help. Measures of poverty are unsuitable for global comparison because of the problem of comparing incomes in countries with different national currencies. Moreover, in many developing countries official data on incomes does not take into account what people earn through cash-in-hand trading and produce in their households without money changing hands (see Figure 3.1 and Table 3.1).

A group of psychologically oriented social scientists have sought to reduce the meaning of welfare to a single goal: life satisfaction or happiness. Sample surveys ask people to give a subjective evaluation of the extent to which they are happy or satisfied with their life (see, for example, Glatzer et al., 2015; Fitjers and Krekel, 2021). The annual World Happiness Report contains Gallup World Poll data from up to 150 countries. The 2022 Report (Helliwell et al., 2022) concludes that the happiest people live in Nordic countries and the least happy in Afghanistan and Lebanon. However, there is a dispute about whether the correlation between individual happiness and national income demonstrates that the level of national income is a major cause of happiness (cf. Easterlin, 2013; Senik, 2017). Moreover, many individuals say that their degree of life satisfaction is primarily determined by relations with family and friends and by their health rather than by income (Ackerman, 2020).

1.2 Making progress nationally

The idea of progress as the continuing improvement of conditions in a society is relatively recent. Ancient philosophers saw history in terms of the fall as well as the rise of nations and empires. In the eighteenth-century Enlightenment, philosophers prescribed ways in which societies could progress. The nineteenth-century Industrial Revolution created dynamic economies that transformed national populations and financed public policies for health, education, and employment. In the twentieth century laws were enacted entitling citizens to claim health, education, and employment services from the state, and in the twenty-first century pressures for more and higher standards of welfare benefits were institutionalized. In countries where levels of welfare are lower, there are political pressures to progress faster and to sooner or later catch up with standards set by global leaders.

Progress in national welfare occurs when there is a positive change in social conditions over a significant period of time. If there is positive evidence of a developing country moving toward the standards of highly developed countries, this is an indication of globalization. If the trend shows a country falling further behind global standards, there will be controversy about who or what is to blame and a demand for the governors to do something to speed up progress. While climate-change activists oppose forms of progress that negatively affect the environment, few go so far as to argue that governments should abandon efforts to raise standards of health, education, and employment.

Progress over decades illustrates what Albert Einstein called the eighth wonder of the world: the big effect produced by compounding a seemingly small annual rate of change over many years. Applying the same percentage increase to an ever-expanding base increases the size of each year's progress. Cumulatively this can create a substantial change (see Chapter 8). For example, the annual increase of a few months in national life expectancy can add about two years of life in a decade and five years in a quarter-century. The shorter the life expectancy in a country, the bigger the impact of the compounding of progress. A five-year increase in life expectancy in a developing African country has a relative impact that is one-third higher than the same absolute increase in a highly developed country.

Time horizons short and long

The time horizon of politicians tends to be short: the period when they hope to be in office. Dictators may claim to rule for life, but this leaves open whether they die in office of old age, by violence, or in exile. Elected politicians must campaign for popular support; the next election sets a time limit on how far most office holders plan ahead. Within an election cycle, a government can make a marginal increase in spending on a welfare policy or enact a law that will take years to have a positive effect. Promising long-term change in welfare can be politically congenial since it allows politicians to claim immediate credit for their intentions without being held to account if their promises cannot be met. All governors risk having their plans for progress disrupted by events such as the coronavirus pandemic. Yet over decades the direction of change in basic welfare measures such as life expectancy and literacy tends to be positive and irreversible.

In contrast to that of politicians, the time horizon of governments is long. Most policies left behind by an outgoing administration do not disappear because of a change in the party in charge: they stay on the statute books. There are government departments with interest in maintaining or expanding the programmes they administer, and their interests are shared by all who benefit from these policies. Programmes are carried forward by political inertia; this is especially true of welfare policies for education and health (Rose and Davies, 1994). While marginal changes in health and education and monthly fluctuations in employment are headlined by the media, most welfare policies carry on unchecked.

Major changes in the health and education of a society do not take place as fast as elections or coups produce a change in government. The turnover of generations is required for raising the age of compulsory education to increase the education level in society as a whole, because such statistics take into account the education that adults had when they left school up to six decades past. Today's estimates of the life expectancy of newborn infants can only be confirmed by empirical evidence in the twenty-second century.

Even when social statistics are reported annually, it takes an accumulation of data over a number of years to show whether a single year-on-year change is the start of a trend. A trend line can be upwards, as is the case with the percentage of youths going to university. By contrast, when monthly unemployment fluctuates, the trend line tends to be flat as increases and decreases cancel out their effect. When there is good news about the reduction of a form of illfare, such as infant mortality, there is a trend line down, while an increase in illfare, such as obesity in the population, is shown by a trend line up.

Comparisons across time involve a dilemma: the shorter the time period, the less progress can be achieved, once a country's level of health, education, and employment change very little from one year to the next. It takes decades to register the evidence of substantial progress. However, the longer the period of time, the more the universe for comparison changes. In the past three-quarters of a century, the boundaries of many countries have altered radically through wars and domestic disruptions, and decolonization has created many new states. When the United Nations was founded in 1945, it had fifty-one member states; today it has 193 members, many of which have undergone changes of their political regime or national boundaries. The great majority of UN member states have yet to achieve global standards of health, education, and employment.

Fixing the global standard of welfare at 1991 provides a robust test of the combined impact on individual welfare of short-term events and the long-term compounding of small annual changes. The period includes changes in national governments, the global economic recession of 2008, and periods of high economic growth. Concurrently there have been revolutions in computing, the internet, and technology.

Concluding the analysis of welfare going global in 2019 avoids conclusions being distorted by the subsequent global coronavirus pandemic that started in early 2020 and ended, according to the World Health Organization, in May 2023. There are many theories about the long-term effect of the pandemic on health, education, and employment. Short-term theories emphasize immediate negative effects, while long-term projections can draw on evidence of the past resilience of societies (Section 10.4). Adequate empirical evidence of the long-term effect of this short-term shock will only emerge in the 2030s (see Section 10.4).

1.3 Globalization is about catching up

The term globalization has many meanings (Roberts and Lamp, 2021). It often refers to national economies becoming interdependent through the increasing international trade in goods, services, and capital, which economists see as a win-win outcome for all countries. Populist politicians characterize globalization differently. A left-wing critique describes it as a process in which the richest and most powerful countries exploit poorer countries. A right-wing critique is that employing workers in low-wage countries to produce goods at a lower cost does so at the expense of workers in high-wage countries. Both sets of critics call for deglobalization on the grounds that the big winners from globalization are not countries but multinational corporations. The Russian invasion of Ukraine has encouraged governments to question global dependence on imports of specific goods as potentially threatening national security.

Since the institutions that influence individual welfare are national, local, and within households, the globalization of welfare is not caused by international interdependence. The local delivery of health care and education is remote from the interests and reach of multinational corporations and foreign governments. In this book globalization refers to processes chiefly occurring within each country. These processes can raise its national level of health, education, and employment, whether it has previously been high or low. Catching up with global standard-setters is a by-product of making national progress.

Global standards of welfare are here defined as the highest mean level of achievement among the seven continental groups described in the following section. Setting the global standard as the mean of countries in the top group avoids the fault of league tables that make a single country the global standard-setter. It also allows for inequalities within every continent, since half the countries in the top group will be above the group's median and half below. Setting standards separately for health, education, and employment leaves open to empirical determination whether highly developed countries set global standards for all forms of welfare. The extent to which countries fall short of a standard is a matter of degree not kind. For example, in Africa, where adult literacy is lowest, nonetheless 65 per cent of adults in the median country are literate.

The analysis of globalization involves comparison. Welfare indicators that show a country making progress by comparison with its own past can appear not good enough when compared with countries making progress at a faster rate. The analysis of globalization requires comparison across national boundaries. The most familiar form of comparison is a league table in which countries are ranked from top to bottom according to their achievement on a given indicator of welfare. A league table transforms information about a country's actual level of welfare into a numerical ranking with no substantive meaning. For example, when the OECD ranks thirty European countries on infant mortality, Britain has only three more deaths per thousand than Estonia. Yet Estonia appears first and the United Kingdom is twenty-seventh (OECD, 2020: 125), as the league table converts an absolute difference of three-tenths of 1 per cent into a very large gap. League tables encourage observers to view comparison like a winner-takes-all competition in which only one country can be the winner and every other country is a loser (cf. Hirsch, 1977). Moreover, league tables ranking countries on a single year's performance ignore the effect of differences between countries in their long-term rate of progress.

Catching up through unequal rates of progress

Catching up is about more than making progress; it is about closing the gap between countries setting global standards of welfare and those falling short. It requires a lagging country to make progress at a significantly faster rate than the countries it is trying to catch up with. The past three decades are full of spectacular examples of this happening. In this period, the welfare of Chinese has been transformed by rapid growth in health and education. If the gap is very large, it can nonetheless be reduced by making progress at a rate that makes catching up in future a realistic goal. In 1991 the infant mortality rate in Africa averaged 161 deaths per thousand and the global standard was 12 deaths per thousand. By 2019 infant mortality in Africa had fallen by almost twelve times the reduction in the already low rate of highly developed countries. The gap between the two groups was thus reduced from 149 to 63 deaths per thousand.

In a globalizing world, there are plenty of opportunities for national policymakers to increase their rate of progress by learning from leaders. Countries below global standards may quickly benefit by adopting practices and policies that have taken leading countries a long time to develop through a process of trial and error (Gerschenkron, 1962; Rose, 2005). A major function of the World Bank is to provide countries with technical assistance and money so that they can speed up their development. Furthermore, the globalization of new technologies through the market can enable developing countries to skip a stage in development. In the year 2000 New York City had more telephones than the whole of the African continent. Today a majority of Africans have a mobile phone that can access the internet without requiring a computer (International Telecommunications Union, 2021).

If a country's policymakers are satisfied with maintaining an annual rate of progress that is below that of global leaders, then national progress will be combined with falling further behind the leaders. For example, in 1991 female life expectancy in the United States was above the average for highly developed countries. However, progress since then has been at half the rate of the average highly developed country; by 2019 life expectancy in the United States had fallen below that of the average highly developed country.

Alternative targets for catching up

The critical issue about whether a country is catching up is political, not statistical: the choice of targets. A fixed target such as abolishing infant mortality can be reached sooner or later as long as a country makes progress. However, if a target is open-ended, such as life expectancy, it is harder for a country below the global standard to catch up, since global leaders are also increasing life expectancy. Thus, a country must make progress at a significantly faster rate than leading countries or fall further behind, since applying the same rate of progress to a higher level of life expectancy will add more months and years to the leader than the time that followers can gain by applying the same rate to their lower level of achievement. For example, since 1991 female life expectancy in the Republic of Korea and in Nigeria grew by the same annual rate, but because it was initially much higher in Korea, this added ten years to the life expectancy of Koreans compared to an additional six years for Nigerians.

Catching up is much easier if a fixed target is chosen. It is not a zero-sum competition in which what one country gains the other loses, as is competition to top a global league table. A fixed welfare goal sets a limit that in principle every country can achieve. The choice of a fixed target means that a country is competing only with its own past. As long as it is making progress annually, sooner or later it will reach a fixed target. How long it takes a country to catch up with a fixed target depends upon its rate of progress and the gap between its starting point and its fixed goal.

Highly developed countries long ago reached the mathematical limit of virtually 100 per cent adult literacy by making primary schooling compulsory and free. There is thus no scope for these countries to increase literacy. However, the later introduction of free compulsory education in most countries means that they have yet to achieve complete adult literacy. Even where national governments have succeeded in establishing free primary education nationwide, this cannot confer literacy after the fact on adults who were born before primary schooling was available where they lived. For example, in Africa in 1991 an average of 36 per cent of adults were illiterate, a gap of 35 percentage points from the global standard. Progress in achieving complete literacy has progressed at a rate twelve times faster in Africa than in highly developed countries. Nonetheless, there remains a gap of 34 percentage points between the mean of African and highly developed countries.

1.4 The Global Welfare Database

To test the extent to which welfare is going global, a multidimensional strategy of comparison is needed. Instead of treating welfare as a single attribute, in this book comparisons are made between progress on multiple indicators of health, education, and the employment of women. To ascertain progress, comparisons are made within countries between their past and present performance on each of the six welfare measures. This is followed by comparisons across countries and continents in order to identify to what extent countries that are not at global standards are catching up or falling behind. The starting point for analysis has been the construction of the Global Welfare Database (see Appendix).

Diving into data without drowning

Because government is good at keeping records, there is a plenitude of data about the welfare of citizens. Basic statistics for health, education, and employment date from whenever these conditions first became the concerns of national policymakers. In highly developed countries, this was usually in the nineteenth century, starting with a national census. Developing countries usually lack such lengthy records, but after joining the United Nations or applying for a World Bank loan their government will be asked to compile a mass of social indicators that are in keeping with international standards set by developed countries, and they will be offered assistance in doing so. Once a measure of health, education, or employment is adopted by a government institution, bureaucratic inertia normally ensures that it is routinely collected henceforth.

National governments are the primary source of data about the welfare of their population. The World Bank's Statistical Capacity Index* shows that the capacity of developing countries to collect data varies substantially. On a scale that runs from 0 to 100, the average developing country has a rating of 67. Among the developing countries in the Global Welfare Database, ratings in the Statistical Capacity Index range from as low as 34 in Iraq and Turkmenistan to as high as 97 in the Kyrgyz Republic.

International organizations are data aggregators rather than originators of data. This book's database has been constructed from publicly available intergovernmental sources, principally the World Development Indicators of the World Bank and specialized agencies of the United Nations (see Appendix). Each institution obtains its data from national statistical offices. In principle, national agencies compile welfare statistics according to internationally agreed standards. However, there are both theoretical and practical difficulties in implementing common measures in countries that differ greatly in their development and resources (see Chapters 3 and 4). Fortunately, these differences are much less for data about social welfare than for the economic statistics often used as proxies for welfare (cf. Stiglitz, Sen, and Fitoussi, 2010).

To avoid drowning in an ocean of data, it is necessary to look before you leap to avoid fishing for data in the misleading belief that more data will invariably produce better results. The theoretical framework in Figure 1.1 and the social resources model in Figure 4.2 identify the key concepts for which statistical indicators are needed for the book's Global Welfare Database.

* https://datatopics.worldbank.org/statisticalcapacity/scidashboard.aspx.

Selecting and grouping countries

While this book is about the welfare of the world's population as it is affected by their national context, it is important to exclude from the Database territories that report data but are not normal states. The World Bank (2022) database includes 218 territories that it describes with the familiar word 'country', while noting, 'The term country, used interchangeably with economy, does not imply political independence but refers to any territory for which authorities report separate social or economic statistics'. The United Nations reports 193 member states; the most populous members, China and India, each has a population more than 1250 times that of the smallest country, Nauru.

Of the territories that report statistics twelve states have been excluded because of internal strife and division that deny them the capacity to account for the whole of their nominal population; for example, this is the status of Ukraine today. Nine states have been excluded because a large proportion of their population are immigrants whose welfare is much influenced by their country of origin—87 per cent in the case of Qatar. In addition, eight states are excluded because key statistics are missing. For further details, see the Appendix. Because it would be misleading to treat the welfare of mini-countries as equal in importance to that of larger countries, fifty-nine countries and territories with fewer than one million people have been excluded.

The Global Welfare Database includes 127 countries with an estimated total population of 7.3 billion people in 2019. This is 95 per cent of the world's population and 99 per cent of the world's population living in independent states that regularly report welfare data. By the time this book is published, the world's population will be above eight billion and still growing (see Chapter 10). Details about the Global Welfare Database are given in the Appendix. An electronic version of the database can be downloaded from www.oup.co.uk/companion/WelfareGoesGlobal.

For clarity in presentation, tables and figures summarize evidence by placing countries into four continent groups and a transcontinental group of highly developed countries. India and China are each included in their own right, as each has a population larger than that of any continent (Table 1.1).

Most of the forty countries of *sub-Saharan Africa* were colonies of the United Kingdom, France, or Portugal until they gained their independence decades after the Second World War. Countries range in population from more than 200 million in Nigeria to a little more than one million each in Mauritius, Eswatini (formerly known as Swaziland), and Equatorial Guinea.

Table 1.1 Countries in the Global Welfare Database

	Population	GDP PPP per capita
China	1.41 bn	$16,092
India	1.37 bn	$6,700
Asian Developing Countries (16 countries) Afghanistan, Bangladesh, Cambodia, Indonesia, Laos, Malaysia, Mongolia, Myanmar, Nepal, Pakistan, Papua New Guinea, Philippines, Sri Lanka, Thailand, Timor, Vietnam	1.14 bn	$8,823
Highly Developed (34 countries) Australia, Austria, Belgium, Bulgaria, Canada, Croatia, Czech Republic, Denmark, Estonia, Finland, France, Germany, Greece, Hungary, Ireland, Italy, Japan, Korea, Latvia, Lithuania, Netherlands, New Zealand, Norway, Poland, Portugal, Romania, Russia, Slovak Republic, Slovenia, Spain, Sweden, Switzerland, United Kingdom, United States	1.24 bn	$44,709
Sub-Saharan Africa (40 countries) Angola, Benin, Botswana, Burkina Faso, Burundi, Cameroon, Central African Republic, Chad, Cote d'Ivoire, Democratic Republic of the Congo, Equatorial Guinea, Eswatini, Ethiopia, Gabon, Gambia, Ghana, Guinea, Guinea-Bissau, Kenya, Lesotho, Liberia, Madagascar, Malawi, Mali, Mauritania, Mauritius, Mozambique, Namibia, Niger, Nigeria, Republic of the Congo, Rwanda, Senegal, Sierra Leone, South Africa, Tanzania, Togo, Uganda, Zambia, Zimbabwe	1.03 bn	$4,869
Latin America (20 countries) Argentina, Bolivia, Brazil, Chile, Colombia, Costa Rica, Dominican Republic, Ecuador, El Salvador, Guatemala, Haiti, Honduras, Jamaica, Mexico, Nicaragua, Panama, Paraguay, Peru, Trinidad and Tobago, Uruguay	0.60 bn	$15,050
Middle East &North Africa (15 countries) Algeria, Azerbaijan, Egypt, Iran, Iraq, Jordan, Kazakhstan, Kyrgyz Republic, Morocco, Sudan, Tajikistan, Tunisia, Turkey, Turkmenistan, Uzbekistan	0.53 bn	$11,937

Source: Global Welfare Database; see Appendix. GDP measured in US dollars adjusted to purchasing power parity at 2017 prices.

A minority has experienced violent conflict since independence, including the three most populous countries, Nigeria, Ethiopia, and the Democratic Republic of the Congo. A majority of African countries are classified as low-income countries by the World Bank, and only four are considered upper-middle-income. As nine-tenths of states in the continent are sub-Saharan, the forty countries included are described as representing the African continent. *Asian developing countries* sprawl across the Pacific and Indian oceans. Indonesia, with 270 million people, is the fourth most populous country in the world; Pakistan is fifth, with a population of 216 million; and Bangladesh is eighth, with 164 million (see Table 9.1). Their twentieth-century histories are diverse. Most are ex-colonies of Britain, France, the Netherlands, or the United States. Eleven of the sixteen Asian developing countries are lower-middle in their income. None is low-income and none is high-income.

In the fifteen countries grouped together in the *Middle East and North Africa* (MENA) region, an average of 94 per cent of the population is nominally Muslim. However, they are associated with different branches of Islam, and six former republics of the Soviet Union and Turkey have had governments that promoted secularization. Egypt, Turkey, and Iran together account for almost half the group's 530 million people. Oil-rich sheikhdoms, including Saudi Arabia, are excluded because their population is below one million and is divided between citizens and a substantial fraction of expatriate workers. Four countries are classified by the World Bank as high-income thanks to wealth from natural resources, nine as upper-middle-income, and two as lower-middle-income.

The countries of *Latin America* have had stable boundaries as independent states for up to two centuries, far longer than many European, African, and MENA countries. However, in many countries competition involving the military, civilian dictators, and democratic groups has resulted in a number of changes in political regimes. Two countries—Brazil and Mexico—together account for more than half of Latin America's population. Chile and Trinidad are both classified as high-income countries; two-thirds of the remaining eighteen countries are classified as upper-middle-income countries and none as low-income. The move of rural populations to cities has facilitated access to health, education, and work in the official economy, while inflation has devalued national currencies.

Although *highly developed countries* are not geographically concentrated, economic interdependence, electronic communication, and rapid intercontinental travel have brought them together as a virtual continent with a global impact. Geographical distance is no obstacle to a country becoming highly developed. The thirty-four countries are spread across Europe and North America and in Asia from the Republic of Korea to New Zealand. Comparisons within this group often ignore continental boundaries. Welfare standards in the United States are often compared with Europe instead of neighbouring Mexico, and the British government makes comparisons with other developed

Anglo-American countries rather than its closest neighbours, France and Ireland. Large economic differences do not lead to similarly large differences in welfare. The per capita GDP of Switzerland is more than four times that of Greece, but the average life expectancy in Switzerland is less than two years more.

Because welfare is in essence about people, not states, the penultimate chapter shifts the analysis to the globalization of welfare among the world's population. This has the effect of greatly boosting the importance of China and India, since together they have more than one-third of the world's population. This contrasts with countries that are usually the focus of welfare studies. The United States has only 4 per cent of the global population, the United Kingdom less than 1 per cent, and the combined population of Scandinavia is less than one-third of 1 per cent of the global population.

Progress enables people and countries on every continent to aspire to catching up with global standards of welfare. However, globalization does not mean that there will be a homogenization of values among people living in cultures from Ireland to India and from Nigeria to Norway. Better health, education, and employment opportunities increase the capability of individuals to choose a way of life that suits them in keeping with their capabilities and values and the institutional resources of their society.

References

Ackerman, C. E., 2020. 'Life Satisfaction Theory & 4 Contributing Factors'. https://positivepsychology.com/life-satisfaction/.

Easterlin, Richard A., 2013. 'Happiness and Economic Growth: The Evidence'. Bonn: *Institute for the Study of Labour Discussion Paper No. 7187.*

Etzioni, Amitai, 1996. *The New Golden Rule.* New York: Basic Books.

Fitjers, Paul, and Krekel, Christian, 2021. *A Handbook for Wellbeing Policymaking.* Oxford: Oxford University Press.

Gerschenkron, Alexander, 1962. *Economic Backwardness in Historical Perspective.* Cambridge, MA: Harvard University Press.

Glatzer, Wolfgang, Camfield, Laura, Møller, Valerie, and Rojas, Mariano, 2015. *Global Handbook of Quality of Life.* Dordrecht: Springer.

Helliwell, J. F., Layard, R., Sachs, J. D., De Neve, J.-E., Aknin, L. B., and Wang, S., eds., 2022. *World Happiness Report 2022.* New York: Sustainable Development Solutions Network.

Hirsch, Fred, 1977. *Social Limits to Growth.* London: Routledge.

International Telecommunications Union, 2021. *Measuring Digital Development 2021: Facts and Figures*. Geneva: International Telecommunications Union.

OECD, 2020. *Health at a Glance: Europe 2020*. Paris: OECD Publishing.

Roberts, Anthea and Lamp, Robert, 2021. *Six Faces of Globalization*. Cambridge, MA: Harvard University Press.

Rose, Richard, 2005. *Learning from Comparative Public Policy: A Practical Guide*. London: Routledge.

Rose, Richard, and Davies, Phillip L., 1994. *Inheritance in Public Policy: Change without Choice in Britain*. New Haven: Yale University Press.

Sandel, Michael J., 1998. *Liberalism and the Limits of Justice*. Cambridge: Cambridge University Press.

Sen, Amartya, 2001. *Development as Freedom*. New York: Oxford University Press.

Senik, Claudia, 2017. 'Wealth and Happiness'. In K. Hamilton and C. Hepburn, eds., *National Wealth: What Is Missing, Why It Matters*. Oxford: Oxford University Press, 67–86.

Stiglitz, J. E., Sen, A., and Fitoussi, J.-P., 2010. *Report by the Commission on the Measurement of Economic Performance and Social Progress*. http://ec.europa.eu/eurostat/documents/8131721/8131772/Stiglitz-Sen-Fitoussi-Commission-report.pdf.

World Bank, 2022. http://datahelpdesk.worldbank.org/knowledgebase/articles/378834-how-does-the-world-bank-classify-countries.

2
The Welfare Mix

For an individual the total amount of welfare is more important than its source. Welfare is not the exclusive result of what is done by the state, what is sold and bought in the marketplace, or what people and families do for themselves. The total welfare of individuals is the product of the welfare mix, that is, the combined activities of three different social institutions—the household, the market, and the state. Because welfare takes multiple forms, it would be wrong to expect individuals to rely exclusively on a single institution of the welfare mix for their health, education, and employment. The German concepts of the *Sozialstaat* (social state) and the *soziale Marktwirtschaft* (social market economy) recognize both the state's provision of health and education services and the contribution of the market, not-for-profit institutions, communities, and households.

Individuals influence the welfare mix that influences their health by the choices that they make about their lifestyle: what they eat and drink and whether they exercise. During the coronavirus pandemic, people could reduce the risk of infection by putting on a mask and limiting their social contacts. They also chose whether to be vaccinated with anti-virus products produced by pharmaceutical companies and distributed by public health services. What an individual learns depends on what they are taught in their household and the extent to which their family supports their efforts to benefit from the education that the state provides. An individual's employment reflects their aptitudes and working habits as well as the market demand for workers and the government's economic policy.

The market makes a double contribution to the welfare mix. It provides money that people need to buy the goods and services that individuals cannot produce for themselves, such as prescription drugs and textbooks. It also provides the tax revenue that the state needs to finance health and education services. Free-market economists argue that the market would be a more efficient institution for providing health and education services than the state (cf. Niskanen, 1971; Besley, 2007: ch. 2; OECD, 2019). People who have the money are free to buy health care privately and pay for private tuition for their children. But many millions of people who have the money nonetheless make use of the state's health and education service, and billions of people don't have the money. Even if politicians campaigning for office promise to cut taxes, if they win control of government they usually preside over increased spending on social policies that voters value rather than jeopardizing their re-election by making big cuts in spending on health and education.

Public finance theories see state provision of welfare services as necessary to correct market failures, and public expenditure on health and education are big-ticket items in the budgets of the world's prosperous states. Politicians of all parties appeal for votes by promising that, if elected, they will make the state's health and education services bigger and better. A Google search finds that there are 50 per cent more references to the welfare state than to individual welfare.

The relative contribution of institutions to the welfare mix varies between the least and the most developed countries. In countries where the capacity of the state is weak and the market provides few jobs with a steady income, individuals must rely for much of their welfare on what can be provided within their household. In a low-income society a household can be a family business in which everyone works. With economic development, individuals benefit from cash-in-hand local markets and from rudimentary public services such as primary schools that promote literacy. In highly developed countries, most people earn an income through wages from employers that are taxed by the state, which then spends much of its revenue on welfare services.

Whatever the amount of public expenditure on welfare services, it is no more than one among many inputs to the welfare mix, and input does not equal output. As Lord Beveridge explained in his classic report recommending social insurance for all Britons,

> Social security must be achieved by co-operation between the State and the individual. The State should offer security for service and contribution. The State in organizing security should not stifle incentive, opportunity, responsibility; in establishing a national minimum, it should leave room and encouragement for voluntary action by each individual to provide more than that minimum for himself and his family. (1948: 7)

The next section explains how the total welfare of an individual in a society reflects the contribution of the state, the market, and an individual's household, and the comparative advantages and disadvantages of each. It is followed by a description of how political choices over two centuries in autocracies as well as democracies have resulted in the welfare mix evolving in highly developed countries and reaching the high level it is at today. The evolution of the welfare mix has yet to reach this level in developing countries. While the globalization of communications has everywhere raised the aspirations of people for health and education, it does not provide the material resources to achieve global standards in most of the world's countries.

2.1 Modelling the welfare mix

The state has a monopoly on the provision of collective goods such as public health but it has no monopoly of the resources that produce of individual health, education and employment. As Figure 1.1 shows, an individual's or a country's total welfare is the result of how the household, the market, and the institutions of the state interact. The coronavirus pandemic has demonstrated the flexibility of the welfare mix. Enterprises selling fast food to busy workers found that much of their business disappeared as their customers turned to working from home and substituted meals they made for themselves in their own kitchen. The closure of schools kept many youths at home, and the result was a combination of schooling by parents and computerized online learning.

The *household* is the primary source of welfare in the least developed societies. When several generations live together, they can exchange services with each other without any money changing hands. Individuals can grow food and prepare meals within their household, spin yarns and make clothes, and rely on do-it-yourself maintenance of their house. Youths can learn from their parents how to do jobs, and if they gain paid employment outside their home, can give part of their earnings to their household. Being employed to work without pay in the household has been common among peasant families in Europe for centuries.

To ignore the importance of the household for welfare because family members do not pay for services they produce and share with each other is to practise anti-social accountancy. If everyone who was too ill to work or go to school had to go to a hospital instead of being cared for at home, public expenditure on health care would greatly increase. Empirical studies of how people allocate their time in highly developed societies show that, in the course of a 168-hour week, family members collectively spend many hours in unpaid household work (Gershuny and Sullivan, 2019). The extent to which household work affects the welfare mix is especially evident for women who are unpaid carers of family members (see Section 7.3).

The market affects individual welfare by the way it is organized and by the amount of cash it generates to finance welfare services that the household cannot provide. In low-income countries, the cash-in-hand economy provides individuals with an income outside the sight of tax collectors. Individuals can use the money they earn to pay for services and products sold by pharmacists and to buy textbooks that schools do not provide for their children. Government can tax imports and exports of centrally provided services such as electricity and buildings. It cannot generate much revenue from taxes on wages because most people are not employees of firms that can deduct taxes before wages are paid. Nor can it collect sales tax routinely when most goods are not sold with a computerized receipt but for cash.

The market is not the sole source of individual income in highly developed societies. Non-market public sector institutions are significant employers. In highly developed countries, the largest groups of government employees are teachers and health workers delivering welfare services. In addition, up to one-fifth of incomes are social security pensions paid to people retired from work. In highly developed countries, households with two or more members are likely to have two incomes, whether from employment, pensions, or both. In addition, a household member may also act as an unpaid carer.

The development of a modern economy in which wages, sales, and cash flow are recorded in audited accounts and bank payments provides a tax handle that the state can turn to secure large sums of revenue. Modern states use their tax revenues to pay for many goods and services that can contribute to individual welfare but that individuals cannot produce at home, such as hospitals, universities, and employment services. If education is compulsory, it must be free and funded by the state, since many families cannot pay the market cost of education.

The totality of health care in a society comes from a mixture of sources. Nurses may be employed in the public sector or in a private clinic, and doctors can be self-employed professionals remunerated by private sector insurance and patients as well as the state. In developing countries individuals may treat their ills with home remedies or what they buy from a pharmacist. In Britain one-fifth of spending on health care is private expenditure, and in the average European Union country one-quarter of health expenditure is private (Table 2.1). In the United States, public as well as private spending on health care is higher than the European Union average, while the achievement of health is less.

There are political limits to what a state can do to influence individual welfare. It can promote popular goals such as reducing infant mortality, but

Table 2.1 Public and private expenditure on health

	Public	(% of GDP) Private	Total
United States	8.0	9.7	17.7
Germany	10.0	1.7	11.7
France	9.4	1.8	11.2
United Kingdom	8.0	2.3	10.3
Italy	6.5	2.2	8.7
European Union	6.2	2.1	8.3
Greece	4.6	3.2	7.8

Source: OECD, 2020b: 161, except the United States (a federal government statistic).

birth rates are immediately due to activities within the household. Government policies can affect the population through public health policies, but only a government with a totalitarian vocation would seek to control family size. In 1979 the People's Republic of China introduced a one-child policy in an attempt to limit what it then saw as an unmanageable population explosion. The government claimed it prevented 400 million births before the policy was relaxed and finally terminated. Now, because it faces the prospect of a long-term contraction of its population of working age, the Chinese government is trying to get houscholds to have more children (Fong, 2015).

Each individual has a personal welfare mix reflecting their needs, resources, and preferences. Youths attend state schools while depending on their family for food and shelter; they may also earn a bit of money through a part-time job as they become active consumers of goods that the market offers teenagers. Individuals make many choices that influence their personal health, such as how much alcohol they drink and whether they smoke. A woman may concentrate exclusively on unpaid work within the household or work as a paid employee in the private or public sector. People are aware of what the state can do when it contributes to their welfare and even more when it does not.

2.2 Evolution of the welfare mix

Fundamental changes in the welfare mix have taken centuries to evolve, to the point reached in high-income societies today in which the state looms large as an influence on individual welfare. The starting point is a traditional society in which the household was the primary source of welfare. Within a village many services were exchanged without money changing hands. When feudal lords demanded payments or the state levied taxes, such demands could be paid by *corvée*, that is, by giving a number of days of labour to the state instead of paying money. The parochial organization of the church gave it an authoritative presence in almost every community. Churches could organize schools and give alms to those they deemed the deserving poor. In cities, artisans and merchants formed guilds and mutual aid societies to provide welfare for their members. When Alexis de Tocqueville visited the United States in the 1830s, he was struck by the way in which Americans met many needs through informal cooperation with friends and neighbours in rural settings in which salaried jobs and the federal government were remote.

Market institutions began to become major contributors to the welfare mix in Europe with the development of cities, industries, and new means of communication and transportation (Mitchell, 1975). The market economy offered an alternative to working for food and shelter within a rural household. People could have jobs in mills, mines, and factories in which they were paid money for their work. Women were no longer confined to working within their households; they could seek employment in shops and mills or be paid to do housework by becoming domestic servants.

In a modern economy the production of many forms of welfare is capital-intensive as well as labour-intensive. Individuals who feel ill no longer expect to rely simply on home remedies; they go to a doctor's surgery for diagnosis and the prescription of internationally marketed drugs or to a clinic or hospital for specialist treatment. Education is no longer about children being taught at home or in a one-room village school. Their schooling becomes increasingly costly and the subject matter more complex as they progress up the educational ladder to universities that have large libraries, many laboratories, and digital facilities as well as teaching staff.

Evolution of the state's role

The European state was not created to meet the welfare needs of its subjects (Rose, 1976). Initially, most public expenditure was devoted to a few classic concerns, especially administering justice and maintaining national security and public order (Flora, 1983). However, the growth of crowded cities created a need for public sanitation and safe drinking water. Increased trade between countries and continents resulted in five nineteenth-century cholera epidemics across Europe, the United States, and Asia. In response, the state began to take responsibility for public health to prevent epidemics threatening its population as a whole. It left individuals to look after their own health as best they could.

The growth of an economy in which money was of primary importance produced a fiscal dividend for the state; it gained much revenue without having to levy high taxes. It promoted nationwide communication through a national postal service and operated or regulated telegraph and telephone services. In parallel, it promoted the construction of a nationwide system of railways and roads. This initially provided the infrastructure for nationwide markets and subsequently for the delivery of welfare services to people wherever they lived.

The state first became a dominant partner in the welfare mix by making education compulsory and free for every household. Education became compulsory in Sweden in 1842 and across Northern Europe in the decades that followed. Governments funded primary education in the belief that a literate population made better workers and better soldiers. In England, compulsory education was introduced three years after a significant expansion of the right to vote with the argument, 'We must educate our masters'. In Southern Europe the state's capacity to deliver education developed more slowly, and on other continents mass public education came much later (see Chapter 6).

Paradoxically, the spread of jobs with weekly wages created income insecurity. Whereas a peasant without money could live at the subsistence level with what the family produced, urban workers who lost a job because of an industrial injury or economic recession were threatened with the loss of money needed to buy food and pay their rent. To protect themselves against the risks of sickness and old age, people began to organize an extension of their household—local mutual aid societies. By the late nineteenth century, cooperative societies and trade unions in Britain promoted benefits for their members; in Germany, by contrast, trade unions pushed for the state to take responsibility for welfare (Heidenheimer, 1969).

The Second World War greatly expanded the state's welfare provision in countries that were not occupied by an invading army. Food rationing was introduced, thereby improving the health of people whose diet had previously been restricted by poverty. To boost morale, governments promised to expand the state provision of welfare once the war ended. For example, in Britain pledges for major developments in education, income security, and full employment were made by a wartime coalition government headed by Winston Churchill and implemented by a Labour government elected when the war ended (Titmuss, 1950). In countries that were occupied, people relied on their household and informal networks for much of their welfare rather than on a state controlled by invaders. Once the war in Europe ended, national governments spent up to a decade rebuilding and expanding institutions that had provided a modicum of welfare before the Second World War.

Treble affluence—simultaneous growth in the national economy, public spending on welfare services, and individual income—occurred in what a French economist called the thirty glorious years between 1945 and 1975 (Fournastié, 1979). Gross domestic product more than doubled in Britain and the United States and more than trebled in France, Germany, and Italy. Public expenditure as a percentage of a much larger national product increased by up to one-third in many countries, and in Sweden it doubled to 54 per cent of the gross national product. Even though taxes increased on wages, the average wage-earner enjoyed a great increase in take-home pay and became a consumer with discretionary income as well as a worker (Rose and Peters, 1978: ch. 2).

The state spent the fiscal dividend of growth primarily on health, education, and income security policies. It financed more of the same—for example, new schools and hospitals—and new programmes such as mass university education, universal health care, and laws to increase the welfare of groups that had previously been discriminated against. By 1975 central government spending on health, education, income maintenance, and related welfare services accounted for three-fifths to three-quarters of general government spending in highly developed countries (Flora, 1983; Dincecco, 2017: 59).

The global recession of 1975 caused national markets to contract and public revenue and households' take-home pay to shrink. By this time, the post-Second World War expansion of the welfare state was sufficiently entrenched for the setback to be temporary and resilience strong enough for long-term progress to continue. Even politicians who rhetorically opposed public expenditure, such as Margaret Thatcher and Ronald Reagan, headed governments that ended up spending more on welfare services to which citizens were entitled by law. Subsequent recessions, especially the global crisis of 2008, led to states adopting austerity measures that challenged but did not reverse the long-term growth in publicly funded welfare services (Hemerijck and Huguenot-Noel, 2022). The coronavirus pandemic and concerns about climate change are fresh reminders that the growth of state support for welfare policies is repeatedly subject to challenge (see Chapter 10).

Today European states no longer spend the bulk of their budget on nineteenth-century activities of the state. By 2020 public expenditure had increased to 53.1 per cent of the gross domestic product in the average European Union member state, and spending on social protection, health, and education accounted for two-thirds of total public expenditure (Figure 2.1).

THE WELFARE MIX   41

[Pie chart showing: Social protection 41%, Health 15%, Education 10%, Economic affairs 11%, Security 3%, General/other 20%]

- Social protection   ▨ Health
- ▨ Education   ▨ Economic affairs
- ▨ Security   □ General/other

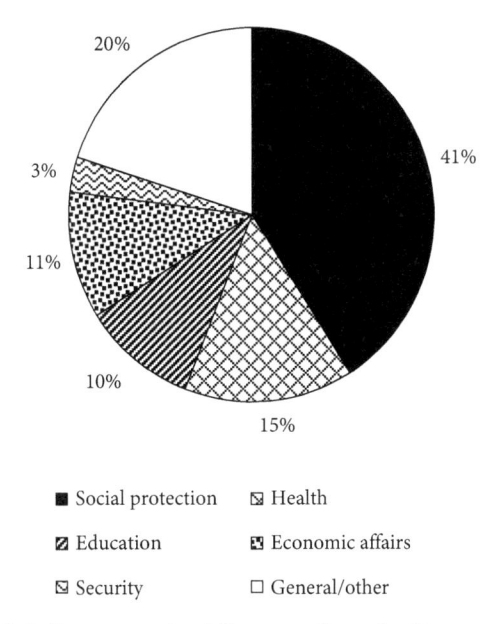

Figure 2.1 Purposes of public expenditure by European states

Source: Eurostat, 2022. General Government Expenditure by Function. https://ec.europa.eu/eurostat/statistics-explained/index.php?title=Government_expenditure_by_function_%E2%80%93_COFOG#

Two-fifths of a country's budget and 22 per cent of its GDP are allocated to spending on health, education, and social protection policies that provide an income to older people, the unemployed, and the disabled.

Concurrently, ordinary individuals in highly developed countries have gained increased resources to expand their welfare. Treble affluence has given people discretionary income, and more education has given individuals the capability to make choices about spending this income. Increased employment opportunities mean that women no longer need to depend on a male breadwinner for their income, and the market and state have expanded care for children and the elderly that was previously provided by the non-waged household work of women. The extension of entitlements from means-tested benefits for a minority to universal coverage given to all citizens has broadened the base of public support for the state's contribution to the welfare mix.

The state today is a substantial, but not an exclusive, source of individual welfare. Good health reflects an individual having a healthy lifestyle; the state is principally responsible for dealing with temporary and chronic problems of poor health. State schools and universities have an essential role in educating youths, who subsequently can advance their knowledge through the internet and experience. In highly developed states, workers no longer need to rely exclusively on the market or their household for income; if they become unemployed, the state may pay an unemployment benefit.

Two centuries of development have altered the welfare mix through processes of addition, subtraction, and substitution. When there is an increase in the number of years that youths spend in school, this is an addition to total welfare. When the state provides a national system of health insurance, the net effect is reduced by the extent to which this substitutes for private-sector health insurance and individual payments. When the state and the private sector provide day care for preschool-age children and for the elderly, this reduces the contribution that non-waged houschold members make to family care.

2.3 Politics shapes the welfare mix

The state is a political institution as well as a part of the welfare mix. Thus, political debate about what it ought to do influences its contribution to the welfare mix. Differences about political values within a country are far less than differences in values between states.

In the 1880s the idea of the social state was used by the German Chancellor Otto von Bismarck to describe the introduction of novel policies in which the state augmented an individual's reliance on the household and the market for their health and employment (Alber, 1982; Saez, 2022). The idea of a social state was an alternative to the liberal idea of a state that left individuals free to pursue their own interests. Bismarck's political goal was to secure working-class commitment to the undemocratic institutions of the Wilhelmine *Reich*. He assumed that a worker who had the promise of a secure income guaranteed by the state would be far more supportive of the existing regime than a worker without such security. The *Reich* did not collapse because of class conflict, as Marxists assumed would happen, but because of military defeat.

Welfare-state authoritarianism was a creation of the Soviet Union (Breslauer, 1978; Rose, 2009: 32 ff.). The communist party state gave priority to establishing an industrial economy; this required an education system that would produce skilled workers indoctrinated with communist values. The mobilization of women as well as men in the labour force was accompanied by the provision of childcare for women, especially in strategic industries. The legacy of the Soviet experiment continues to influence the welfare of people who had been subject to a communist system (cf. Chapters 5–7).

The idea of a social market combining economic efficiency and social justice was promoted by Christian Democratic parties in Europe after the Second World War as a justification of a welfare mix in which the state gave financial support to the health and educational institutions of the Catholic Church, as well as to state-owned and -managed institutions. With the decline in church attendance, these parties and their allies have altered their names. In 1999 the Christian Democrat International changed its name to the Centrist Democrat International; it has members on five continents and is the largest party in the European Parliament. The term 'social market' is frequently used in Germany by all mainstream parties (cf. Mau, 2004).

The use of technical expertise to decide the contribution of the state and the market to the welfare mix dismisses the importance of political values and political bargaining. Technocrats can write as if they were Plato's philosopher-kings, promulgating what ought to be the optimal allocation of the state's budget among welfare services. Free-market economists argue that the optimum is the state making the minimum contribution to the welfare mix. Social policy experts often prescribe that the state should pursue policies to equalize incomes in the belief that this will achieve the optimum of health and education in society. In making such recommendations, technocrats are practising the politics of the apolitical, excluding from consideration those who value forms of welfare differently from themselves and politicians who have an electoral mandate to decide the welfare policies of the state.

In democracies freedom of speech encourages debate about the role of government in the welfare mix. Whatever a democracy's resources, politicians can compete for votes by offering to spend more money on welfare programmes, by promising to cut taxes, or by claiming that they will do both, whether or not they can deliver on such a promise. In undemocratic regimes, autocrats do not need to worry about losing votes, but they are concerned with losing authority because of a failure to respond to the needs of their subjects for basic health, education, and employment.

While the values of those who control the government of the day may be immediately important, they are not all-important. The great majority of the public policies that contribute to the welfare mix today are not decided by the government of the day. They are the cumulative legacy of decisions taken by previous governors over a period of generations (Rose and Davies, 1994). In countries such as France, Germany, and Russia they are also the consequence of decisions taken by politicians in previous regimes.

2.4 Aspirations global but resources national

Globalization has spread the aspirations for welfare expressed in the founding documents of the United Nations. A lack of resources does not stop politicians from voicing aspirations. The constitution of the Republic of India proclaims that it is a socialist state committed to the state's promotion of welfare and justice. However, these notional rights are not enforceable by the courts, and the policies of successive Indian governments have not provided the resources to realize a high standard of welfare for all Indians. For a majority of Indians, the household remains the basic source of welfare, augmented by what the resources of the market and the policies of governments can provide.

There are multiple reasons why states have not caught up with global standards of welfare since aspirations began to go global more than half a century ago. The economic resources important for financing welfare services are very unequally distributed worldwide. According to the World Bank's classification of countries, just over one-third are high-income countries having a per capita income of $13,205 a year after adjustment for purchasing power parity (World Bank, 2023). There are big differences between countries within this category; the highest high-income countries generate about four times more income per person than the lowest high-income countries. High-income countries are expected not only to provide a high income for their own populations but also to provide money that the World Bank can use to make loans and grants to increase welfare in developing countries.

Among the hundred-plus developing countries that qualify for World Bank assistance because they are below the high-income threshold, there are income differences of more than ten to one. They are divided into three groups according to their gross national income per capita. In the twenty-eight countries and territories where per capita income is equivalent to less than $1,085 a year, the household is invariably the most important source of welfare. In lower-middle-income countries with per capita incomes of up to $4,096, many households can buy some basic health services in the market, and their children are likely to receive a free primary education. In upper-middle-income countries, households have more money to spend on treatment for ill health and to help their children. In addition, the state has more resources to provide welfare services that will help its population catch up with global standards of welfare sooner or later (see Section 10.1).

Whatever the resources of a country, there is competition for their use between government ministries responsible for the economy, the environment, national security, and welfare policies. Moreover, however much money is allocated to welfare, there is competition for funds between departments of health, education, and social security. Within a ministry responsible for education, there is competition between spending on preschool education, on special education for disadvantaged children, and on universities. States may also influence the welfare mix by enacting or repealing laws that give the state or individuals the final decision about such matters as abortion and same-sex marriage.

While almost all countries have made progress in welfare in the past three decades, there remain substantial differences in welfare between high-income and developing countries. For example, Mexico is an upper-middle-income country with a per capita income that has more than trebled in the past three decades. However, it is still less than half that of people in the average high-income country. Even though Mexico's public expenditure on education as a percentage of GDP is close to the OECD average, the actual amount spent on educating youths is less than half the OECD average. Nor can a big majority of Mexicans compensate for the state's low spending by paying for private education for their children, because they too lack the money to pay education fees (OECD, 2020a: 270, 284).

The formidable gap in income between continents does not translate into a similar gap in welfare. Even though the mean income of countries in sub-Saharan Africa is barely one-tenth that of the average highly developed country, the gap in different forms of welfare is much less. The life expectancy of African women is three-quarters that of the average highly developed country, and the percentage of literate adults is two-thirds that of the global standard. There is a difference of 8 percentage points in the proportion of females in employment, and female employment is higher in Africa than in highly developed countries.

In countries all over the globe, money is not the only resource that is lacking. If public employees responsible for delivering education, health, and other public services at the grass roots are corrupt, then citizens will be short-changed of welfare services. Wars between states and ethnic groups and competition for power between civil and military leaders can reduce the state's contribution to the welfare mix. Ten of the twelve most populous developing countries in the world have been involved in cross-border or internal wars since 1945, and the combination of corruption and civil strife devalues the state's contribution to the welfare mix.

References

Alber, Jens, 1982. *Vom Armenhaus zum Wohlfahrtsstaat: Analysen zur Entwicklung der Sozialversicherung in Westeuropa*. Frankfurt: Campus.

Besley, Timothy, 2007. *Principled Agents? The Political Economy of Good Government*. Oxford: Oxford University Press.

Beveridge, Lord, 1948. *Voluntary Action*. London: George Allen & Unwin.

Breslauer, George W., 1978. 'On the Adaptability of Soviet Welfare-State Authoritarianism'. In Karl W. Ryavec, ed., *Soviet Society and the Communist Party*. Amherst: University of Massachusetts Press, 3–25.

Dincecco, Mark, 2017. *State Capacity and Economic Development*. Cambridge: Cambridge University Press.

Flora, Peter, 1983. *State, Economy and Society in Western Europe 1815–1975*. Frankfurt: Campus.

Fong, Mei, 2015. *One Child: The Past and Future of China's Most Radical Experiment*. Boston: Houghton Mifflin Harcourt.

Fournastié, Jean-Paul, 1979. *Les Trente Glorieuses, ou la révolution invisible de 1946 à 1975*. Paris: Fayard.

Gershuny, Jonathan, and Sullivan, Oriel, 2019. *What We Really Do All Day*. London: Pelican Books.

Heidenheimer, Arnold, 1969. 'Trade Unions, Benefit Systems and Party Mobilization Styles', *Comparative Politics*, 1, 3, 313–42.

Hemerijck, Anton, and Huguenot-Noel, Robin, 2022. *Resilient Welfare States in the European Union*. Newcastle upon Tyne: Agenda Books.

Mau, Steffen, 2004. *The Moral Economy of Welfare States*. London: Routledge.

Mitchell, B. R., 1975. *European Historical Statistics 1750–1970*. London: Macmillan.

Niskanen, W. A., 1971. *Bureaucracy and Representative Government*. Chicago: Aldine-Atherton.

OECD, 2019. *Government at a Glance 2019*. Paris: OECD Publishing.

OECD, 2020a. *Education at a Glance 2020*. Paris: OECD Publishing.

OECD, 2020b. *Health at a Glance: Europe, 2020*. Paris: OECD Publishing.

Rose, Richard, 1976. 'On the Priorities of Government: A Developmental Analysis of Public Policies', *European Journal of Political Research*, 4, 3, 247–89.

Rose, Richard, 2009. *Understanding Post-Communist Transformation: A Bottom Up Approach*. London: Routledge.

Rose, Richard, and Davies, Phillip, 1994. *Inheritance in Public Policy: Change without Choice in Britain*. New Haven and London: Yale University Press.

Rose, Richard, and Peters, B. Guy, 1978. *Can Government Go Bankrupt?* New York: Basic Books, 1978.
Saez, Emmanuel, 2022. 'Understanding the Social State', Finance & Development (March 2022), 23–5.
Titmuss, Richard M., 1950. *Problems of Social Policy*. London: HMSO.
World Bank, 2023. 'Income countries grouped by income'. http://datatopics.worldbank.org/world-development-institute

3
Welfare about More than Money

Understanding welfare requires numbers. Without numbers we lack a sense of proportion about how much welfare there is in a society, whether there is progress, and how a country's national welfare compares with other societies. Equally, we need words and concepts to understand what numbers mean. Without words numbers are mute and without concepts they are meaningless. Social statistics provide quantitative evidence about the condition of people; economic statistics refer to activities that involve the production of goods and services. The term 'statistics' emphasizes the relevance of numerical data to the activities of the state. Sophisticated economists recognize this. Robert Lucas, who won a Nobel Prize for building economic models, told his University of Chicago students that economists are 'basically storytellers, creators of make-believe economic systems'.

Modern governments are dependent on statistics because governors are responsible for social welfare and economic activities on a scale that is far beyond the comprehension of personal observation. It is impossible for a Minister of Health to assess a nation's health by visiting every hospital or home. In the absence of statistical indicators, policymakers are reduced to basing policies on personal experience, anecdotes, or an ideology that confirms what they have already decided to do.

The statistics that we use as indicators of welfare are not timeless instruments given by nature; they are social constructs that represent what policymakers considered important at a particular moment in time. Babylonian emperors carried out headcounts of the population to estimate their need for food, and Egyptian pharaohs to identify the supply of labour for building pyramids. The Roman Empire used censuses of people and their property to identify people liable for taxation. Censuses in the modern sense began in Prussia in 1725; in the United Kingdom and United States at the start of the nineteenth century; and in India in 1882. Population censuses informed governors of the number of men who could be conscripted for military service. Statistics on birth and death gained importance in the nineteenth century as the need for public health policies increased with urbanization.

Late nineteenth-century social reformers such as Beatrice and Sidney Webb, co-founders of the London School of Economics, were pioneers in using statistics about social conditions as evidence to support their campaigns for policies to improve the welfare of the British people. The use of statistics for international public policy began in the nineteenth century to stop merchant ships from spreading contagious diseases as they sailed from country to country (Cooper, 1989: 237). Even though statistics have been separately compiled about male and female labour force participation for a century or more, only in recent years has data on gender equality in employment become a political issue.

While governments collected data on specific forms of economic activity such as imports as part of the process of taxation, a system of national accounts that covered the whole of a country's economic activity only began to develop in the 1930s. When the British government rather than the market controlled the allocation of goods and services in the Second World War, national accounts were necessary to identify the total resources and needs of a society at war. The United States published the first system of national accounts in 1947, and the United Nations its first proposals for internationally comparable national accounts in 1952. National accounts provide data that can be used to test economic theories and hypotheses.

Many parts of national accounts referred to the production and consumption of physical goods and services rather than to people. Theories of public finance and welfare economics combine an interest in money and in people; which is given priority depends on political values. Keynesian economists tend to emphasize the full employment of people, whereas followers of Milton Friedman give priority to the supply of money.

The globalization of finance has given increased importance to money as national governments have become dependent on borrowing money from abroad, sometimes in foreign currencies, and to the foreign exchange value of their national currency. Cross-nationally comparable economic statistics are important for the activities of the International Monetary Fund, the European Central Bank, and international bankers and currency traders. The World Bank and government agencies giving aid to developing countries use national accounts to monitor and evaluate the economies of recipient countries. Social statistics primarily feed into a national government's health, education, and employment ministries; they are also referenced in political debates about the welfare of a country's population.

Because of the political relevance of statistics, their collection can face political resistance. The introduction of censuses in many colonies was initially resisted because of a belief that the information would be used to increase social controls. In multi-ethnic Nigeria the census has been described as a weapon that politicians use to maximize their power by inflating the number of people who live in their region (Bamgbose, 2009; Fawehinmi, 2018). Policymakers may choose to ignore inconvenient statistical evidence. After the collapse of the Soviet Union the director of the International Monetary Fund, Michel Camdessus (IMF, 1994: 97), justified IMF aid to Russia on 'very strong personal assurances' from the Russian Prime Minister and from religious leaders who 'expressed their confidence that Russia's traditional spiritual values would enable the Russian people not only to cope with the difficulties of the transition process but also to make it more human'.

In response to the theoretical development and policymaking applications of national accounts, in the 1960s a group of American social scientists started a movement to develop a parallel system of accounts focused on the social conditions of people. It was very relevant to Lyndon Johnson's Great Society programme, and in 1969 the Department of Health, Education and Welfare published a pioneering report on social indicators (HEW, 1969). The American initiative was quickly followed by European governments (Rose, 1989; Land and Michalos, 2018). The OECD now publishes a set of social indicators, and the World Bank (2021) has produced *Data for Better Lives*, a guide showing developing countries how to use social as well as economic statistics to improve their national welfare.

This chapter explains why progress in global welfare should be measured with social indicators rather than economic indicators. The next section explains how economic statistics influence public expenditure and the evaluation of the costs and benefits of welfare policies. It is followed by a description of soft spots in official economic statistics. Unofficial shadow economies omitted from official statistics are particularly important in developing countries, and unpaid work in the household is important in every society. Multiple social indicators directly measure individual welfare in ways that are comparable across time and across national boundaries.

3.1 Money as an input to the welfare mix

A late Victorian founding father of economics, Alfred Marshall, described money as the measuring rod of economic science. While economic theory may be written in calculus, when its concepts are applied to public policies the basic unit is money. Economic indicators are considered hard data because they are expressed in precise numerical terms and money is fungible; it can be used for anything from paying schoolteachers to buying military aircraft. While most people cannot comprehend the billions spent by government, they do know what the money they earn will or will not buy.

The official economy

The system of Standard National Accounts that is used to produce such familiar statistics as the gross domestic product gains authority because it is official, that is, produced by national governments. Businesses that have registered offices, factories, and hundreds or thousands of employees are required to report their activities to government periodically. The activities of public sector institutions are also a significant part of most economies, and customs officials monitor trade with other countries. Because these activities are known to the government, they are readily accessible as sources of tax revenue.

Statistics about economic growth show whether a country is fulfilling promises made by politicians to promote prosperity and whether a developing country is making enough progress to catch up with countries that are materially better off. An economic recession is defined as two successive quarterly periods in which the gross domestic product contracts instead of growing. National accounts are used to make forecasts about the likely trajectory of the economy in the months and years ahead. These forecasts are relevant not only to business investors but also to politicians concerned about their electoral future. Forecasts carry a qualification in fine print—all other conditions remaining equal.

Economic indicators of growth, unemployment, and inflation make headline news. If the news is good, governors will want to claim credit whether or not their actions are the cause of good news. If the news is bad, opposition politicians will use economic indicators as a stick with which to beat the government of the day. Economic statistics are often treated as indicators of welfare too. Policymakers who would not describe themselves as Marxists sometimes talk like economic determinists. President Bill Clinton's election campaign manager, James Carville, identified the key issue as 'It's the economy, stupid'. This encourages the simple hypothesis: more economic growth produces more welfare.

Although economic indicators are policy-relevant, they are not prescriptive; that is, they do not tell politicians what to do. When statistics show that unemployment is rising, there are demands to 'do something'. More than one policy response is possible and can be justified by economic theory, because there is a two-party system in economics. A group of economists associated with the University of Chicago favour free-market policies, while a transatlantic Cambridge–Harvard–MIT network favour government management of the economy. The international eminence of these economics departments attracts students from around the world, thus giving their theories a global reach. Yet before an economy can run on a course set by economy theory, politicians must choose between their competing prescriptions.

Public expenditure as an input to welfare

The government's budget links public expenditure to policy handles, that is, measures that a government can turn one way or another in order to steer the economy in the direction that it prefers. They are more immediately useful to policymakers than social indicators that government can do little about, such as birth rates. There is no assurance that revenue will be directed to social policies. For example, although Pakistan has a gross domestic product per capita that ranks in the bottom quarter globally, the share of its GDP that the government spends on military defence places it among the top 10 per cent of the world's countries.

Public expenditure allocated to such social services as health and education is an input to the welfare mix; it is not an output. The money spent on building hospitals directly benefits the enterprises constructing them. Likewise, the wages and salaries paid to doctors and nurses buy the services of people who treat patients with health problems, but do not buy health per se. Whether the efforts of health workers are effective in restoring health depends less on what they are paid than on what the patient's problem is. A 2 per cent rise in public expenditure on health is not the same as a 2 per cent increase in the health of a national population.

Valuing welfare

Welfare economics uses microeconomic techniques to calculate a social welfare function that shows how government should allocate public expenditure in order to maximize utility. Utility is an abstraction; it does not refer to anything in particular. To evaluate welfare policies in terms of utility risks the production of 'a stream of logical deductions that are not about anything at all' (Little, 1963: 81 f.).

Cost–benefit analysis can be used to evaluate a specific policy by comparing the money it costs with the estimated cash value of its benefits. If the sum of economic benefits is greater than the costs, the policy is worthwhile, but if the costs are greater than the benefits, the assessment is negative. The analysis can also be used to compare competing policies: it favours the policy with the greater net monetary benefit. However, while the costs of spending on education and health can be directly verified, many inputs to education and health, such as reading or exercising, are not bought but undertaken in free time.

Economists estimate costs and benefits of goods and services that are not bought and sold in the marketplace by creating shadow prices. In theory a shadow price is what individuals would be prepared to pay for a public service; it is not what they are willing to pay in taxes needed to pay for these services. Furthermore, the relation of costs and benefits is not stable. The benefit of a restaurant meal is likely to differ depending on whether it is eaten alone or with friends or family.

In a cost–benefit evaluation of a university education, direct money costs including tuition, the purchase of books, food, and lodging can be set against the shadow benefit of gaining new social experiences and independence from the family. The long-term individual benefit is conventionally estimated as the additional income that a graduate gains compared to a non-graduate over a period of four decades or longer, less the net cost of earnings foregone by a youth when attending university rather than being employed. The cash benefit of a state university education to government includes the tuition that students pay and the tax revenue generated by student and faculty expenditure. This must be set against the direct cost of government payments to a university to bridge the gap between the total cost of the institution and a student's tuition. The long-term shadow benefit to government is the increased tax revenue generated from graduates' higher earnings and from the boost to the country's gross domestic product that graduates are assumed to give. The procedure can give students and policymakers a cash estimate of the net cost or benefit of studying for a degree. However, the gain or loss is not real money.

A trade-off cannot be made between costs and benefits when absolute values are involved. For example, if the right to life is regarded as absolute, then the state cannot execute a serial killer in order to save the cost of keeping the killer in prison for decades. Government decisions about dealing with the coronavirus pandemic involved cost–benefit analysis between two competing values of protecting lives and protecting the economy. Saving lives involves restrictions that reduce economic activity, while protecting the economy from recession increases social contacts that spread a sometimes fatal virus. The benefits of saving lives are priceless to the households benefiting, while the cost of doing so is felt by government in reduced tax revenue and by businesses in reduced profits. An independent review of British government COVID-19 decisions associated with many deaths and with the quick discovery and dissemination of an effective vaccine concluded:

> This picture is very different from what our national accounts will show, where the vaccine will scarcely feature. That is entirely consistent with the idea that national accounts and GDP tell us about our economic product but not about our wellbeing. (Weale, 2021)

3.2 Soft spots in hard numbers

Constructing official statistics

Nothing could appear harder than a country's gross domestic product, yet the figures routinely produced are not hard in the tangible sense. Key economic indicators such as GDP are constructed by combining a large number of variables about national economic activity. The calculation of GDP is not as simple as adding up purchases at the checkout counter of a supermarket. It combines verifiable data and estimates from disparate sources with different degrees of reliability and validity. GDP's sources include the enterprises that deduct taxes and social security contributions for payment to the government; the manufacturers of hard goods such as bricks; management consultants offering soft services; and artificial constructs such as the notional basket of goods used to estimate inflation.

The calculation of gross domestic product is a process. The first published estimate of GDP is widely used in decision-making by the government, financial institutions, and foreign exchange markets. Since it is calculated on the basis of data available at the time of publication, it is subsequently revised as fuller and more accurate data becomes available over the following year or two. Detailed analysis of the revision of the United Kingdom's GDP over more than a decade finds that there is no consistent bias in the direction of error. Revisions sometimes lead to an increase in GDP and sometimes to a decrease in GDP. The size of the correction fluctuates within a range of 1 per cent, a small proportion but in absolute terms an error margin of up to £25 billion

(Robinson, 2016). There are similar margins of error in the initial GDP figures that American and German policymakers use. Leading economists warn, 'If our measurements are flawed, decisions may be distorted' (Stiglitz, Sen, and Fitoussi, 2010: 7).

Annual publications of economic statistics contain many official warnings about soft spots in official data. Footnotes and appendices qualify the accuracy and reliability of what is published. To arrive at a figure for the UK's gross domestic product, statisticians estimate it in three different ways. Since all three approaches are considered theoretically equal, the headline figure of GDP is an average of the three approaches. Such is the misinterpretation of GDP that the UK Office of National Statistics (2020: ch. 3) cautions:

> GDP can often be described as a measure of wealth, welfare, or wellbeing. It is none of these and has not been designed to be an all-encompassing indicator for these concepts. GDP is a measure of economic activity and, whilst there may be a link between this and wealth and welfare, such a link is complex.

While inflation can be directly experienced by every shopper, the official measure of inflation on which policymakers rely is an abstract concept. To avoid annual political debates about how much pensions and other benefits should be raised or what interest rate must be paid on government bonds, changes in spending can be linked to changes in an index of inflation. The value of any adjustment depends on the index that is chosen. Official indexes are based on annual changes in the price of each item in a notional basket of goods. When the French government wanted to keep its inflation index down years ago, it kept the price of candles in the basket rather than do what French households did, use electricity.

There are more than a dozen price indexes in the United Kingdom (Economic Affairs Committee, 2019). Chief among the 700 items in the retail price index are spending on housing, food, and automobile transport. New items are added annually, such as spending on electric cars. The consumer price index was subsequently introduced for calculating increases in welfare payments, with the claim that it would put the whole welfare system on a more sustainable and affordable footing. It did this by changing the formula for calculating inflation by reducing the importance of housing costs. This produced an estimate of annual inflation about 1 per cent below the retail price index, cutting the increase in social security payments by more than £2 billion annually.

Inflation increases the nominal value of the goods and services that constitute the annual calculation of gross domestic product. It is thus necessary to control for its effect when examining economic growth. Otherwise, the economy of a country with a high inflation rate could appear to be growing by 10 to 50 per cent annually. This can readily be done by applying one or another inflation index so that each year's GDP is stated in terms of the value of money at the starting point of the evaluation of growth over time. Inflation-adjusted trend figures are often referred to as measures of real income, even though they are the product of an artificial construct that depends on the choice of an inflation index as well as on the actual production and exchange of goods and services.

Statistical capacity

Official statistics are not facts given by nature but data aggregated by national statistical agencies from a variety of governmental and non-governmental sources. To construct measures of the official economy requires agencies that are part of a government with the effective authority to collect financial data from households and businesses. It also requires a substantial staff with the technical skills to turn the data collected into a set of Standard National Accounts that meet high international standards. Furthermore, the globalization of the economy and of the use of economic statistics is putting pressure on statistical agencies in developing countries to catch up with rising international standards (World Bank, 2021).

The World Bank continuously engages with more than 140 developing countries. It uses their statistics to identify the economic and social needs of a country and the extent to which World Bank-funded projects meet or fail to meet their objectives. Because of this reliance, the World Bank has created a Statistical Capacity Indicator of a government's ability to collect economic and social data (http://www.worldbank.org/en/data/statistical-capacity-building). The Statistical Capacity Indicator combines twenty-five different indicators. The ten indicators of Methodology focus on whether the procedures used to construct national accounts follow international rules. The Sources of Data indicators focus on censuses of the population, agriculture, poverty, and the registration of births and deaths. Measures of Timeliness are indicators especially relevant to the Millennium Development Goals of the United Nations.

A substantial majority of national statistical agencies are given favourable evaluations by the 2020 Statistical Capacity Index (http://bbs.worldbank.org; cf. Jerven, 2014). The median countries—Côte d'Ivoire, Ecuador, and Bolivia—had scores of 70 on a 0 to 100 scale. The highest-ranking Latin American country was Mexico, with a score of 93. The Statistical Capacity of

India, with a history of data collection going back to late nineteenth-century British rule, was 91. The sixteen countries with a Statistical Capacity rated below 50 were a mixture of countries that have a very small population, are very low in development, or have been disrupted by internal armed conflict. The capacity of Libya was the lowest, with a score of 29, and Somalia was a close second.

For professional economists, the crucial concern is not the capacity of national statistical agencies in low-income countries to provide high-quality data, but whether the data fits the theoretical system of Standard National Accounts. However, gains in theory have their limitations: 'formal elegance by itself is not enough to extend the accounts into a wider welfare sphere' (Horn, 2008: 71).

Constructing a global currency

In the absence of a global central bank issuing a global currency, cross-national comparisons of currency need a common unit of account to control for some currencies being 'heavier' than others: that is, the currency used to buy an iPad in New York City has fewer zeros than the currency used to purchase the same object in Rio de Janeiro or Beijing. Transactions in foreign currencies show buyers that the purchasing power of their national currency is not the same in other countries as it is at home. The foreign exchange market for currencies continuously measures the value of currencies such as the dollar and the euro. *The Economist*'s Big Mac currency index shows that a standard McDonald's hamburger costs two-fifths more in Switzerland than in the United States, while costing two-fifths less in South Africa.

To make comparisons between national economies, gross domestic product statistics must be converted into a common currency and per capita GDP calculated to control for very substantial population differences between countries. The currency most in use internationally is the United States dollar. A fundamental flaw in converting dozens of national currencies into dollars is that the conversion rate only reflects fluctuating values in foreign exchange markets without regard to differences between countries in the cost of living. In a world of fixed exchange rates, this would be of limited consequence. However, exchange rates are no longer fixed: the value of the dollar in relation to other currencies floats up and down daily as it is speculatively traded in foreign exchange markets around the clock around the globe.

To control for differences in the cost of living, the OECD has created an index of purchasing power parity (PPP) to take into account cross-national differences in the cost of the same basket of goods in different currencies. The use of a basket of goods is logical but does not take into account differences in consumer tastes between countries in matters such as food, and differences in needs such as spending more on heat in Northern European countries than in Africa. Moreover, major cross-national differences in the government provision of such welfare services as health care affect the amount of money that people need to spend in order to look after their welfare.

Since the cost of living tends to be lower in less developed countries, an income that appears low by American or European standards buys a lot more if spent in the markets of a low-income country, and vice versa. In purchasing power parity terms, Swiss per capita income drops by almost one-quarter compared to the United States and that of Japan drops by one-third. Purchasing power per capita GDP rises by almost a quarter in Portugal, and in Mexico the domestic purchasing power of the peso can be two and a half times greater than its international exchange rate value.

On the assumption that income is the primary determinant of an individual's welfare, poverty is often cited as a measure of illfare. However, there is no agreed measure of poverty. The World Bank (2020) defines poverty as lacking an income from the official economy sufficient to purchase a given basket of goods and services. However, this approach ignores the extent to which people with low incomes or living in low-income countries earn money in the unofficial shadow economy or can produce a significant portion of what they need within their own household.

An alternative approach is to define poverty in relative terms. The relative approach assumes that the higher the standard of living in a country, the more money an individual needs in order to avoid being considered poor (Jolliffee and Prydz, 2017). Relative poverty can be defined as 40, 50, or 60 per cent of the average income in a society; official definitions differ between national governments and between intergovernmental organizations. Measures of relative poverty can show poverty rates in high-income countries that are double or almost treble absolute measures of poverty. Moreover, measures of relative poverty in Northern Europe can represent a lifestyle that can be considered satisfactory or even luxurious in many developing countries.

3.3 Unofficial economies add to the welfare mix

The official statistics on which policymakers and investors rely have multiple strengths: they are quantitative, expressed in money terms, and have the imprimatur of the state and of economic science. However, official statistics also have limitations: they leave out two economies that provide resources supporting individual welfare in many parts of the world. In the shadow economy, money changes hands in the marketplace without being recorded in national accounts. In the household economy, the value of the work done by family members cannot appear in the national accounts because it is unpaid.

The significance of differences in official, shadow, and household economies varies over time. Economic activity was happening for thousands of years on every continent before government began compiling official economic statistics. Thus, economic historians must make up estimates of the condition of the national economy by relying on the available numerical evidence, by estimating activities for which there is no written evidence or from a combination of both approaches. As a basic rule, the further back in time one goes, the less adequate are written records for tracking cash-in-hand transactions and the production of goods and services within the household.

The significance of unofficial economies varies over space too. Economic activity in which money changes hands in the marketplace without any official record is much more important in countries with governments that are administratively weak, a condition more often found in developing countries than in high-income countries. Unpaid household work is significant in the daily lives of people everywhere, while varying in the extent to which it is a primary source of the necessities of life or complemented by earnings from employment in the official economy.

The shadow economy

In poorer countries of the world, the shadow economy is the real economy, because it is where people earn cash in order to buy what they cannot produce within their own household. Money is important in the shadow economy but because people are paid cash in hand rather than by bank transfer, their earnings are off the books. This keeps such earnings out of the hands of tax authorities and out of official economic statistics.

Shadow economy activity is labour-intensive (OECD, 2017: ch. 1). The sale of goods in street markets is conducted cash in hand rather than electronically, and buyers in street markets and small shops in developing countries are much more likely to have cash in their pockets than a credit card. Construction workers can be paid in cash by bosses who prefer to do this rather than file paperwork and pay employment tax for their workers. Plumbers and electricians can combine work in the official economy with after-hours work for cash in hand whatever the level of the economy. Shadow economy activity is not capital-intensive. Practitioners of traditional medicine do not need hospital equipment; by contrast, a surgeon needs hospital facilities that are capital-intensive and visible to the tax authorities.

The variety of methods used to estimate shadow economy activity produce similar findings; they show that its importance tends to be much higher in developing than in developed countries (Medina and Schneider, 2018). In sub-Saharan Africa and Latin America in the 1990s the shadow economy increased the money value of what was produced in the official economy by more than two-fifths. Moreover, it was twice as large in national significance as the shadow economy of OECD countries (Figure 3.1). By 2015 the shadow economy of these developing countries had grown less than their official economy; nonetheless, it added more than one-third to the money value of the official economy on average. The shadow economy is much less important in OECD countries that have become highly developed by relying on capital-intensive activities and services produced by large enterprises. In the 1990s the shadow economy added almost one-fifth to the official gross domestic product of highly developed countries; by 2015 it added less than one-sixth to the measure of the official economy.

Shadow economy size compared to official GDP

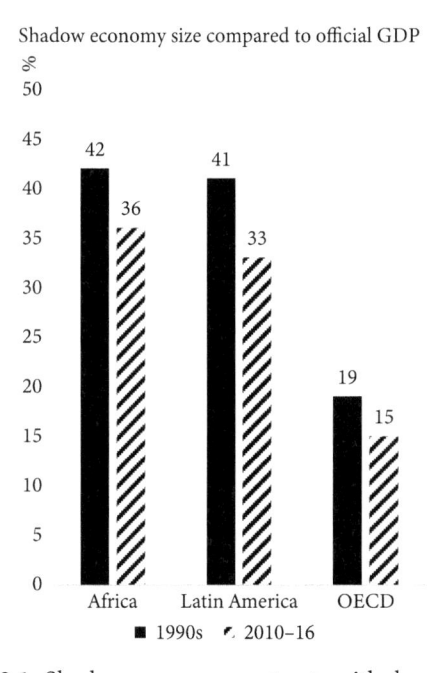

Region	1990s	2010–16
Africa	42	36
Latin America	41	33
OECD	19	15

Figure 3.1 Shadow economy contracts with development
Source: IMF Working Paper by Medina and Schneider, 2018.

The effect of the shadow economy on welfare tends to be greatest in less developed countries where skilled doctors and good schools are hard to come by. People feeling ill may rely on traditional remedies bought in the marketplace. Parents of children going to overcrowded schools may use cash-in-hand earnings to buy second-hand books and to pay teachers for private tuition. In a highly developed economy, the shadow economy is less relevant to welfare services. Employment in the official economy provides not only a regular wage but also welfare benefits through taxation and state-mandated social security contributions.

Unpaid work

The term 'economy' is derived from the Greek word for the management of the household, including activities essential for the welfare of its members. The word 'occupation' initially referred to the main activity that occupied a person's time, whether it was being a housewife, a peasant, or an accountant. Similarly, the original meaning of 'work' is an activity intended to produce a particular result, whether it is a meal, a good examination score, or an automobile.

Work is an economic activity even if it is unpaid, as long as whatever is produced could in principle be sold. For example, caring for an ill person is work whether it is done by another family member or by a nurse employed in a hospital. Whereas physical exercise to take care of one's health involves effort, it is not work in the economic sense, since a person cannot sell their exercise to another person. If taking exercise involves paying a trainer, the trainer is a worker but the person paying for a physical workout is not.

The value of unpaid work can be multiplied when it directly benefits more than one person. This is particularly the case when welfare benefits are provided by unpaid family members for others in their household. A parent looking after a preschool child is not only contributing to the child's preschool education, a job that could be done by an employee of a childcare firm, but also giving affection to their child and receiving it in return (Stanford Children's Health, 2021).

Because work can be measured in units of time, there is no need to decide an hourly rate of pay when comparisons are made. Insofar as unpaid work does not require much more equipment than knitting needles, a stove, or a lawnmower, there is little capital cost involved and the resources needed may be produced without money—for example, collecting firewood from a nearby

Table 3.1 Paid and unpaid work

	Paid Work	Unpaid Work	Total
(Average minutes per week)			
Mexico	302	265	567
China	315	159	474
India	272	190	462
United States	251	196	447
United Kingdom	235	198	433

(Unpaid work includes housework, looking after other family members, and home maintenance).
Source: Time-use budgets of Centre for Time Use Research (CTUR, 2021).

forest. Social scientists study how individuals use their time by asking a sample of individuals to keep a twenty-four-hours-a-day record of what they do during a week or longer. Researchers create time budgets showing the time devoted to sixteen activities ranging from sleeping to paid employment (CTUR, 2021). Statistical accounts of unpaid work are comparable across national boundaries because, unlike money, hours are constant units of measurement.

Sleep takes up the largest portion of an individual's time; on average it claims more than eight hours a day. Even if it is regarded as an investment of time to maintain energy and health, sleep is not an economic activity because one cannot sell or exchange one's sleep to another person. Paid work is second in importance, but takes up much less time since it is not a seven-days-a-week activity, nor does everyone in society work for money (CTUR, 2021). Paid work is more important than unpaid work but the difference is a matter of degree, not kind (Table 3.1). Unpaid work accounts for more than two-fifths of working time in the United States and the United Kingdom, as well as in Mexico and India. Mexicans are high in both unpaid and paid work because the economy is sufficiently developed to support regular employment at low wages complemented by a lot of unpaid work.

Time-use diaries identify many types of unpaid work that in principle could be provided by paid workers. Within every household many meals are produced without hiring domestic servants to cook and serve them. Much daily household maintenance is done by its members, and simple do-it-yourself repairs too. In households with children, mothers and to a lesser extent fathers give hours daily to childcare; in highly developed countries the employment of a nanny to look after children is very limited because of its cost. In households with older people with infirmities of age members of the family can provide care; the cash value of this becomes evident only when family members cannot provide care and it must be paid for by the financial resources of the infirm person and/or by publicly funded carers.

Countries become more developed through growth in the official economy, because capital-intensive production in the official economy can result in more goods and services than the great bulk of labour-intensive unpaid work. Nonetheless, the contribution of unpaid work to the national economy remains significant in highly developed economies. In 1975 unpaid work was valued as adding 24 per cent to the GDP of the United Kingdom. In the decades since, the official economy has grown substantially. Nonetheless, unpaid work is still estimated to add up to 24 per cent to the value of the UK's gross domestic product (Gershuny and Sullivan, 2019: fig. 6.2).

3.4 What social indicators add

Social indicators make people count because they are direct measures of individual health, education, and other conditions influenced by the welfare mix. By contrast, official statistics about the national economy are *asocial*; they are not about people but about the production and consumption of all kinds of goods and services. Statistics about health, education, and employment refer to objective phenomena rather than the subjective feelings of individuals as happiness indicators do. This does not mean that social indicators are mere facts; they are meaningful because they are signs of welfare or illfare within society. In the words of the innovative American government paper, *Toward a Social Report* (HEW, 1969):

> A social indicator may be defined as a statistic of direct normative interest which facilitates concise, comprehensive and balanced judgments about the conditions of major aspects of a society. It is in all cases a direct measure of welfare.

Social indicators turn attention from examining the inputs of the welfare mix to the condition of the people who are meant to benefit from those inputs. A change in perspective can produce a strikingly different conclusion. For example, the United States spends more than twice as large a share of its national product on health services than the average European country. However, the actual health of Americans is not up to the standard of Europeans. The life expectancy of women in the United States is lower than that of two dozen

European countries, and infant mortality is higher than in any European country except Bulgaria and Romania (see Chapter 5).

Social indicators show that the globalization of welfare is much more advanced than the globalization of national incomes. After controlling for differences in purchasing power, the gross domestic product per capita in China and Latin America is little more than one-third that of the average developed country. The GDP of India and the average African country is barely one-sixth that of developed countries. By contrast, cross-national differences in basic welfare measures such as adult literacy tend to be marginal (Figure 3.2). The proportion of literacy among Chinese adults is only 2 percentage points lower than that in highly developed countries. Even where adult literacy is lowest, majorities of Indians and African adults are literate.

While the cross-continental gap in gross domestic product has been widening in the past three decades, countries on all developing continents have been

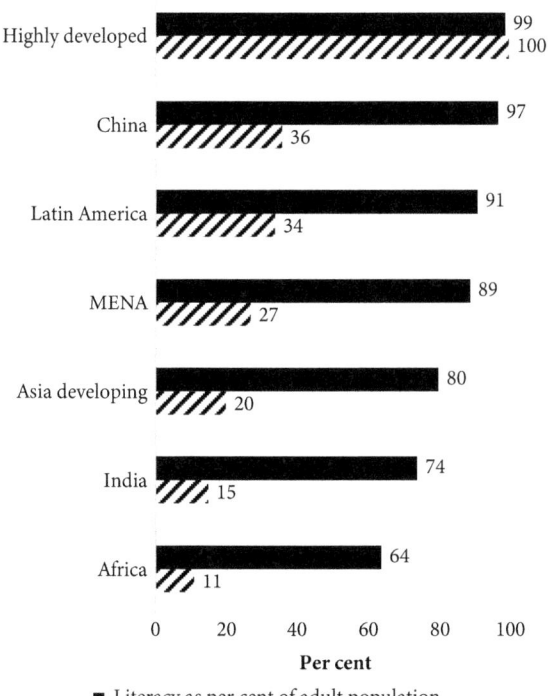

Region	Literacy (%)	GDP (%)
Highly developed	99	100
China	97	36
Latin America	91	34
MENA	89	27
Asia developing	80	20
India	74	15
Africa	64	11

■ Literacy as per cent of adult population
▨ GDP: Per cent of GDP per capita in highly developed countries

Figure 3.2 Gross domestic product and literacy contrasted
Source: Global Welfare Database.

reducing their distance from global leaders in welfare. The distance in adult literacy has been reduced by 16 percentage points in the average African country and 26 per cent in India. By contrast, the already large gaps in the purchasing power GDP of highly developed and Latin American countries has widened to more than $8,000, and the gap with the average African country has grown to more than $14,000.

Welfare indicators

This book reflects the pluralism of social indicators by examining multiple measures of welfare in three different domains—health, education, and employment. For a century or more, national governments have collected data about a variety of social indicators on birth, death, education, and other social conditions. Each indicator can be quantified without any need to give it a notional money value. Social indicators that reveal negative conditions, such as an increase in the percentage of youths dropping out of compulsory education, reveal faults in welfare policies.

Social indicators can be compared across national boundaries without the problems that bedevil economic comparisons when foreign exchange values of national currencies are misleading and purchasing power parities problematic. Eschewing money values also facilitates direct comparison between social conditions in different economic systems, such as market economies, poor countries where much activity does not involve money, and a Soviet-style non-market economy with a low 'moneyness' of money (Grossman, 1977). Because social indicators are not denominated in money, there is also no need to worry about controlling for the effects of inflation on a notional basket of goods constructed three decades earlier.

The total welfare of a national population cannot be summarized in a single social indicator because direct measures of individual welfare are incommensurable; that is, they have different metrics. Life expectancy is measured in years; infant mortality in the number of deaths per thousand; and education by different types of educational qualifications. By contrast, the United Nations Human Development Index is a minestrone soup. It is constructed by converting health, education, and income indicators into standardized scores using the same measurement, thereby making them commensurable. The standardized scores are then added together to produce an Index number ranging from 0 to 100. While a country's singular number can give it a ranking in a league table, the Index itself provides no meaningful information about the particular conditions of health, education, and income that go into producing it.

Most social indicators refer to conditions that change slowly from year to year. A youth must spend a decade or more in school to obtain an educational qualification; thus, it can take up to two decades for a new educational policy for preschool children to register an effect in the number of university graduates. Since an individual's age at death reflects an accumulation of influences from the time of their birth, national figures for life expectancy tend to change by only a few months from one year to the next.

Social indicators cannot prescribe what individuals or governments ought to do. However, by calling attention to social conditions nationally and internationally, social indicators can and do stimulate debates about the performance of government policies and the need for change. Controversy shows that social indicators meet a more robust test than statistical significance: they are politically significant.

References

Bamgbose, J. Adele, 2009. 'Falsification of Population Census Data in a Heterogeneous Nigerian State', *African Journal of Political Science and International Relations*, 3, 8, 311–19.

Camdessus, Michel, 1994. 'Camdessus Expresses Confidence in Russian Economic Reform', IMF Survey (4 April 1994), 97–8.

Cooper, Richard N., 1989. 'International Cooperation in Public Health as a Prologue to Macroeconomic Cooperation'. In R. N. Cooper et al. (ed.), *Can Nations Agree?* Washington DC: Brookings Institution, 178–254.

CTUR (Centre for Time Use Research), 2021. http://www.timeuse.org. London: University College.

Economic Affairs Committee, 2019. 'Measuring Inflation'. London: House of Lords Fifth Report of Session 2017–19 HL paper 246.

Fawehinmi, Feyi, 2018. 'The Story of How Nigeria's Census Figures Became Weaponized'. https://qz.com/africa/1221472/the-story-of-hownigerias-census-figures-became-weaponized/ (accessed 26 March 2020).

Gershuny, Jonathan, and Sullivan, Oriel, 2019. *What We Really Do All Day*. London: Pelican.

Grossman, Gregory, 1977. 'The Second Economy of the USSR', *Problems of Communism*, 26,5, 23–40.

HEW (Health, Education and Welfare), 1969. *Toward a Social Report*. Washington, DC: Department of Health, Education and Welfare, Government Printing Office.

Horn, Robert V., 2008. *Statistical Indicators for the Economic & Social Sciences.* Cambridge: Cambridge University Press, 2nd edition.

Jerven, Morten, 2014. *Poor Numbers: How We Are Misled by African Development Statistics and What to Do about It.* Ithaca: Cornell University Press.

Jolliffee, Dean, and Prydz, Espen Beer, 2017. *Societal Poverty: A Relative and Relevant Measure.* Washington DC: World Bank Policy Research Working Paper 8073.

Land, K. C., and Michalos, A. C., 2018. 'Fifty Years after the Social Indicators Movement: Has the Promise Been Fulfilled?' *Social Indicators Research*, 135, 835–68.

Little, I. M. D., 1963. *A Critique of Welfare Economics.* Oxford: Clarendon Press.

Medina, Leandro, and Schneider, Friedrich, 2018. *Shadow Economies around the World.* Washington, DC: International Monetary Fund Working Paper 18/17.

OECD (Organization for Economic Cooperation and Development), 2017. *Shining Light on the Shadow Economies.* Paris: OECD.

Office of National Statistics, 2020. 'A Guide to the UK National Accounts'. https://www.ons.gov.uk/economy/nationalaccounts/uksectoraccounts/methodologies/aguidetotheuknationalaccounts.

Robinson, Lee, 2016. 'Rewriting History: Understanding Revisions to UK GDP'. *Bank Underground.* https://bankunderground.co.uk/?s=Rewriting+History%3A+Understanding+Revisions+to+UK+GDP.

Rose, Richard, 1989. 'Whatever Happened to Social Indicators? A Symposium'. *Journal of Public Policy*, 9, 4.

Stanford Children's Health, 2021. 'Why the Family Meal is Important'. Stanford, CA: Lucile Packard Children's Hospital, http://www.stanfordchildrens.org/en/topic/default?id=why-the-family-meal-isimportant-1-701 (accessed 4 April 2022).

Stiglitz, Joseph E., Sen, Amartya, and Fitoussi, Jean-Paul, 2010. *Mismeasuring Our Lives: Why GDP Doesn't Add Up.* New York: New Press.

Weale, Martin, 2021. 'How Much Are the Covid-19 Jabs Actually Worth to Us All?' Financial Times, 26 March 2021.

World Bank, 2020. *Poverty and Shared Prosperity 2020: Reversals of Fortune.* Washington, DC: World Bank.

World Bank, 2021. *Data for Better Lives.* Washington, DC: World Bank World Development Report.

4
The Development of Welfare

The globalization of welfare is a long-term process of change in society. There are big cross-national differences in the degree to which changes have enabled societies to reach global standards of health, education, and employment. To explain these differences as having a single cause—differences in national development—raises the question: What is meant by the abstract term 'development'? (cf. Baland et al., 2020.)

The concept of development gained its current significance after the Second World War. European nations did not want to restore their pre-war economies and political institutions but wanted to develop their economies and institutions and attain a much higher level of welfare. This process was boosted by economic aid from the Marshall Plan, followed by the formation of the Organization for Economic Cooperation and Development (OECD) in 1961. In parallel, the World Bank was created to promote economic development in the majority of the world's countries, which were far from the level of OECD countries.

The focus on a lack of economic resources has resulted in development often referring narrowly to economic development. Policies concentrated on investment in infrastructure that directly and visibly could contribute economic growth, such as electricity-generating plants and roads. These activities were designed by engineers, evaluated by economists, and built with equipment financed by foreign aid. The focus on economic development encouraged the use of a single macroeconomic indicator, a country's officially measured gross domestic product, as evidence of development. However, this is an incomplete indicator of a society's economic activity and even less suited as a measure of social welfare (see Figure 1.1). While admitting that national income is not a direct measure of welfare, a World Bank (2021) publication asserts, 'It has proved to be a useful and easily available indicator that is closely correlated with other non-monetary measures of the quality of life'. However, correlation with welfare is not causation.

This study of welfare provides an alternative measure of the development of a society: the health, education, and employment status of people in a society. From a social perspective, the institutions needed to produce welfare—schools, clinics, and fair employment practices—are different in kind from the dams and airports that aid economic development. All three institutions that constitute the welfare mix—the household, the market and the state—are involved in the process of changing lives that results in economic development (see Figure 1.1).

Theories that use an economic indicator to represent a country's development assume that a country low in national income will be similarly low in urbanization and freedom and high in corruption. Insofar as this is the case, it would be sufficient to rely on gross domestic product per capita to explain cross-national differences in health, education, and welfare. However, an alternative theory takes into account the fact that countries below global standards of welfare can and do differ in their level of resources; they may be very high in urbanization but low in gross domestic product, as is India, or they may have a relatively high GDP but not a high level of freedom, as is the case for China. Theories of unbalanced growth suggest that in such cases a country may use its strongest resource, whatever it may be, to break out of an equilibrium that maintains a low level of welfare and begin to make progress toward increased welfare (Hirschman, 1958; Cramer, Sender, and Oqubay, 2020: ch. 6).

However defined, development presents a chicken-and-egg problem to social scientists. Which comes first, economic development or social development? It takes money to build the schools and clinics that provide welfare to masses of the population, but it also takes educated and trained people to develop a subsistence economy in which output is limited to what illiterate and unhealthy workers can produce. Economists have emphasized the critical role of investment in creating structural changes that produce economic development and social development in their wake (Todaro and Smith, 2020: ch. 3). Political scientists have emphasized the importance of political institutions and practices as setting the conditions needed for markets to function (for example, Almond and Coleman, 1960; Rostow, 1960). Marxists have emphasized the importance of power. The power of the Communist Party was used without constraint in the Soviet Union to develop an industrial economy in what had been a largely rural and illiterate society. Marxists have also argued that the power of highly developed capitalist states has been used to distort and exploit development of weaker states with fewer resources (Frank, 1974).

This chapter starts by reviewing each of four crucial resources that can influence the welfare of a country's population: gross domestic product, urbanization, low corruption, and individual freedom. Since the elements are highly correlated statistically, they can be combined into a single Index of Development. The construction of the Index is explained in the second section. Since development is not the only influence on a nation's health, education, and employment, in the third section hypotheses specify three additional potential influences on different forms of a country's welfare: its history, culture, and public expenditure. The chapter concludes by describing the statistical methods used to empirically test their actual influence on measures of health, education, and male and female employment.

4.1 Multiple resources for development

Development is a construct that refers to a multiplicity of economic and political resources that may collectively influence a country's welfare. They include a high level of urbanization, a low level of corruption, and a democratically accountable government. There are major differences globally in the distribution of resources, though the extent of difference varies between continents and between resources (Table 4.1), Highly developed countries have a gross domestic product that is more than three times that of Latin America but there is only a difference of 3 percentage points between them in urbanization. There are also major differences between continents of developing countries. While in Africa the gross domestic product averages less than half that in Middle East and North African countries, the level of corruption is much higher in the MENA region. The world's two most populous countries—China and India—differ substantially on three measures of development, while being equal in their negative corruption rating.

Table 4.1 Continental differences in resources

	GDP per cap in $'000	Urban in %	Transparency 0–100	Freedom 0–100
Highly developed	44.7	75	66	90
Latin America	15.0	72	37	69
MENA	11.9	58	31	25
Africa	4.9	43	32	45
Asia developing	8.8	38	33	46
China	16.1	60	41	11
India	6.7	35	41	75

Source: Global Welfare Database. Variable captions described in text. Transparency is Corruption Perceptions Index; 100 equals least corrupt.

Gross domestic product

The conventional measure of a country's economic development is the gross domestic product of its official economy. Up to a point, the problem of comparing GDP figures calculated in different national currencies can be offset by evaluating national income in terms of purchasing power parity (PPP) in US dollars (see Chapter 3). Since costs such as the pay of teachers and health workers are lower in less developed countries, taking purchasing power into account reduces the substantial difference between continents in the pay of people who deliver welfare services. If there were global statistics for earnings in the shadow economy, this would further reduce the cross-continental difference in real incomes. However, such allowances do not close the gap between countries with very different levels of per capita income.

Countries that can be described as highly developed have an average income of $44,700 per capita; however, they vary significantly from each other. Even after controlling for differences in purchasing power, Swiss citizens enjoy almost three times the income of Bulgarians. While the United States and Russia are each in their own way highly developed, the average American has an income more than double that of the average Russian. These differences reflect the legacy of the Soviet Union relying on a politically controlled non-market economy for development.

There are major differences too in income between and within developing continents. In Latin America, there is an extreme difference between Panama and Haiti. The Canal Zone gives Panama a per capita income ten times higher than Haiti, where a corrupt government exploits its people rather than its resources. Africa has the lowest mean national income of any continent; it is one-tenth that of highly developed countries. Yet sub-Saharan African countries can be divided into two categories equal in number—countries that are in the lowest income bracket globally and those that have a middling income.

Asian countries are extremely heterogeneous. Japan and Korea have the per capita income of highly developed countries. China's gross domestic product is more than double the combined GDP of twenty Latin American countries, although the per capita GDP of China is much the same as the Latin American average. Similarly, the GDP of India is more than double the combined product of forty African countries, but its per capita income is only one-third higher than the average African country. A majority of developing Asian countries from Indonesia to Pakistan have an average gross domestic product per capita similar to India, while Malaysia and Thailand have national incomes per capita higher than China.

Urban population

Cities concentrate the national resources that sustain development through the supply of goods and services, skilled labour, and professional expertise, and institutions that deliver welfare services (Zenghelis, 2017). There are technical colleges and universities, clinics, and hospitals. By contrast, residents in rural areas lack ease of access to these institutional providers of welfare services. Back-breaking work in agriculture does not contribute as much to development as work in factories or with computers. While living in a village may give an individual a secure identity within the community, traditional norms can be obstacles to change. By contrast, a city offers opportunities to develop in new ways; in the words of a German saying, 'City air makes for freedom' (*Stadtluft macht frei*).

Each national government sets its own definition of urban population; it may refer to a single local government unit, an urban agglomeration, or a large labour market that includes rural as well as built-up areas. By any measure, most of the biggest cities in the world are in developing countries. Of the thirty-three cities that the United Nations (2018) estimates have a population of more than 10 million people, twenty-seven are in developing countries. China has six cities with more than 10 million people each, led by Shanghai, and India has five, led by New Delhi. Among highly developed countries, only Moscow and Paris are credited with having more than 10 million people within their boundaries.

The urban population of continents averages 54 per cent, but there are differences in degree between continents. In high-income countries, three-quarters of the population live in urban areas. The positive resources for national development are not at global standards in cities as well as rural areas of the large majority of developing countries. While many Brazilians who move from rural areas to big cities such as Rio de Janeiro live in *favelas* (slums and shanty towns), the opportunities that cities offer households to improve their welfare are better and closer at hand than in rural and jungle areas. Official statistics record three-fifths of Chinese living in cities. However, this is likely to be an underestimate because a significant number of rural people work in a city without being legally resident there. India is distinctive in that barely one-third of its population lives in cities.

Freedom

The state makes a significant contribution to development by what it does not do as well as by what it does. In countries where the government respects freedom from the state, individuals are free within the limits of their capabilities to make many decisions about their own health, education, and employment (Berlin, 1958; Sen, 2001). While freedom is a priceless resource to individuals, it is not cost-free to the political elite, when citizens can use their freedom and democratic institutions to hold their governors to account.

An international non-governmental organization, Freedom House, produces an Index evaluating the extent to which governments grant civil liberties and political rights to their citizens. Each country is scored on twenty-five criteria that cover such topics as freedom of speech, belief and association, civil society, and market institutions. There are also criteria emphasizing freedom from arbitrary actions by the state and the right to elect or eject the government in free and fair elections. The Freedom House Index scores countries on a 100-point scale and groups them into three categories: free, fifty-three countries; partly free, forty-one countries; and unfree, thirty-three countries (http://freedomhouse.org/reports).

Citizens in high-income countries usually enjoy a high degree of freedom from the state as well as a high level of welfare services. The average high-income country has a score of 90, and Finland, Norway, and Sweden receive the maximum rating of 100. Eight countries with a legacy of communist rule are in the top category of freedom, while Hungary is characterized as partly free and Russia as unfree. There are big variations in freedom within continents of developing countries. In Latin America, the average Freedom House score is 69, and five countries have Index ratings as high or higher than the United States during Donald Trump's presidency. In the MENA region, country scores range from 69 for Tunisia to 2 for Turkmenistan. African governments have varied greatly in their regard for civil liberties and political rights: seven counties are classified as free, nineteen as partly free, and the remainder as unfree.

Corruption in the delivery of welfare services

National governments enact laws that entitle citizens to receive health, education, and employment services, and billions of people do so. Governments also enact bureaucratic regulations about how public employees ought to deliver welfare services to everyone who is entitled to receive them. Whether they do so is an empirical issue.

To evaluate the actual practice of these employees, Transparency International's Global Corruption Barometer conducts nationwide sample surveys in more than 100 countries. Each survey asks people who report contact with a service in the past year whether they have had to pay a bribe to get the service to which they are entitled. The likelihood that individuals pay a bribe varies between continents (Rose and Peiffer, 2019: ch. 4). Only 2 per cent of West Europeans have paid a bribe for a public service, but the proportion paying bribes rises to 23 per cent in the Middle East and North Africa region and 61 per cent in India. In China, there are two ways for people to get what they want without regard to the law: They can use *guanxi* (informal connections through personal or Communist Party networks) or pay a bribe. Bribes are most likely to be paid for using health services because it is the only service with which a majority of people have contact during the year (see Figure 1.2).

While welfare is directly influenced by bribery at the grass roots, national development is especially vulnerable to corruption at the top level of government, where national politicians and high-ranking officials make decisions about big-bucks contracts for building everything from roads and power stations to hospitals. Transparency International's Corruption Perceptions Index (CPI) evaluates political systems on a scale in which the most honest governments can be rated as high as 100, and the most corrupt assigned a low rating (http://www.transparency.org).

The 2019 Corruption Perceptions Index gave the average highly developed country a rating of 66 on the 100-point scale. Scores ranged from 87 for Denmark to a low of 43 for Bulgaria. In developing continents corruption is widespread, but there are a minority of countries that are exceptions to this generalization. In Latin America the range is between 71 in Uruguay and 18 in Haiti. The average CPI score for an African country is 32, with a 45-point difference between Botswana and Equatorial Guinea.

Globally there are consistent differences in resources between highly developed and developing countries, but the size varies among the four measures of resources. The average gross domestic product of highly developed countries is four times that of the average developing country after controlling for purchasing power. By contrast, the urbanization of highly developed countries is only half again that of the average developing country; moreover, there are thirteen developing countries with a higher level of urbanization than the average highly developed country. On the Corruption Perceptions Index, the average highly developed country has a rating twice as favourable as that of the average developing country, but the average rating of every developing continent is higher than that of the most corrupt highly developed countries. Differences in freedom among highly developed countries tend to be limited to matters of degree, while there is substantial variation among developing countries. The median developing country is evaluated by Freedom House as partly free, while thirty-two developing countries are considered unfree, and twenty-one are considered free.

4.2 A Global Index of Development

Theories that use an economic indicator to represent a country's development assume that a country low in national income will be similarly low in urbanization and freedom and high in corruption. Insofar as this is the case, it would be sufficient to rely on gross domestic product per capita to explain cross-national differences in health, education, and welfare. Even if there is a substantial correlation between a country's GDP and its level of welfare, this does not explain the actual process by which more money results in a country making progress toward global standards.

Since resources take multiple forms, it would be logical to test the effect that each kind of resource has on welfare by including all four in a single multivariate regression equation. However, this is unsuitable because reliable statistical results can be obtained only if measures are not correlated with each other. This is not the case: a country's urbanization, corruption, and freedom ratings are significantly correlated with each other and with its gross domestic product. This does not mean that they are equal, since differences in the way each is measured make them incommensurable (Table 4.1). It is, however, in keeping with development being a high-level concept that covers multiple manifestations of national development.

The Index of Development

As the welfare mix emphasizes, the health, education, and employment of a society are not the result of a single cause but reflect the interaction of multiple resources (Figure 1.1). Thus, there are good theoretical and methodological reasons for creating a multi-item Index of Development that takes into account the four resources reviewed in the preceding section. Doing so for 127 countries ensures substantial reliability in comparing countries within and across continents.

Table 4.2 Development Index: principal component analysis

Variable	Factor loading	Communality
GDP per capita	0.53	0.84
Urban percentage	0.44	0.60
Freedom House	0.49	0.74
Corruption Index	0.53	0.87
Eigenvalue		3.05
Variance explained		76%

Source: Global Welfare Database.

The empirical extent to which multiple indicators form related facets of an overarching concept can be assessed by principal component analysis, a statistical technique that calculates the relationship of different indicators to an underlying dimension. The extent to which multiple indicators form a single dimension is shown by related statistics: the factor loading and commonality measures; the eigenvalue shows the strength of the association and the amount of variance accounted for by the principal component. Because the four indicators differ in how they are measured, in the statistical analysis each is standardized on a scale ranging from 0 to 100.

The principal component analysis shows that gross domestic product, urbanization, freedom, and corruption are so closely linked that they can be combined in a single Index of Development (Table 4.2). The eigenvalue accounts for 76 per cent of the variance among the four resources, and the factor loadings show that each of the four indicators has a strong relationship with the principal component.

To achieve a high Index of Development score, a country must not only have a high GDP per capita but also be high in urbanization, have a government that respects its citizens' freedom, and have public officials who respect the law rather than administering services corruptly. Reciprocally, a low Index score reflects a country not only being low in per capita income but also being more rural, corrupt, and authoritarian. For clarity in describing how countries differ on the Index of Development, their principal component scores have been transformed into an Index in which the country with the most resources for development, Norway, has a score of 100, and the country with the fewest, Burundi, has a score of 0.

The principal component analysis locates each of 127 countries on the Index of Development according to its resources for development. The global mean for the Index of Development is 43, and the median country has an Index rating of 37. This demonstrates the extent to which most of the world's countries are relatively low in their resources for development. There is a substantial gap between the mean Index rating of highly developed countries and developing continents, and within every continent there is a substantial variation too in national Index scores (Figure 4.1).

Among highly developed countries, Norway is the global leader with an Index rating of 100. Both the United States, with an Index of Development of 89, and the United Kingdom, with 88, are above the mean for highly developed

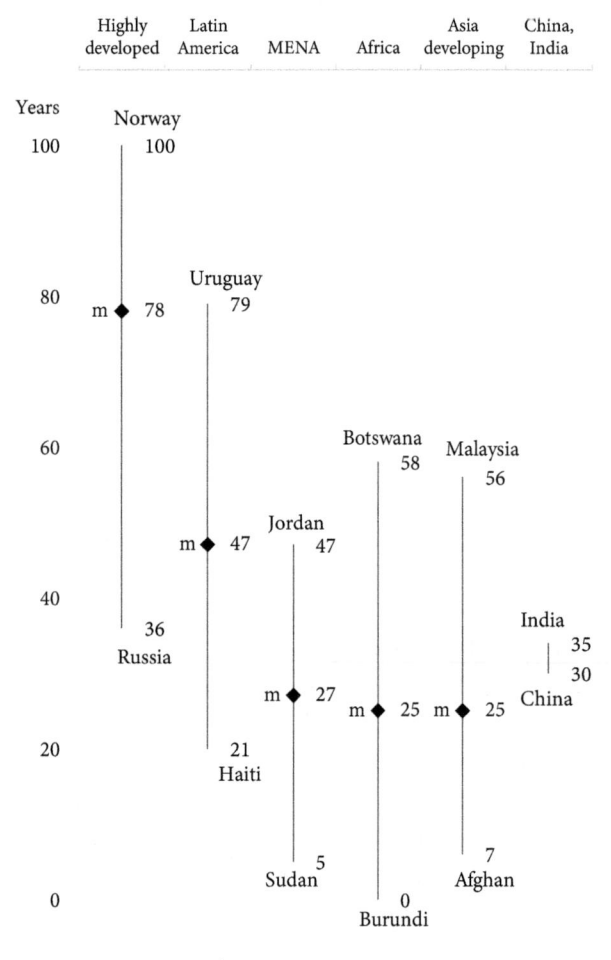

Figure 4.1 Development varies within and between continents

Source: Global Welfare Database.

countries. However, fifteen European Union member states are below the group's mean Index value of 78, including four Mediterranean countries from Greece to Portugal. The unbalanced character of Russia's politics and economy produces an Index of 36, virtually the same as that of India. The closeness is due to India's high rating on freedom offsetting its low GDP, while Russia's relatively high GDP is offset by its low level of democracy and high level of corruption. Latin American countries also have a continental Index of Development mean that is above the global level, but not by much. Uruguay has an Index score that is higher than that of the average highly developed country, while Haiti has an Index score lower than the continent with the lowest average.

Differences in the Index of Development within developing continents are greater than differences between continental means. There are only small differences in the mean Development Index for India, Africa, and Asian developing countries, while Africa has four countries above the global Index mean and Asia includes two developing countries above the mean Index.

4.3 Accounting for global differences in welfare

Given this book's focus on the welfare of individuals, it would be logical to account for global differences in welfare by conducting a statistical analysis of a representative sample of the world's population. National surveys are now conducted in more than 100 countries by a variety of academic and market research networks that differ in how much data they collect about the welfare of individuals as distinct from their opinions, and in the reliability of their statistical methods. Moreover, simply pooling respondents in more than 100 national surveys for statistical analysis would result in a database that was very unrepresentative of the world's population since national samples occur in countries that are more than one hundred times different in population. In a global survey that fairly represented the world's peoples, almost one-third of the respondents would be Chinese or Indian, given their weight in the world's population, and seven very populous countries would constitute a majority of respondents (see Chapter 9).

Welfare is not the exclusive product of an individual's characteristics; it reflects the interaction between an individual's attributes and the national resources and market institutions that collectively constitute the welfare mix. Thus, understanding the sources of welfare requires a model that takes into account the variety of a society's resources that may influence the welfare of

```
Resources
Development ─────────╮
Culture     ─────────┼──► National
History     ─────────┤    welfare
Public expenditure ──╯
```

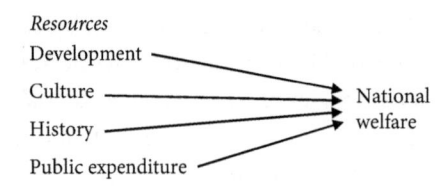

Figure 4.2 A social resources model of national welfare

individuals (Figure 4.2). In addition to the Index of Development, the level of national welfare can also be influenced by its culture; the legacy of its history; and public expenditure on welfare. Each of these characteristics can be hypothesized to affect one or more forms of a country's welfare. Since the 127 countries in the Global Welfare Database include 95 per cent of the world's population, it provides appropriate evidence for statistically testing hypotheses about what influences differences in measures of welfare within and between countries and continents.

In order to confirm whether societal resources have the same effect on different forms of welfare, we separately test the effect of four hypotheses on six indicators of health, education, and female employment. For each pair, one is more subject to short-term change and the other to long-term change. For health, the dependent variables are the life expectancy of women and infant mortality. For education, the dependent variables are the percentage of the adult population that is literate and the percentage of youths enrolled in secondary education. The indicators of female employment are the proportion who participate in the labour force and the degree of gender equality in employment. The characteristics and cross-national distribution of each of these welfare indicators are detailed in the chapters on health, education, and work for women that follow in Part II.

Theories of development hypothesize: *the higher a country's level of development, the higher its welfare*. The components of the Index of Development emphasize characteristics in societies that are already at or approaching global standards of welfare, such as its officially recognized economy (see Chapter 3). They do not take into account the important role of the cash-in-hand shadow economy and the household economies, which tend to be much more important in developing countries. To take into account the potential effect of this difference, while the Index of Development is included as an influence on health and education indicators, in the analyses of female employment it is replaced by an indicator of the percentage of the population working in agriculture.

In the study of a single country, a unique culture may be used to explain its welfare. While there are many differences between national cultures, religious beliefs can influence cultures in dozens of, but not all, countries. In the contemporary world, distinctive Islamic values may be held by citizens of dozens of countries across continents, and such values are independent of a society's level of development. Muslims who do not drink alcohol may live longer; youths whose early education emphasizes memorizing sacred texts may be less interested in further education; and women may be less likely to be employed in work outside the home. The hypothesis that follows is: *if a country's culture includes distinctive Muslim norms, this will significantly influence its level of welfare.* In thirty countries more than half the population is Muslim.

The influence of the historical experience of authoritarian rule can persist for decades after regimes have collapsed. Beginning in the 1920s, the Communist Party of the Soviet Union pursued development through the total mobilization of the population in ways that were bad for health but increased education and female employment (cf. Cook, 1993; Rose, 2009). After the Second World War, communist systems were imposed by Soviet force on societies throughout Eastern and parts of Central Europe. Three decades after communist regimes collapsed, in eighteen countries in the Global Welfare Database the majority of the population had been born and often educated in a communist-controlled society. Insofar as early socialization has a lifetime effect on individual welfare today, in countries with the legacy of a communist regime people are more likely to have worse health but a higher level of education, and women are more likely to participate in employment than would be expected given their level of development. The generic hypothesis is: *if a country has been subject to a communist government for decades, this will significantly influence its level of welfare.*

Public policy studies of highly developed countries often treat public expenditure on welfare as influential because it is an intervening variable that modifies how much of a country's gross domestic product is spent on public services. A national government can spend a larger share than the global average on a priority welfare measure or less because it gives priority to a non-welfare policy such as defence. In this way, public expenditure can influence individual welfare independently of any influence by the gross domestic product. *The greater the proportion of a country's gross domestic product that a government spends on welfare, the higher its level of welfare.*

Many more influences on welfare have been documented in studies of variations within a single country or groups of highly developed countries belonging to the European Union or OECD. Theories of political agency emphasize the lasting influence that actions by national leaders can have on many conditions within a society (Miller, 2005). This has particular resonance in developing countries in which elite leadership is free from constraints incorporated in Freedom House indexes of democracy. In the words of Kwame Nkrumah, the first president of Ghana, 'Seek ye first the political kingdom and all things shall be added unto you'. Although a country's level of development limits its resources, within its parameters political elites can make choices that influence health, education, and the employment of women. However, since the influence of national leaders is confined to a single country, their influence cannot be included in a statistical analysis of 127 countries. However, country-specific influences may be reflected in its being an outlier with a level of welfare much higher or lower than can be accounted for by the four generic influences included in statistical analyses (see Section 8.4).

Many influences can only be measured by indicators that are not available for all developing countries. For example, income inequality is often cited as a major negative influence on many forms of welfare. However, the Gini Index, used as the measure of national inequality, is calculated from statistics of the official economy that ignore a substantial portion of household economic activity in many developing countries (Figure 3.1). The World Bank describes the sources of data used to calculate the Gini Index as not suitable for comparisons that include developing countries.*

Because many developing countries were once colonies, studies of the welfare of a single postcolonial society often emphasize the influence of the legacy of its former imperial ruler. However, imperial rulers differed in their character, in their colonial policies, and in the length of time they ruled different colonies. Likewise, the dozens of countries that were colonies for much of the past century have differed in the way in which they achieved independence, in their resources for development, and in the priority and form of policies influencing the welfare of their population. For these reasons, it is not feasible to take the varied legacies of imperial governors into account in a study of global welfare.

Statistical analysis

Different forms of welfare (W) can be a function of five independent variables: the Index of Development (D), a majority of a society's population

---

* https://www.indexmundi.com/facts/indicators/SI.POV.GINI/rankings.

being Muslim (M), the legacy of a communist regime (ExCom), public expenditure on a specific welfare service (Pexp), and the error term (e), which represents other influences that cannot be included in the global statistical analyses such as the actions of a particular national politician. The generic equation accounting for national differences in health, education, and female employment is:

$$W(f) = D, M, ExCom, Pexp + e$$

Ordinary least squares (OLS) regression analysis tests statistically whether and to what extent hypothesized influences have a significant effect on cross-national differences in health, education, and employment. The extent to which these independent variables collectively account for the global variance in welfare is measured by its R^2, which can range between 0 and 100 per cent. The measure of statistical significance shows the probability that results are not due to chance but are reliable; that is, they would be repeated if many regressions were conducted. In the chapters that follow, the influence of an independent variable is considered to be reliable if it is statistically significant below the 0.01 level. This shows that there is a less than a 1 per cent chance that a statistical association is due to random causes.

Statistical significance says nothing about the size of the effect that an influence has on a particular measure of welfare. A statistically significant indicator does not necessarily have a big effect; it may give a boost of only a few percentage points to a particular measure of welfare. Moreover, two significant effects can push in opposite directions. For example, the effect of a communist regime in promoting mass education may to some extent offset the negative impact of the regime on political and economic development. The beta coefficient and standard error show the size of the effect of a significant independent variable on a given measure of welfare.

The three chapters that follow in Part II test statistically how much of the global variation in welfare can be accounted for by a society's resources. Chapter 5 examines influences on multiple measures of life and death. Chapter 6 focuses on the literacy of adults, how much secondary education youths have, and how the learning of youths differs between cultures. The analysis in Chapter 7 is about whether women participate in employment and do so on equal terms with men. Part III of the book compares how the influence of resources differs between forms of welfare and how much of the world's population is at global standards of welfare and how much is not. The conclusion (in Chapter 10) looks at future prospects for the globalization of welfare to billions more people.

References

Almond, Gabriel A., and Coleman, James S., eds., 1960. *The Politics of Developing Areas*. Princeton: Princeton University Press.

Baland, Jean-Marie, Bourguignon, F., Platteau, J.-P., and Verdier, T., eds., 2020. *The Handbook of Economic Development and Institutions*. Princeton: Princeton University Press.

Berlin, Isaiah, 1958. *Two Concepts of Liberty: An Inaugural Lecture*. Oxford: Clarendon Press.

Cook, Linda J., 1993. *The Soviet Social Contract and Why It Failed*. Cambridge, MA: Harvard University Press.

Cramer, Christopher, Sender, John, and Oqubay, Arkebe, 2020. *African Economic Development*. Oxford: Oxford University Press.

Frank, Andre Gunder, 1974. *Capitalism and Underdevelopment in Latin America*. New York: Monthly Review Press.

Hirschman, Albert O., 1958. *The Strategy of Economic Development*. New Haven: Yale University Press.

Miller, Gary J., 2005. 'The Political Evolution of Principal–Agent Models', *Annual Review of Political Science*, 8, 203–5.

Rose, Richard, 2009. *Understanding Post-Communist Transformation: A Bottom Up Approach*. London: Routledge.

Rose, Richard, and Peiffer, Caryn, 2019. *Bad Governance and Corruption*. London: Palgrave Macmillan.

Rostow, W. W., 1960. *The Stages of Economic Growth*. New York: Cambridge University Press.

Sen, Amartya, 2001. *Development as Freedom*. New York: Oxford University Press.

Todaro, Michael P., and Smith, Stephen C., 2020. *Economic Development*. New York: Pearson, 13th ed.

United Nations, 2018. *The World's Cities in 2018*. New York: United Nations, Department of Economic and Social Affairs, Population Division.

World Bank, 2021. 'Why use GNI Per Capita to Classify Economies into Income Groupings?' https://datahelpdesk.worldbank.org/knowledgebase/articles/378831.

Zenghelis, Dimitri, 2017. 'Cities, Wealth and the Era of Urbanization'. In Kirk Hamilton and Cameron Hepburn, eds., *National Wealth: What Is Missing, Why It Matters*. Oxford: Oxford University Press, 315–34.

PART II
BASIC FORMS OF WELFARE

5
Health

Living Longer and Avoiding Death

Health is of utmost importance for the welfare of every individual everywhere. Moreover, health is important at every stage of the life cycle from infancy to old age, not least when it is taken for granted by individuals in the prime of life. People prefer good health to bad health, yet billions of people have a lifestyle that tends to shorten their life. If people experience ill health, they look for help from whatever resources are available in the welfare mix in their society.

Until the advancement of medical science in the twentieth century, the household provided the great bulk of health care. Childbirth was almost invariably at home and remained above 50 per cent of births until the Second World War in Britain and the United States, before falling to 1 per cent in the 1990s. Germany began state-mandated health insurance for employees in the late nineteenth century. The entire population of Britain became entitled to health care in 1948. Similar trajectories were followed elsewhere in Europe. The United States is exceptional among highly developed countries in the persistence of a debate about whether to have a national health system.

The health of a country's population today is very much the product of the welfare mix. Individuals influence their health daily by the choices they make about what they eat and drink, by smoking or not smoking, or by whether they cycle to work or go by car. Children are influenced to adopt healthy or unhealthy habits by the household in which they grow up. A large majority of people certified as too ill to work are treated at home rather than being hospitalized, and elderly people are more often cared for at home than by institutions of the market or the state. The market provides individuals with an income and range of goods and services that affect their health for better or for worse. Most health expenditure by the state provides medical and hospital treatment for individuals, while public health policies dealing with pollution and epidemics make for better health in the population as a whole.

Welfare Goes Global. Richard Rose, Oxford University Press. © Richard Rose (2024).
DOI: 10.1093/oso/9780198908463.003.0006

Differences in national health vary between and within continents. In highly developed countries, state-of-the-art health care can be met from public revenue and household income. In countries lacking resources for development, individuals cannot rely on health care from the state and can afford to buy little from the market. If households grow their own food, there is no assurance that this will provide a healthy diet, and the absence of labour-saving devices may lead to exhaustion through undernourishment and overexertion.

A country's health involves making progress towards open-ended goals such as longer life and towards fixed goals such as getting rid of infant mortality. Across and within continents, there has been substantial progress in raising life expectancy in the past three decades. However, making progress does not ensure that a developing country is catching up with the standard set by highly developed countries. Moreover, while scientists agree that individual lifestyle choices about drinking alcohol, eating, and smoking can have negative effects on health, there is little political agreement about what the government should do to minimize health-damaging choices of individuals.

This chapter starts by comparing the life expectancy of men and women across continents. Everywhere men have a shorter life expectancy than women. Because eradicating infant mortality is a fixed goal that gives leading countries little scope for progress, developing countries can catch up with leaders sooner or later, depending upon how far they currently are from global standards. The third section examines cross-national differences in choices of lifestyles that can have fatal consequences, such as using tobacco or ignoring road safety laws. The final section summarizes the substantial progress in the globalization of health.

5.1 Life expectancy increasing

Long life is everywhere a major goal of individuals and supported by government policies. In highly developed societies it is valued as giving people more time to enjoy life in retirement; in developing societies it is valued so that people do not have their working life cut short by death. Retirement creates a need for a subsistence income and, if old age creates infirmities, there is a need for care in the household or in an institution. Life expectancy figures are valued by national governments and insurance companies as important information influencing the cost of health care and pensions.

Women living longer everywhere

In 1993 the World Bank declared, *'Health conditions across the world have improved more in the past 40 years than in all of previous human history'* (1993: 23; italics in the original). In the 1870s life expectancy for women was high in Sweden at 49 years, but it was only 39 years in Italy and lower in developing countries (Mitchell, 1975: table B.5; Flora, Kraus, and Pfenning, 1987: 93 ff.). Women born in developed countries could expect to live about 50 years in 1900, 70 years in 1950, and rising to 79 years in 1991. In the past century, life expectancy in developing countries has progressed greatly, but from a lower starting point. In sub-Saharan Africa in 1950 women were estimated to live 37 years; by 1991 life expectancy had risen to 54 years.

The life expectancy of women has continued to show progress in the past three decades in every country covered in this book, but significant differences remain between and within continents (Figure 5.1). Today, life expectancy averages 83 years in highly developed countries and reaches higher still in Japan and South Korea, while Russia and Bulgaria have the lowest life expectancy, 79 years. China and three developing countries in Asia plus Turkey are above the threshold for highly developed countries set by the two ex-communist countries Russia and Bulgaria. Sub-Saharan Africa has the lowest average life expectancy for women, 64 years, and Nigeria, the most populous country on the continent, has a life expectancy for women of only 53 years. In Asian developing countries mean life expectancy is ten years higher than in the average African country, and in India eight years higher.

Even though life expectancy has risen by an average of five years where it was already highest, continents where it was lowest are beginning to catch up with highly developed countries. In 1991 there was a life expectancy gap of twenty-five years between women in Africa and in highly developed countries. By making progress at a compound annual growth rate more than two and a half times that of highly developed countries, the average African country reduced the gap in life expectancy by six years. India, where life expectancy was also low, reduced the gap in life expectancy with highly developed countries by seven years. Progress was not so fast where life expectancy was already higher. Latin American countries made progress at only a slightly faster rate than highly developed countries, thereby reducing the gap in life expectancy by only two years.

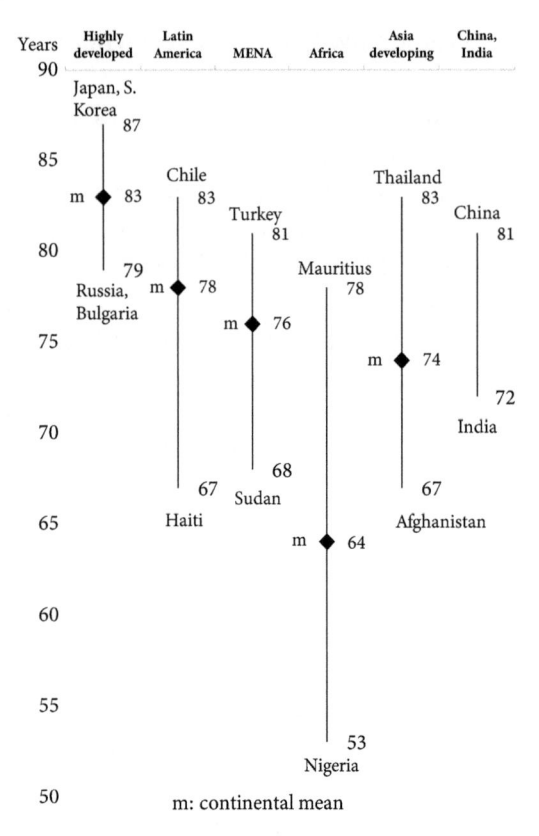

```
Years   Highly      Latin                      Asia        China,
        developed   America   MENA    Africa   developing  India
  90
        Japan, S.
        Korea
              87
  85
                    Chile              Thailand
        m ◆ 83       | 83               | 83
                             Turkey              China
                              | 81               | 81
  80          |
              79             Mauritius
        Russia,  m ◆ 78       | 78
        Bulgaria
                      m ◆ 76
  75
                                        m ◆ 74
                                                    | 72
  70                                              India
                              | 68
                        | 67             | 67
  65                   Haiti  Sudan    Afghanistan
                                m ◆ 64
  60

  55
                                | 53
                               Nigeria
  50                  m: continental mean
```

Figure 5.1 Life expectancy of women
Source: Global Welfare Database.

Resilience and COVID-19

Short-term shocks interrupt but do not reverse long-term trends, because people are resilient. In the course of their life, people usually recover from bouts of ill health, and chronic ill health can affect a person's lifestyle without being fatal. Public health statistics integrate the effect of short-term shocks, such as an economic recession, with the subsequent resilience of a country's population. A shock that causes many deaths such as COVID-19 can immediately reverse average life expectancy from one year to the next. Nonetheless, such occurrences need not reverse the cumulative effect of many years of progress in the lengthening of life.

In the three decades that preceded the COVID pandemic, the year-on-year change in female life expectancy shortened at least once in 103 of 127 countries. In the average country, life expectancy declined in three of twenty-eight years, and there were four years in which there was an insignificant positive or negative change of less than one-tenth of a year. The resilience of countries in response to these setbacks resulted in progress promptly resuming after a setback.

The COVID pandemic infected almost 800 million people from early 2020 to May 2023, when the World Health Organization (2023) officially declared that virus infections were no longer at the scale of a pandemic. In the first year of the epidemic, female life expectancy fell in ninety countries, while showing a change of less than one-tenth of a year in ten countries and rising in twenty-seven countries. In subsequent years there was a decrease in the number of countries in which life expectancy fell as countries demonstrated resilience. By the time WHO declared the COVID pandemic at an end, it had accounted for less than 4 per cent of worldwide deaths in the period.

Men making progress but not catching up

Male life expectancy tends to follow the same cross-continental pattern as female life expectancy (Figure 5.2). The average is highest in highly developed countries—78 years. Its low threshold is set by Russia, at 67 years, and in the 1970s male life expectancy was even falling in Russia. Today, men in forty developing countries have a higher life expectancy than in Russia.

Male life expectancy at birth is everywhere lower than that of women (Figure 5.2). The global average life expectancy for women is five years higher than that for men. At the continental level there is a difference of up to six years in the life expectancy of men and women in China and three developing continents. The gap in India is least two years, as women as well as men have a relatively low life expectancy (Figure 5.2).

Progress in male life expectancy tends to be higher in less developed countries, thereby reducing cross-continental differences. In the past three decades the gap in life expectancy between men in highly developed countries and in Africa has been reduced by three years and in India by four years. It nonetheless remains substantial—eighteen years for African men and eight years for Indian men. The average gap between highly developed countries and the MENA region, Asian developing countries, and China has been reduced by about two years. Latin American countries have hardly reduced their gaps in male life expectancy with highly developed countries. Even though there has been significant progress in raising the life expectancy of both men and women in the past three decades, globally the gender gap remains constant.

92 WELFARE GOES GLOBAL

Female/Male inequality in life expectancy

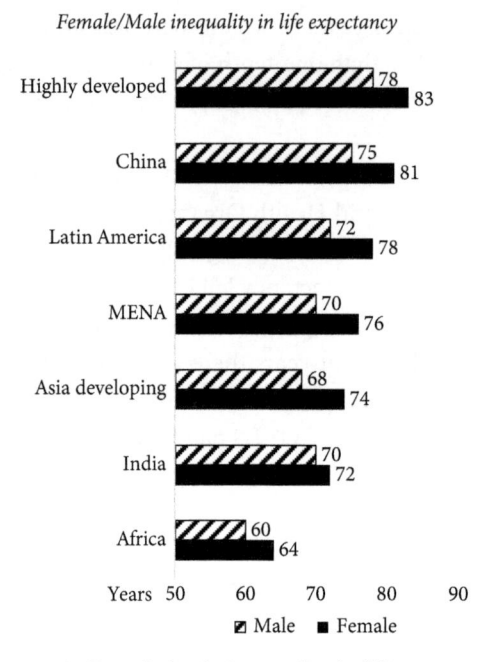

Region	Female	Male
Highly developed	78	83
China	75	81
Latin America	72	78
MENA	70	76
Asia developing	68	74
India	70	72
Africa	60	64

Figure 5.2 Female/male inequality in life expectancy
Source: Global Welfare Database.

Development makes for longer life

An ordinary least squares regression analysis supports the development hypothesis: the more developed a country is, the longer people live. Moreover, the effect is virtually the same for men and women (Table 5.1). People enjoy a substantially longer life in countries that are higher in per capita income, are higher in urbanization, deliver public services without corruption, and are free of authoritarian influences on people's daily lives. After controlling for other influences, every 1-point increase in the 10-point Index of Development* adds an average of 2.4 years to a woman's life and the same amount to the shorter life of men. The regression analysis accounts for virtually the same amount of variance in the life expectancy of men, 63.5 per cent, as for women, 66.8 per cent.

The legacy of a communist regime has a complex effect on life expectancy. The Index of Development is lowered by a legacy of corruption and authoritarianism, thus reducing the overall effect of development on life expectancy. However, communist economies gave many women employment

---

* The original 100-point Index is shortened here and in subsequent tables to 10 points to increase clarity in assessing impact.

opportunities and more health care; this legacy has a positive effect on the life expectancy of women. By contrast, these regimes have failed to give a significant boost to men (Table 5.1). This suggests that in communist regimes men were likely to work in industries subject to 'storming', heavy physical and mental stress to meet monthly production quotas with resources inferior to what was normal in highly developed countries.

The dynamics of the life expectancy of German women demonstrates the impact on welfare of the political division between communist and non-communist states. When Germany was divided into two political systems in 1949, the life expectancy of women in what became East Germany was 69 years and that in West Germany 2 years lower. In the subsequent four decades both states made progress, but at different rates. In 1989 life expectancy was 79 years in West Germany and 76 years in East Germany. After German reunification in 1990, the government invested substantial resources to assist people in the former communist state to catch up with West Germans. While life expectancy for women rose in all parts of Germany, progress was faster in East Germany, and the legacy of inequality from the past has ended (Rose, 2009: table 3.2).

Theories of the welfare state often assume that public spending on health has a major positive effect; such spending as a proportion of a country's gross domestic product reflects the priority that the state gives to promoting the health of its citizens. The amount spent on health care in highly developed countries today is especially large both in the absolute sense and as a proportion of GDP (see Table 2.1). However, spending on health care

Table 5.1 Development lengthens lives of women and men

	Female	Male
Development Index	2.36***	2.41***
	(0.23)	(0.20)
Ex-communist	4.12**	1.78
	(1.32)	(1.17)
Muslim	0.25	1.32
	(1.15)	(1.03)
Health expenditure	0.06	0.00
	(0.22)	(0.19)
Variance explained R^2	63.5%	66.8%

** $p < 0.01$, *** $p < 0.001$
Source: Ordinary least squares regression analysis of Global Welfare Database. Standard errors in parentheses.

has no statistically significant effect on the life expectancy of women or of men (see Table 5.1). What matters for longer life is not the relative priority given to health services in a country's overall expenditure but the resources for development that give people large urban hospitals and specialist clinics, health staff who do not seek bribes, and the freedom to choose a lifestyle that affects their life expectancy.

5.2 Infant mortality decreasing

Infant mortality is a direct measure of health in society since it shows the number of newborn infants who survive to the age of 5, whereas life expectancy reflects concerns extending up to four-fifths of a century. The incidence of infant mortality in a society reflects the welfare mix: the physical health of the mother, the care and nourishment an infant receives in the home, and perinatal care provided by the public and private sectors. It is thus possible to reduce infant mortality relatively quickly through public policies applying social technologies that improve perinatal care, support the diet of infants, and give parents more time and resources to devote to childcare in smaller families. As Mark G. Field notes (1994: 183), 'Infant mortality is first and foremost a social rather than a medical problem; as an indicator it is a good measure of the social, economic and political wellbeing of a population.'

At the beginning of the last century, infant mortality was everywhere a substantial and unwelcome fact of life. In 1900 more than one-fifth of infants died before the age of 5 in Britain and the United States. Infant mortality was higher in Europe and higher still on other continents where records of home births were incomplete. Notwithstanding the world depression, by the 1930s advances in medical care and public health had halved infant mortality in Britain and the United States. In the decades after the Second World War, there were large absolute falls in infant mortality in highly developed countries, bringing it down to twenty-six deaths per thousand in 1960. While rates in developing countries were declining too, infant mortality was 100 to 200 deaths per thousand or even higher (United Nations, 1950).

Making progress towards a fixed goal

The eradication of infant mortality is a fixed goal, with zero deaths per thousand its limit. It is in principle possible for every country in the world to reduce

HEALTH: LIVING LONGER AND AVOIDING DEATH 95

infant mortality to virtually zero. Since infant mortality today varies by up to sixty-three deaths per thousand between continents and even more between countries within some continents, this goal is hardly achievable in the near future. Nonetheless, insofar as countries have the resources and the population has the will to apply known methods to reduce infant mortality, by making progress they can slowly catch up with global standards. Countries setting the global standard have little scope for progress, since they have already reduced infant deaths to an average of four per thousand births.

The dynamics of catching up with a fixed target are shown by cross-continental progress in infant mortality (Figure 5.3). Highly developed countries that set the global standard in 1991 were already close to the limit;

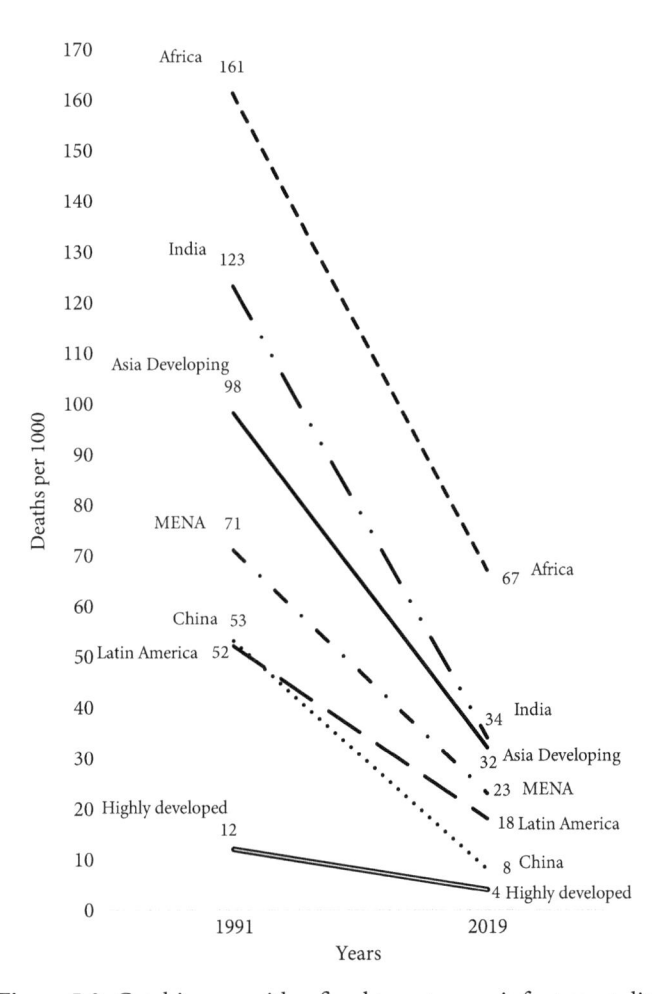

Figure 5.3 Catching up with a fixed target: zero infant mortality
Source: Global Welfare Database.

on average there were twelve deaths per thousand. At the other extreme, in Africa official records showed infant mortality averaging 161 deaths per thousand. Within Africa there were also big variations: nine countries reported an infant mortality rate below 100 per thousand, while eleven reported death rates above 200 per thousand. Infant mortality in India, Asian developing countries, and the MENA region were from six to ten times the rate in highly developed countries.

Since getting rid of infant mortality is a fixed target, the early success of highly developed countries in reducing infant mortality meant that in recent decades there was an average decrease of only eight deaths per thousand. This has resulted in almost complete success in eliminating what had once been a common household risk to an average of 996 infants per thousand surviving to age 5. Moreover, progress towards the elimination of infant mortality is going global. In the past three decades continents with the highest rates of mortality are making fastest progress. Infant mortality is falling by as much as ninety-four deaths per thousand in the average African country and eighty-nine deaths per thousand in India. Progress puts China within four deaths per thousand of the global standard set by highly developed countries.

Accounting for infant mortality

As is the case for life expectancy, statistical analysis supports the development hypothesis. The resources in the Index of Development have a significant and substantial effect on infant mortality (Table 5.2). For every 10-point increase in the Index of Development, the number of infant deaths falls by seven per thousand, and the effect is to reduce infant mortality between the most and least developed countries by seventy-one deaths per thousand. Ex-communist countries again show a higher standard of health care than other countries with a similar mediocre Index of Development. A communist legacy of providing maternity and perinatal care reduces infant mortality by twenty-one deaths per thousand, significantly offsetting the negative effect of communist systems on development.

Total public expenditure on health care has no significant effect on infant mortality. This reflects infant mortality claiming a very small part of public spending on health. Developing countries where infant mortality is highest are good candidates for receiving foreign aid for perinatal policies that produce prompt and visible benefits. Moreover, the development of the economy gives households more resources to avoid infant deaths through improved

Table 5.2 Development reduces infant mortality

Development Index	−7.19***
	(0.94)
Ex-communist	−21.61***
	(5.50)
Muslim	5.81
	(4.81)
Health expenditure	0.18
	(0.91)
Variance explained R^2	51.7%

** $p < 0.01$, *** $p < 0.001$
Source: Ordinary least squares regression analysis of Global Welfare Database. Standard errors in parentheses.

childcare practices in the household and what they can buy in an expanding market.

5.3 Lifestyles and avoidable deaths

Whereas deaths from infirmities of old age are likely to reflect natural causes, avoidable deaths are due to choices that individuals make about their lifestyle—for example, whether they smoke or whether they drive carefully or recklessly. The lifestyle that individuals choose, whether healthy, unhealthy, or a mixture of both, is influenced by the institutions of the welfare mix. Tobacco is sold in the market and subject to government taxes and regulations. Automobiles are sold and serviced in the market, and the government taxes cars and the fuel they consume. There are standard international measures to capture the extent of national variations: the percentage of the adult population that smokes and the number of fatal motor vehicle accidents. By contrast, national differences in whether people drink alcohol, what and how much they drink, and how often they drink are so great that this lifestyle cannot be reduced to an internationally meaningful metric.

Smoking differs by gender

By the beginning of the twentieth century, habit-forming cigarettes were being marketed worldwide, and tobacco taxes made a significant contribution to public revenue in many countries. During the Second World War governments gave free or cheap cigarettes to their military forces in the belief that it would help relieve wartime stresses. By 1950 smoking was established in countries on every continent. More than 60 per cent of British men and 40 per cent of British women were smokers. In the United States smoking peaked at 45 per cent of adults in 1954. In communist systems, the state-controlled economy manufactured and sold cheap cigarettes with a high content of tar and nicotine (Ritchie and Roser, 2022).

Medical researchers in Britain began publishing research in the late 1940s showing that smoking was a cause of death from lung cancer and heart problems. In 1964 the United States Surgeon General's Report *Smoking and Health* identified tobacco use as a major source of illfare. In the decades since, governments around the world have adopted policies to reduce smoking through taxes increasing its cost, banning it in public places, and educating youths about its adverse effect on health. However, governments have not sought to ban the import and sale of tobacco or declare its possession a criminal offence. The World Health Organization estimates that more than 8 million people worldwide die annually from the effects of smoking.

While there has been a scientific consensus for half a century that smoking can cause ill health or death, there is no behavioural consensus: in every country on record a significant minority continue to smoke, and as older smokers die they are replaced by youthful smokers. Today more than one in five of the world's adult population smokes, notwithstanding more than half a century of publicity about the potentially fatal effect it has on health (Lancet, 2021). Smoking tends to be an addictive habit formed in youth and maintained throughout a lifetime. Differences in smoking between countries are greater than the differences between continents. Among highly developed countries, there is a big range between 39 per cent of adults smoking in Bulgaria and Greece; 25 per cent in the United States, which has been a leader in publicizing smoking as a source of illfare; and 13 per cent in Norway. In Africa an average of 14 per cent use tobacco, with a range between 5 per cent in Ethiopia and a high of 31 per cent in South Africa.

Because smoking is an avoidable cause of death, progress is shown by a decline in the proportion of smokers in the population. In the past three decades smoking has declined on every continent as awareness of the harmful effects of smoking has become global. Smoking has fallen most where it was previously high (Lancet, 2021). In China 61 per cent of men smoked in 1990; this figure has since fallen by 11 percentage points, though it is still the highest in the world. In highly developed countries smoking by men has fallen by 12 percentage points, while smoking by women has fallen by only half that amount. The decline in smoking has been least where it has been lowest, sub-Saharan Africa, a reduction of 3 percentage points.

On all continents there is a consistent pattern: men are much more likely to smoke than women; globally, an average of 28 per cent of male adults smoke compared to 10 per cent of females. The gender difference is greatest in developing countries; in India men are seven times more likely to smoke than women, and in China smoking by men is more than ten times the rate of women. By contrast, the gender difference is least in highly developed countries: 31 per cent of men report smoking and 21 per cent of women. Moreover, there are four countries—Sweden, Norway, Ireland, and the United Kingdom—where the proportion of women who smoke is much the same as that of men.

Influences on smoking are radically different between men and women. A multiple regression analysis of female smokers accounts for six times as much of the cross-national variation in smoking as a similar regression for male smokers (Table 5.3). Development has a substantial effect on women smoking but no significant effect on whether men smoke. The higher a country's Index of Development, the greater the likelihood that a woman smokes. After controlling for other influences, women in highly developed countries are 20

Table 5.3 Development increases female smoking but not male

	Female	Male
Development Index	2.02*** (0.23)	0.90 (0.51)
Ex-communist	8.10*** (1.34)	7.84** (2.96)
Muslim	−3.20** (1.17)	3.00 (2.59)
Health expenditure	0.28 (0.22)	−0.73 (0.49)
Constant	−1.37 (1.39)	27.01*** (3.06)
R^2	0.664	0.100
N	127	127

** $p < 0.01$, *** $p < 0.001$
Source: Ordinary least squares regression analysis calculated from Global Welfare Database. Standard errors in parentheses.

percentage points more likely to smoke than women in the least developed countries. The big effect may be due to the Index of Development including a measure of individual freedom. Whereas men tend to be free to indulge themselves whatever a country's development, restrictions on the behaviour of women tend to be fewer in more developed countries. This gives women the opportunity to choose for themselves whether to smoke rather than having the choice dictated by cultural norms about how women ought to behave.

There is a significant political effect too: living in a society that was formerly communist-controlled significantly increases the likelihood of smoking by 8 percentage points for both men and women. In the Soviet Union there were no restrictions on smoking, and cigarette sales provided a ready source of revenue for the state; similar policies were followed in other communist-controlled countries. When these regimes collapsed after the fall of the Berlin Wall in 1989, a substantial portion of men and women were nicotine-addicted and had not been exposed to information about smoking as a threat to health (Shkolnikov et al., 2020).

Consistent with the absence of any Islamic prohibition of the use of tobacco, there is no significant influence on men smoking if they live in Muslim societies. While women are significantly less likely to smoke in Muslim societies, the effect is small, a 3 percentage point decrease in female smoking. Public expenditure on health, which is a primary source of public information about the dangers of smoking, has no statistically significant influence on the national level of smoking.

Road traffic deaths

Automobiles are a ubiquitous feature of highly developed societies today. They add to the welfare of individuals by greatly extending their ability to choose where to work and how to spend their leisure time. They are a product of the welfare mix. Individuals use automobiles for their own benefit, the market provides a choice of vehicles that can be run at different levels of cost, and the state provides the roads that cars use. Notwithstanding global demands to reduce pollution, the climate change recommendations of the United Nations COP26 conference did not suggest banning the use of high-polluting cars but recommended switching to vehicles that produce less pollution, such as electric cars.

Car ownership increases with development, but at uneven rates. Vehicle ownership grows relatively slowly at the lowest levels of per capita income, then about twice as fast as income at middle-income levels, and finally about as fast as income at higher income levels, before reaching saturation at the highest levels of income (Dargay, Gately, and Sommer, 2007: 4). Car ownership in the United States was 411 per thousand population in 1960, and almost doubled by 2002, while in Mexico it more than trebled from a low base of 22 per thousand in 1960. Car ownership grew relatively more in India but from an even lower base, rising from one to sixteen cars per thousand in four decades.

The globalization of car ownership is progressing. Because highly developed countries have been close to saturation, developing countries have been catching up. Vehicle ownership now averages more than 540 per thousand people in highly developed countries and 210 per thousand in China. It appears lowest in Africa, at 37 vehicles per thousand, and in India, at 28 per thousand. Since developing countries have five-sixths of the world's population, almost two-thirds of the world's motor vehicles are today in developing countries.

Fatal car accidents are an unwelcome by-product of increased traffic. Deaths from road accidents totalled 1.2 million in 2019. The extent of road deaths in a country reflects the behaviour of individual motorists and pedestrians; the cost and variety of safety features in cars; and the extent to which governments regulate traffic, build safe roads, and license motorists. In principle, road deaths are to a great extent avoidable, if all involved in the welfare mix follow best practices. However, of five procedures that can reduce road deaths, requiring seat belts is the only one that is mandatory in a majority of countries. Four safety features are absent in countries with more than two-thirds of the world's population (WHO, 2018: 5 ff.).

The proportion of fatal accidents, six deaths per hundred thousand, is lowest where car ownership is highest, in highly developed countries (Figure 5.4). Where vehicle ownership is lowest, fatal accidents are highest. In the average African country there are twenty-nine fatal accidents per hundred thousand people, and in Zimbabwe the rate rises to forty-one deaths. Fatal accidents are higher still in the Dominican Republic. In the United States and Russia the fatal accident rate is double that of the average highly developed country. In both countries geography leads to motorists driving more miles and having more accidents.

Progress in reducing fatal accidents is the result of a learning process involving both motorists and pedestrians. When development is in its initial stages, the number of first-time drivers of motorbikes and unsafe second-hand cars increases along with traders transporting goods to street markets in ageing vans. This results in more inexperienced motorists and more pedestrians at risk because they are unaccustomed to taking precautions against motor traffic. Both groups can learn to take precautions by witnessing or being involved in accidents, and car manufacturers and governments can build

102 WELFARE GOES GLOBAL

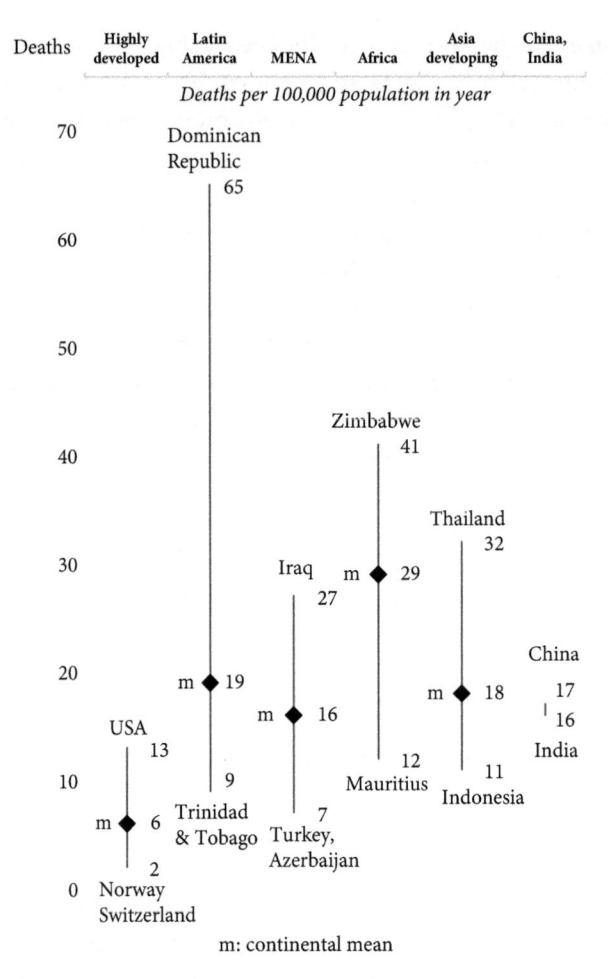

```
Deaths   Highly      Latin                      Asia       China,
         developed   America   MENA    Africa   developing India
              Deaths per 100,000 population in year

  70            Dominican
                Republic
                  65

  60


  50
                                 Zimbabwe
                                   41
  40
                                          Thailand
                                            32
  30              Iraq     m ◆ 29
                            27
                                                     China
  20      m ◆ 19                                       17
                    m ◆ 16                    m ◆ 18 | 16
        USA                                         India
         13                              12      11
  10              9                   Mauritius  Indonesia
              Trinidad   7
        m ◆ 6 & Tobago Turkey,
              2         Azerbaijan
   0   Norway
       Switzerland
                 m: continental mean
```

Figure 5.4 Deaths from road accidents
Source: Global Welfare Database.

more safety features into vehicles and roads. As experience accumulates, this leads to a fall in fatal accidents, notwithstanding a higher level of vehicle ownership.

The resources of the Index of Development and the experience of communist regimes together account for 56.6 per cent of the global variance between countries in fatal road accidents. Even though development gives a big boost to vehicle ownership in a society—there is a very high positive correlation of 0.88 between the two variables—this does not appear to increase fatal road accidents (Table 5.4). Instead, the higher a country's Index of Development, the lower its rate of fatal road accidents. Being at the highest rather than the lowest level of development tends to decrease fatal accidents by twenty-nine

Table 5.4 Development reduces fatal road accidents

Development Index	−2.94*** (0.32)
Ex-Communist	−8.44*** (1.86)
Muslim	−3.75 (1.63)
Health expenditure	0.11 (0.31)
Variance explained R^2	56.6%

** p<0.01 *** p< 0.001
Source: Ordinary least squares regression analysis of Global Welfare Database. Standard errors in parentheses.

deaths per hundred thousand. In addition, the legacy of communist regimes causes a reduction of eight deaths per hundred thousand. This reflects communist governments giving priority to rapid industrialization that relied on the use of heavy-duty vehicles in industry and agriculture. This accustomed the population to living with vehicles, even though they often needed to wait years or have party connections to buy a car for their private use.

5.4 The globalization of health

Multiple influences on health

The regression equations confirm the importance of a country's development for many forms of health. In the countries that are highest in the Index of Development, men and women have a life expectancy that is more than a third greater than in the least developed countries, and newborn infants are almost certain to live into childhood and beyond. Notwithstanding the proliferation of motor vehicles, fatal accidents are a rarity. The only negative effect of development concerns smoking: women are much more likely to smoke if they live in highly developed countries.

The legacy of communist regimes has had a long-lasting effect on health too. Denial of freedom and corruption distorted development to an extent that could not be fully compensated for by the achievement of economic growth and urbanization. Thus, Russia has an Index of Development that is well under half that of leading highly developed countries (see Figure 4.1). Nonetheless, communist societies did institutionalize national systems of health care. This legacy boosts female life expectancy and reduces infant mortality. Prioritizing motor vehicles for economic development has left a legacy of a low level of fatal road accidents in a country where roads stretch for hundreds or thousands of miles. The legacy also has the negative effect of significantly increasing the likelihood of women and men smoking. By contrast, living in a Muslim society has virtually no statistical effect on health. In the six regressions, it is only a significant influence in reducing women smoking by 3 percentage points.

The only indicator that consistently fails to show a significant influence on health is public expenditure as a percentage of gross domestic product. This does not mean that a country's economy is irrelevant, since gross domestic product is an integral part of the Index of Development. A higher income means that people do not have to rely exclusively on home remedies to maintain their health. People can spend money for modern health care in the market and make the co-payments required in many national health services.

In today's world globalization is a matter of degree, not kind. This is especially true of health. Focusing on differences between countries and continents obscures the extent of similarities in the achievement of health. For example, the difference between the life expectancy of the average woman in India, 71 years, and in a highly developed country, 83 years, is a substantial difference but not a difference in kind. In both groups the average woman can expect to live at least 71 years.

The degree of globalization today can be shown by calculating the percentage to which a continent's standard on a particular measure of welfare approaches the standard of the continent with the best achievement. The global standard is set at 100 to make it possible to compare achievements across different forms of welfare (Table 5.5). On this basis, the life expectancy of the average African woman, 64 years, is 77 per cent that of the average woman in highly developed countries, 83 years. The difference is substantially less on other continents. The average life expectancy of women is 93 per cent of the global standard in Latin America and 97 per cent in China. There is a similar difference in male life expectancy between developing continents and the average male life of 78 years in highly developed countries.

The degree of globalization is greatest for the prevention of infant mortality. In highly developed countries 99.6 per cent of infants born alive survive to the age of 5, and the survival rate is equally high in China. Four developing continents are within 3 per cent of the global standard. Infant survival is less high in sub-Saharan Africa, yet the survival rate is still only six percentage points less than the global standard (Table 5.5).

Table 5.5 High degree of globalization in health

	High D	Lat Am	China	MENA	Afr	AsiaD	India
Continental welfare as percentage of global leader
Life Expectancy
Women	100	93	97	91	77	88	87
Men	100	92	97	90	77	87	89
Infant survival	100	99	100	98	94	97	97
Non-smokers
Men	87	100	63	82	99	74	97
Women	81	94	100	99	99	97	100
Road deaths	100	86	88	90	76	87	90

Source: Global Welfare Database.

Notwithstanding the efforts of tobacco companies to globalize the habit of smoking, abstention from smoking is almost completely globalized. The global standard is set by women in India and China, where almost 97 per cent of women are non-smokers. In the other four developing continents, non-smoking is within 6 per cent or less of the global standards. Highly developed countries are deviant; the proportion of non-smokers is almost one-fifth below the global standard. The globalization of non-smoking is more uneven for male smokers than for any other indicator of health in Table 5.5. In China this results in the rate of non-smoking being 37 per cent below that of the Latin American level, and the average Asian developing country is 26 per cent behind the global leader. Highly developed countries are close to the global average for male non-smoking rather than being the leaders on this count.

There are far more motor vehicles and far more miles driven in highly developed countries, yet they set the standard for road safety by having only six fatal vehicle accidents annually for every 100,000 people. The much lower percentage of motor vehicles in developing countries ought to keep road accidents low, but the opposite is the case. Nonetheless, the difference in fatal accidents remains a matter of degree, not kind. While the number of motoring fatalities is more than four times as high in Africa as in highly developed countries, in absolute terms the difference is far less dramatic. Among every 100,000 Africans, the population not subject to a fatal accident totals 99,971 and rises to 99,994 per 100,000 people in highly developed countries.

The gap between global standards and the continent with relatively least welfare is at 6 per cent for infant survival after childbirth, and no continent is more than 37 percentage points distant on any indicator of welfare (Table 5.5). The average gap from global standards for continents that have not yet caught up is as small as 3 per cent for infant survival and 6 per cent for female non-smokers, and at its relative highest—16 per cent—for male non-smokers. On all continents the glass of global health is closer to being completely full than being half full or completely empty.

References

Dargay, Joyce, Gately, Dermot, and Sommer, Martin, 2007. 'Vehicle Ownership and Income Growth, Worldwide: 1960–2030', *Energy Journal*, 28, 4 (October 2004), 143–70.

Field, Mark G., 1994. 'Postcommunist Medicine'. In J. R. Millar and S. L. Wolchik, eds., *The Social Legacy of Communism*. New York: Cambridge University Press, 178–96.

Flora, Peter, Kraus, Franz, and Pfenning, Winfried, 1987. *State, Economy and Society in Western Europe 1815–1975: Volume II*. London: Macmillan.

Lancet, 2021. 'Spatial, Temporal, and Demographic Patterns in Prevalence of Smoking Tobacco Use and Attributable Disease Burden in 204 Countries and Territories, 1990–2019: A Systematic Analysis from the Global Burden of Disease Study 2019', *The Lancet* (10292), 2337–60.

Mitchell, B. R., 1975. *European Historical Statistics 1750–1970*. London: Macmillan.

Ritchie, Hannah, and Roser, Max, 2022. 'Smoking', *Our World in Data*, https://ourworldindata.org/smoking (accessed 22 April 2022).

Rose, Richard, 2009. *Understanding Post-Communist Transformation*. London: Routledge.

Shkolnikov, V. M., Churilova, E., Jdanov, D. A., et al., 2020. 'Time Trends in Smoking in Russia in the Light of Recent Tobacco Control Measures', *BMC Public Health*, 20, 378.

United Nations, 1950. *United Nations Demographic Yearbook, 1949–50*. New York: United Nations.

WHO (World Health Organization), 2018. *Global Status Report on Road Safety 2018*. Geneva: World Health Organization.

WHO (World Health Organization), 2023. *WHO Coronavirus (COVID-19) Dashboard*. https://covid19.who.int/ (accessed 6 June 2023).

World Bank, 1993. *Investing in Health*. Washington, DC: World Bank World Development Report, https://worldpopulationreview.com/country-rankings/smoking-rates-by-country (accessed 14 November 2021).

6
Education

Quantity and Quality

Education contributes to individual welfare as an end in itself and because it increases a person's capability to act on their own behalf (Sen, 2005). More educated people tend to live longer and to get more satisfying and better-paid jobs. Citizens who are illiterate or have only a basic education may fatalistically accept what they have rather than try to improve their lot. Education is a collective asset for society too; it increases the capacity of institutions of all kinds. In a society in which most people have only a minimum of education, there is likely to be a shortage of skilled workers needed for economic growth and to deliver health and education. The World Bank (2018: 38) summarizes the multiple advantages of education for individuals and society with the dramatic statement 'Education is freedom'.

Education is very much a product of the welfare mix. Governments on every continent show their commitment by making education compulsory, building schools and paying teachers. Since the cost of education is beyond the income of most parents in almost every country, compulsory education is free, and voluntary further education is state-subsidized. The market provides training by employers, and in developing countries up to one-fifth of pupils are in private education (World Bank, 2018: 176). Parents start a child's education in the household before schooling begins and influence a youth's study habits and educational aspirations. Not least, youths must devote years of effort to learning whatever their schools offer and as adults continue to learn as the world changes around them.

Making progress in the education of a country's population is a two-step process. A government with sufficient resources can immediately increase the education of young people by making an extra year of schooling compulsory. As youths reach the age at which schooling becomes voluntary, national systems provide advanced secondary education in ways that differ in purpose and duration. In turn, an increase in youths with secondary school qualifications will increase the proportion of young people enrolling in one or another institution for tertiary education. However, it takes generations before an increase in the education of today's youths can affect the whole of a country's adult education. This cannot be achieved until after the death of the last cohort that left school before the length of schooling was increased, or in the case of most developing countries, before free compulsory primary schooling ensured that each new cohort of adults was literate.

To describe the three-tier complex of educational institutions, experts have developed the three-digit International Standard Classification of Education (ISCED). The first digit distinguishes between nine levels of education, ranging from preschool institutions socializing very young children up to research institutions for PhD students. The second digit distinguishes between types of education: general, vocational, professional, or academic. A final distinction is whether a given type of schooling is accepted for entering a higher-level tertiary institution (http://uis.unesco.org/en/topic/international-standard-classification-education-isced).

The cost of education makes a significant claim on a country's gross domestic product, and the cost per pupil tends to rise with each step up the educational ladder. In developing countries that have limited resources to spend on education, there can be difficulties in finding sufficient teachers to provide secondary education for all, and classes may be double the desirable size due to a lack of money and teachers. In highly developed countries, more years of schooling may have little effect if youths do not apply themselves to meet more demanding standards as they progress up the educational ladder.

While there is an international consensus about the purpose of basic primary education, there is no consensus about the purpose of further education. Should it be to give students enhanced vocational skills or to advance their intellectual development, or can it do both for all pupils? Institutionally, there are divisions between vocational schools and academic institutions, and the rising cost of mass education is encouraging greater emphasis to be placed on the economic return from more education and on the choice of subjects at university level. Within every country young people differ in whether they leave school with an academic diploma, with a vocational qualification, with both, or with neither.

This chapter examines how the quantity and quality of education vary within countries, between countries and across continents. The first section reports how far adult literacy has spread around the world and how near or far from this fixed goal some developing countries are. The global expansion of secondary education and the choices involved between vocational and academic skills are discussed in Section 6.2. The quality of academic learning is shown by international tests in mathematics reported in Section 6.3, and of instrumental learning by the spread of a common lingua franca—English as a foreign language. The concluding section documents how the globalization of education is increasing through the turnover of generations.

6.1 Literacy goes global

Literacy is the first target in the process of educating a nation's population. Historically, the promotion of basic education varied with a country's religious context. In the early sixteenth century Martin Luther began advocating universal literacy so that people could read the Bible in German. A century later Lutheran regions of Germany began introducing mass education, and Puritans promoted literacy in New England in the seventeenth century.

Government is the main institution with the authority and the resources to advance mass literacy by making primary education free and compulsory. Even if the length of compulsory schooling is only six years, this is enough to make pupils literate. In the nineteenth century the value of a literate population for the economy and military forces led the most developed countries to introduce compulsory education. Sweden introduced compulsory primary education in 1842, and by 1914 compulsory primary education was the norm in Europe. More than 90 per cent of Western Europeans were literate by the 1930s. However, in Mediterranean countries literacy ranged from below three-fifths in Greece and Portugal to just over three-quarters in Spain and Italy (United Nations, 1950; UNESCO, 1988). By the 1950s the population of most of the world's highly developed countries were more than 90 per cent literate (Lindert, 2021: chs. 4–5).

Literacy on every continent

Because literacy is important for economic growth, the governments of developing countries give compulsory primary education a priority as they gain the resources to meet the cost. The Soviet Union did so in the 1930s and the People's Republic of China introduced compulsory primary education in 1986. The median African country did not begin reporting adult literacy statistics until 2000, and this was often the case in Latin America too. Today, the fixed target of reporting literacy has been reached globally.

In every developing continent a significant amount of progress has been made since 1991, albeit from different starting points. India has advanced the most, 26 percentage points; this has made three-quarters of adults literate, leaving one-quarter illiterate, while China's 19 percentage-point progress has made the country almost totally literate. Literacy rose by an average of 12 percentage points in both Africa and Asian developing countries.

Today, a majority of adults on every continent are literate, but the percentage literate differs. Since highly developed countries introduced compulsory education generations ago, most have reached the fixed target's limit, with 99 per cent of adults literate, and many governments have stopped collecting statistics about illiteracy (Figure 6.1). Portugal, the lowest-ranking country,

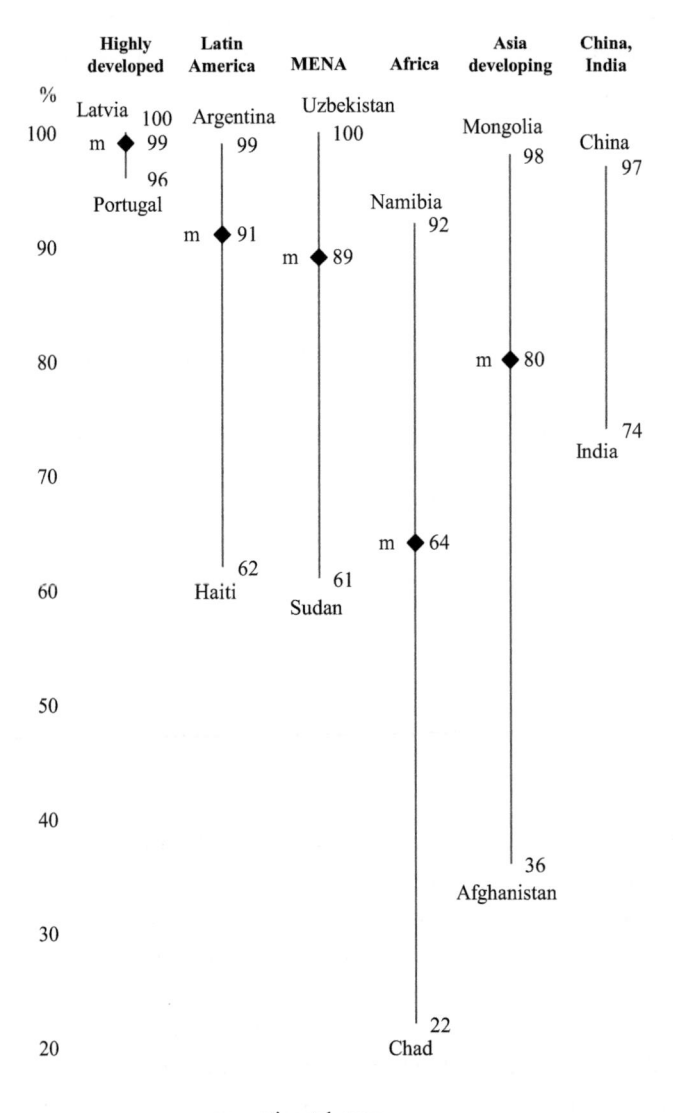

Figure 6.1 Adult literacy across continents

Source: Global Welfare Database.

reports 96 per cent adult literacy. The average literacy rate in Latin America is only 5 percentage points below Portugal, and every Latin American country except Haiti reports that at least four-fifths of its population is literate. Notwithstanding China's complex ideographic script and later start in delivering education in rural as well as urban areas, 97 per cent of Chinese adults are now literate.

Literacy falls below nine-tenths of adults in four continents, and there are significant differences in the degree of literacy within continents. The difference is as high as 70 percentage points in sub-Saharan Africa, and in eleven African countries a majority of adults are still illiterate. Only a small number of scattered island states in the Pacific Ocean do not have laws making education compulsory for all youths.

The achievement of complete adult literacy requires the education of females as well as males. In less developed countries there has historically been a tendency to favour males getting an education. Even when legal barriers are absent, religious and social norms can obstruct the education of girls. In India in 1991 adult males were almost twice as likely to be literate as females. Rapid progress in basic education for young girls has since reduced the gender gap in literacy to 16 percentage points. In China the proportion of women to men who are literate has risen from 91 per cent in 2000 to almost complete parity with men in 2018.

Literacy due to multiple influences

Primary schools, the chief institutions capable of making the whole of the population literate, require the resources that accompany development: schools need to be readily at hand in rural as well as urban areas, and money needs to be available to pay teachers so they do not rely on bribes to supplement their official salary. A country's level of development has a significant and substantial effect on national literacy. For every 1-point increase in the Index of Development, literacy increases by more than 3 percentage points (Table 6.1). However, it is not the only influence.

Communist regimes left a mixed legacy to post-communist states. The need for literacy and skills useful for rapid industrialization encouraged mass education. However, in a global setting this effect is countered by formerly communist states having an Index of Development depressed by restrictions on freedom and corruption in services such as education. Because of communist regimes promoting education for generations born three-quarters of a century ago, in ex-communist systems the literacy of adults is 18 percentage

Table 6.1 Influences on achieving adult literacy

Development Index	3.79***
	(0.51)
Ex-Communist	18.41***
	(3.59)
Muslim	−8.80**
	(3.18)
Constant	65.96***
	(2.88)
Variance explained R2	50.4%

** $p<0.01$ *** $p< 0.001$
Source: Ordinary least squares regression analysis of Global Welfare Database. Standard errors in parentheses.

points higher than would be predicted solely on the basis of their Index of Development.

Adults who live in thirty societies with a majority of Muslims are less likely to be literate. In Muslim societies extending from Morocco to developing countries in Asia the mean level of adult literacy was 72 per cent, while in non-Muslim developing societies the average level of literacy was 80 per cent in 2018. The regression analysis shows that, in societies in which Muslims are a majority of the population, literacy is 8 percentage points lower than would otherwise be the case. However, Muslim countries that have the legacy of former membership in the Soviet Union gain a boost to literacy that is more than twice the negative effect on literacy of their distinctive culture (Table 6.1).

Public expenditure on education as a percentage of gross domestic product produces the same results as public expenditure on health: it has no statistically significant influence on literacy. This is likely to reflect literacy varying substantially between countries, whereas the difference in public spending on education varies little around the global average of 4.4 per cent of a country's GDP. It is 4.4 per cent in sub-Saharan Africa and 4.7 per cent in high-income countries (United Nations, 2020: 364).

National differences in collecting and reporting literacy separately for men and women result in data being available for only fifty-seven countries; highly developed countries are the main under-represented group. Separate regressions of literacy for men and women report results similar to the analysis of 127 countries reported in Table 6.1. It finds that the culture of Muslim societies has a significant negative effect on female literacy but not male literacy.

6.2 More education

Increasing the number of secondary schools is assumed to improve what the OECD calls 'the learning environment' (OECD, 2020: chs. C, D). After making primary education compulsory, governments around the world have made basic secondary education compulsory by raising the school-leaving age. In England it was raised from 12 to 14 in 1918, to 15 in 1947, and to 16 in 1972. In highly developed countries today, ten or more years of full-time education are normally compulsory, and in India and sub-Saharan African countries at least eight years are often compulsory (OECD, 2020: 155 ff.; World Bank, 2018: 58 ff.). Moreover, in the great majority of countries youths have the option of voluntarily continuing their education free of charge beyond the required minimum. The nomenclature used to describe secondary schools differs. For example, an American high school usually teaches pupils to a lower standard than an English grammar school. Eton College offers secondary schooling up to the standard of the first year or two of an American Ivy League college. A German *Gymnasium* is not a place for exercising the body but an academic secondary school where the minds of pupils are given a vigorous workout.

Different purposes, different paths

There comes a point when enough is enough. This becomes evident when youths reach the age at which further attendance in secondary education is voluntary. At this point they face a pair of questions: What kind of course do I follow if I continue in secondary education? What kind of a job can I get with a minimum of education?

Institutions for secondary education differ in the qualifications offered to youths differing in aptitudes and interests. On every continent pupils who complete primary education are either required by law or can volunteer to enter what is technically called lower secondary education and Americans call junior high school. In this book it will be referred to as *basic secondary education*. It typically lasts three years and offers a wider and more specialized range of subjects than primary schools. For generations virtually all youths in highly developed countries have continued into compulsory basic secondary education, and this is now usually the case in China and Latin America. By contrast, an average of one-quarter of African children are not qualified to enter secondary education because they have not completed primary education. Among Africans who complete primary education, four-fifths continue into secondary education.

Secondary education offers pupils a choice of academic and vocational alternatives. An academic course involves a continuation of classroom study leading to examinations that qualify individuals for university entrance. A vocational course gives a specialized education linked to a particular occupation, such as automobile repair or hairdressing, or more general training in information technology. Occupations differ by the amount of education and training required to become a lawyer, a desk-based secretary, or a hands-on chef. They also differ in the extent to which they emphasize written questions, such as accountancy, or handwork, such as laying bricks. Vocational studies may be provided on a full-time basis or as a work-based apprenticeship that is accompanied by part-time classroom instruction. In European Union countries, almost half of male and female pupils in upper secondary education follow vocational courses.

Net enrolment in secondary education is the indicator that the UNESCO Institute of Statistics uses to estimate the percentage of teenagers who continue education. It is the percentage of youths of compulsory school age who are actually enrolled in school. This allows for cross-national differences in the age at which youths are required to remain in education. In highly developed countries net secondary school education enrolment was 93 per cent in 2018, while the mean for developing countries was 62 per cent. China, Latin American, and Middle East and North African countries report enrolment above the mean, and India is at the mean for developing countries. While enrolment in secondary education in Africa has increased by more than three-quarters over three decades, it still only accounts for less than two-fifths of African youths.

There is no certainty that whenever youths leave school they will want to go straight to work. Official labour market statistics classify those between 18 and 24 who are not in education or employment as NEETs (not in education, employment, or training). In highly developed societies an average of 14 per cent of youths are NEETs. In developing countries the proportion is much higher. In Brazil 31 per cent are not in the official economy or education, and in South Africa the proportion rises above two-fifths (OECD, 2020: 64). This does not mean that these young adults are economically inactive in the broader sense (see Section 3.3). They may earn an untaxed income working in the informal shadow economy or do unpaid work in their household.

The Index of Development has an even stronger influence on enrolment in secondary education than on adult literacy. In countries that have an Index of Development 2 standard deviations higher than the global average, the percentage increase in secondary school enrolment is almost double the level of adult literacy (cf. Tables 6.1 and 6.2). The lesser effect of development on

Table 6.2 Influences on enrolment in secondary school

Development Index	7.32***
	(0.55)
Ex-Communist	24.24***
	(4.01)
Muslim	−5.41
	(3.73)
Constant	30.27***
	(3.12)
Variance explained R2	69.0%

** $p<0.01$ *** $p< 0.001$
Source: Ordinary least squares regression analysis of Global Welfare Database. Standard errors in parentheses.

literacy suggests that it is seen everywhere as a necessity, so that youths and their parents will make every effort to enrol in primary school. However, in societies low in development there are fewer secondary school places along with a greater need for youths to start contributing to the household income rather than invest in secondary education.

The communist emphasis on education as a means towards rapid economic growth has left a legacy. After controlling for its Index of Development, the communist legacy gives a boost bigger by one-third to the number of youths attending secondary school than to the achievement of literacy (cf. Tables 6.1 and 6.2). While living in a Muslim society lowers a country's literacy, it does not have an additional effect on enrolment in secondary education.

Tertiary education requires voluntary study at a higher level than secondary education, while also being a broad category that covers courses differing in purpose, academic content, and institutional form. The ISCED definition of tertiary education combines vocationally oriented short courses that lead to a higher vocational qualification and courses conferring a university degree. Some subjects taught at tertiary level, such as law and medicine, have both academic and vocational features. National governments differ in how they organize and describe institutions of tertiary education and can change labels while leaving their content relatively unaltered. For example, after creating polytechnics as tertiary institutions offering vocational qualifications to large numbers of students, the British government renamed them universities so it could claim it had greatly increased the quantity of British university graduates.

The United States has three types of tertiary institutions at three different levels. The top institutions are large research universities, some operated by American states, such as the University of Michigan, and some private, such as Harvard and Yale. They educate students up to PhD level and also offer high-level professional degrees in subjects such as law and medicine. Smaller private colleges offer a four-year general academic education leading to a bachelor's degree, while mass public universities emphasize bachelor's degrees with a vocational focus on such subjects as business and agriculture. Two-year junior colleges offer vocationally oriented training that can lead to employment or to entering the final two years of a four-year bachelor's degree at a state university.

There are substantial differences between and within continents in the percentage of adults with a tertiary education at a level equivalent to a bachelor's, master's, or PhD degree. Differences in nomenclature and duration of study make comparisons only approximate, but the pattern is clear. In the average European country 32 per cent have a qualification equivalent to at least a bachelor's degree, and the same is the case in the United States (OECD, 2020: 50). There are big differences between developing continents in the percentage of adults with some form of tertiary education. The average for Africa is 8 per cent of adults with post-secondary education, while for Latin America the proportion is 19 per cent. Among Muslim countries where Islamic cultural values are widespread, 23 per cent of adults have a post-secondary education in Iran but it is only 9 per cent in Pakistan.

There are both within-nation and cross-national differences in the level of education that adults receive in youth. In highly developed countries, the median adult has enough secondary education to obtain a white-collar vocational qualification. Less than one-fifth have only a minimum of compulsory education, and very few are illiterate. Among the six relatively developed Latin American countries for which there is OECD data (2020: 50), adults are divided into four groups almost equal in size. One-quarter have had a university education and just over one-quarter an advanced secondary education. Further down the ladder, one-quarter have had only a lower secondary education and little more than one-fifth only a primary education. Asian countries show two different patterns. Among adults in India, low education means being illiterate, whereas in China it means having at least an elementary education and being literate. In both countries those with an upper secondary or university education are in a minority. Yet given the massive size of their populations, China and India each have a larger number of educated people than any single highly developed country.

6.3 More learning

In public policy analysis the value of learning is often reduced to quantified estimates of the income gained by individuals in return for the money and time they invest in education. However, there is no one-to-one correlation between the number of years that youths are in school and the quality of what they learn. In the succinct judgment of a World Bank review (2018: 4), 'Schooling is not the same as learning'. Even if all pupils in a class receive a certificate of attendance, they do not receive the same grade. Moreover, much learning does not take place in school but in the home or on the job. It is not validated by examinations but by use in daily life; for example, the knowledge a taxi driver acquires to get around a city efficiently or to charge a fare to a foreign tourist.

Classroom learning

Examinations are the conventional way in which schools assess pupils and national education ministries assess schools. The Programme for International Student Assessment (PISA) was created in the 1990s to produce tests for comparing student learning across national boundaries (http://www.oecd.org/pisa; cf. Woessmann, 2016; Zhao, 2020). Triennial examinations in mathematics, science, and reading are set by multinational teams of experts and national education administrators and coordinated by the OECD. To verify that questions can be understood across continents, three dozen countries pilot a draft questionnaire. Within each participating country the tests are administered to dozens of schools that differ in their curriculum, pupil intake, and location.

Mathematical reasoning is particularly apt for comparison across continents because tests can use the global language of mathematical notation. Moreover, mathematics is a compulsory subject in both primary and secondary schools and does not require the investment in laboratory equipment needed to teach science. The 2018 PISA mathematics test was administered to 600,000 secondary school pupils in seventy-eight countries and cities, of which sixty are included in the Global Welfare Database.

Asian countries produce the best mathematics results (Figure 6.2). Across all continents, the seven highest scores come from Chinese cities, followed by Singapore, Macau, Hong Kong, Taipei, Japan, and Korea. The leading European country is Estonia, ranked eighth. The United Kingdom is just above the mean for highly developed countries, while the United States ranks fifth from the bottom.

Even though Latin American youths have had a similar amount of education as those in highly developed countries, there is a substantial gap between the two groups in the PISA mathematics test. The mean score for eleven Latin American countries is one-fifth below that of highly developed countries. Moreover, none of the highest-ranking Latin American results was up to the level of the lowest result in highly developed countries. This is consistent with Spain, which had initially set standards for its many Latin American colonies, likewise having a low PISA maths score. The average PISA score in Asian developing regions was virtually the same as in Latin America except for Vietnam (Figure 6.2).

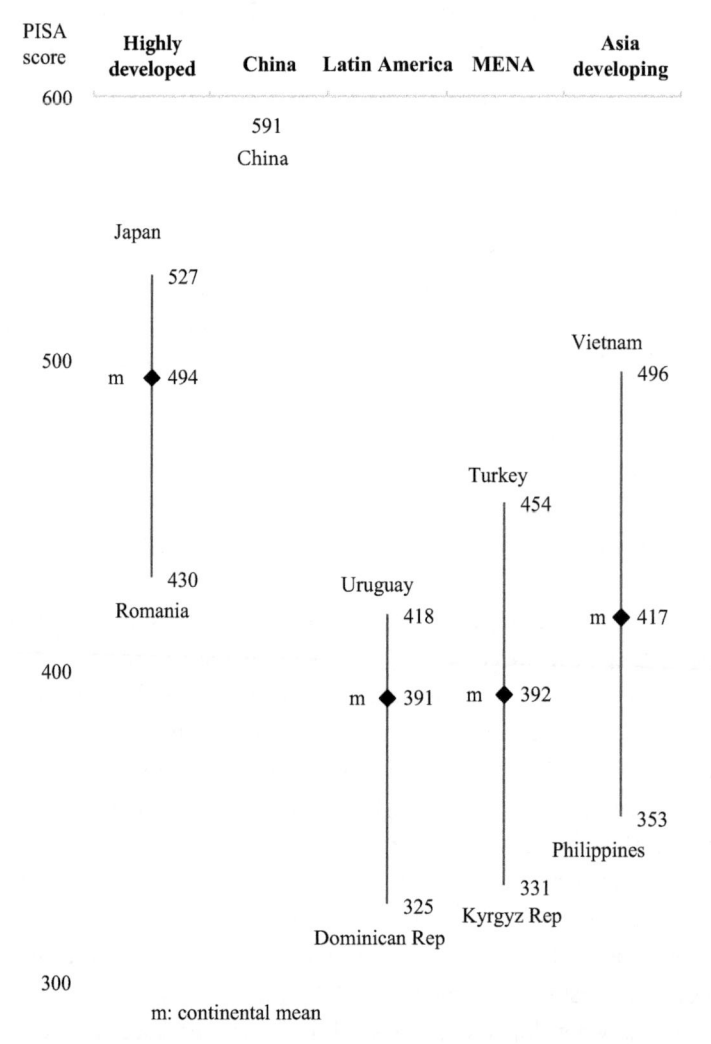

Figure 6.2 Countries differ in mathematical skills

Source: PISA Mathematics Skills 2018 (www.oecd.org/pisa) Number of countries: 34 for highly developed, 11 for Latin America, 8 for MENA, 5 for Asia developing.

The sole African country covered by PISA, Mauritius, scored at the same level as the Latin American mean. It was also the leading country in a similar mathematics test organized in thirteen countries by the Southern and Eastern Africa Consortium for Monitoring Educational Quality (SACMEQ). The median African country's test score was one-quarter lower than that of Mauritius.

Influences on learning mathematics cannot be compared with influences on other welfare measures because PISA tests have only been conducted in less than half the sixty countries included in the Global Welfare Database, and there is a big over-representation of the most developed countries and under-representation of developing countries. Since China, Japan, the Republic of Korea, Vietnam, and Malaysia appear to share a culture that cultivates mathematics skills (Leung, 2017), two regressions are run to test influences on PISA scores. One includes Muslim societies as an independent variable, since it is significant for literacy, and the other replaces that group with a variable for five East Asian countries.

The regression analysis of PISA mathematics scores with the same independent variables as for adult literacy accounts for 44.2 per cent of the variance in PISA mathematics scores; only the Index of Development is significant (Table 6.3). When East Asian countries—China, Japan, Korea, Malaysia, and Vietnam—are substituted for Muslim countries as an alternative measure of culture, a much fuller account is given. This regression raises the variance

Table 6.3 Two models of influences on PISA mathematics scores

Culture	Muslim	East Asia
Development Index	14.37*** (3.10)	19.59*** (2.15)
Ex-Communist	34.36 (14.0)	51.61*** (11.5)
Muslim	−28.15 (18.50)	-
East Asian	-	105.63*** (17.60)
Constant	360.10*** (23.40)	308.84*** (15.93)
Variance explained R2	44.2%	64.6%

** $p<0.01$ *** $p<0.001$
Source: PISA Mathematics Skills 2018 (http://www.oecd.org/pisa). Ordinary least squares regression analysis. Standard errors in parentheses. Number of countries 60, of which East Asia 5 and Muslim 8.

accounted for to 64.6 per cent, and all three independent variables become statistically significant. After controlling for other influences, students in the East Asian group of countries have a PISA score that is 105 points more than would be expected. Moreover, the impact of the Index of Development and of the communist legacy is also increased.

Instrumental learning

Children start learning to talk in their household before they start school. Their motive is instrumental: it is to communicate with others. In a globalizing world adults are increasingly under pressure to learn a foreign language in order to communicate with others in their job, whether they work as an airline pilot, a dealer in foreign currency, or a waiter. Dozens of countries are today officially bilingual. The Republic of India is an extreme example; the eighth schedule of its constitution recognizes twenty-two ethnic languages and makes Hindi and English the official languages of the state.

In an era of globalization, the existence of more than a hundred languages spoken by at least a million people creates a demand for a lingua franca, that is, a common language that can be used to communicate by people speaking different home languages (Rose, 2008). In medieval Europe this was Latin; it became French when France became the most powerful state in Europe. In East Africa Swahili combined Bantu languages and Arabic to become the lingua franca of that region. The spread of the British Empire across the Indian subcontinent and Africa made it a working language over much of the globe. Esperanto, an easily learned amalgam of European languages, was devised in the 1880s but was unable to supplant the use of languages backed by populous and powerful states.

English is today the chief lingua franca in use for communication between people who have different native languages. The global use of English as a lingua franca reflects the contemporary hard and soft power of the United States (Nye, 2004) and the legacy of the British Empire. Even though Spanish is the official language of more than a score of states and is spoken by more than half a billion people, it is not a global lingua franca because Spain is no longer the global power it was when it spread the use of Spanish in the western hemisphere five centuries ago.

The European Union is an extreme example of the instrumental use of English. French was initially its lingua franca, and after the United Kingdom joined it gradually supplanted French as the EU's lingua franca. Since the departure of the United Kingdom, English has remained the official language of only two small member states, Malta and Ireland. Nonetheless, among EU staff who have more than a score of first languages it has remained the institution's primary working language for communication between pairs of people who have different Eropean first languages, such as Spanish, Danish, or Latvian.

Estimates of the globalization of English vary according to the method used, but there is a consensus that more than one billion people make instrumental use of English, and there are more EFL (English as a foreign language) speakers than there are native speakers of English (Eberhard, Simons, and Fennig, 2022). The United States is the country with the largest number of English speakers, because it is the world's third most populous country and English in its American form is its official language (Figure 6.3). However, because its population includes many immigrants from other continents, especially Spanish-speaking countries of Latin America, up to one-quarter of Americans do not speak English as their first language.

While the United Kingdom is second in the number of native speakers of English, it is only sixth in the total number of people who speak English. Because English is the lingua franca of choice for hundreds of millions of people, British people lack the instrumental incentive to learn a foreign language to communicate because they can use their native language. They also lack the incentive to understand how Europeans live, while for continental Europeans such understanding is part of instrumentally learning English (Rose, 2008).

In four of the six countries that have the most English speakers, English is a lingua franca rather than the first language of the hundreds of millions of

United States 315
India 136
Pakistan 109
Nigeria 105
Philippines 69
UK 66

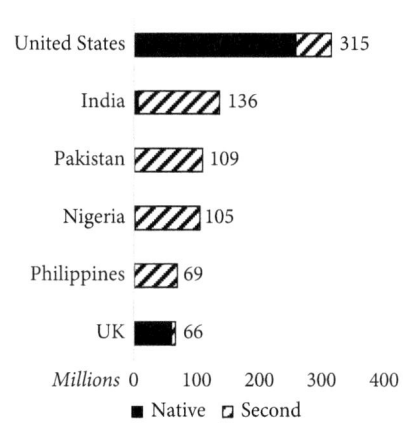

Millions 0   100   200   300   400
■ Native ☐ Second

Figure 6.3 Countries with most English speakers

Source: https://en.wikipedia.org/wiki/List_of_countries_by_English-speaking_population. Accessed 27 May 2023.

EFL speakers. India, Pakistan, and Nigeria each have more than 100 million people using English. This is due not only to the legacy of the British Empire but also to each being a polylingual country, and English is a neutral language that avoids favouring one or another native language over others. This is also the case in the Philippines, a polylingual former American colony.

6.4 The globalization of education

Education becomes globalized insofar as the average country on each continent reaches the level of achievement of the leading continent. Since educational goals tend to be fixed, there is no intrinsic obstacle to the total globalization of educational achievements sooner or later if countries continue making progress to global standards. Table 6.4 shows the extent to which the mean level of education on each continent approaches the mean for the continent with the highest achievement.

The globalization of literacy, the basic requirement for participating in educational progress, is well advanced. In China and the average country in Latin America and the MENA region nine-tenths or more adults are already literate. In India literacy has increased by more than half in three decades, but one-quarter of Indian adults are still illiterate. African countries started from the same low base as India but have not been making progress at the same pace as India. Hence, more than one-third of African adults remain below the global standard for literacy.

Because statistics on primary education show the effect of current national policies, there is a much higher degree of globalization than for adult literacy, which reflects the education or lack of education in preceding generations. In highly developed countries an average of 99 per cent of children complete at

Table 6.4 Globalization of education

	HiDev	LatAm	MENA	China	Africa	India	AsiaDev
Continental education as percentage of global leader							
Adult literacy	100	92	90	98	65	75	81
Primary	99	95	96	100	73	93	97
Secondary	100	78	80	71	38	66	64
Tertiary	100	65	52	66	13	36	34
PISA	84	66	66	100	47	n.a.	71

Source: Global Welfare Database. Primary completion rate. Secondary and tertiary school enrolments as per cent of relevant age group.

least six years of primary schooling. China reports a similar level. In all other continents bar one more than 90 per cent of today's children are enrolled in primary school. Africa is the outlier: more than one-quarter of children do not finish primary school. This group's size is increased if account is taken of those who do not enter primary education.

The difference between highly developed and developing countries is greater in secondary education. By comparison with highly developed countries, only Latin American countries and those in the MENA region show statistics that place them within 25 percentage points of the standard for secondary school enrolment in highly developed countries. Enrolment of youths in secondary education falls to two-thirds of the global standard in India and Asian developing countries. In sub-Saharan Africa the enrolment of youths in secondary education is less than half the global standard, a consequence of its low level of participation in primary education. In the PISA mathematics test, China and Asian developing countries set the global standard for learning. The mean test score in highly developed countries is one-sixth below that of China. It would be lower still if Japan, Korea, and other East Asian countries were not treated as highly developed countries.

The globalization of tertiary education has been progressing rapidly on all continents and in many forms ranging from vocational instruction in information technology to university degrees in the arts and sciences, while trend statistics show the gap between highly developed and developing countries widening. Developing countries have been expanding tertiary education at a higher rate than the global leaders, but their starting point was a level of enrolment only two-fifths that of the leaders; this has produced less increase in tertiary education than the 43 percentage-point increase in highly developed countries. At best, enrolment in tertiary education in Latin America and in China is two-thirds the average in highly developed countries.

Demographic change ensures more globalization of education

The starting point for progress in education is an increase in the education of the youngest cohorts in society. In the great majority of countries, older adults were educated when there was significantly less provision of education than youths get today. The educational profile of a country's population today thus reflects cohorts with significantly different levels of education. In such circumstances, generational turnover in the population will gradually replace the less educated cohorts with younger and more educated cohorts, thereby raising its overall standards. Because both adult literacy and secondary school enrolment are fixed targets, a society can attain both, but the length of time differs: schools can be built faster than the time it takes for cohorts of less educated adults to die.

Table 6.5 shows the extent to which the level of education differs between young and old cohorts in developing as well as highly developed countries. On all continents, those with a low level of education or no education are contracting. In developing countries this results in a significant increase in those with a secondary school certificate and a tertiary level qualification as well. In highly developed countries it actually produces a fall in those completing their education at the secondary level because of the substantial portion of younger cohorts who go from secondary to tertiary institutions. On every continent death removes from the population people who were of school age up to three-quarters of a century ago when schooling was limited. Table 6.5 actually understates the degree of intergenerational change because the older generation is defined as the oldest cohort of working age rather than retirees up to a decade or more above the age of 65.

Global progress in education has occurred in both adult literacy and net enrolment in secondary education, but it has not occurred at the same

Table 6.5 Generational turnover creates progress everywhere

	University	Upper Secondary	Lower or none
Highly Developed	%	%	%
Young	47	41	12
Old	30	46	24
Change	+17	−5	−12
Latin America			
Young	30	37	33
Old	18	21	60
Change	+12	+16	−27
China			
Young	18	18	64
Old	4	8	88
Change	+14	+10	−24
India			
Young	20	13	67
Old	7	5	89
Change	+13	+8	−22

Source: https://stats.oecd.org/, as summarized in OECD, 2020. Total number of countries, 41: highly developed, 33; Latin America, 6, plus China and India.

tempo. It has been faster in secondary education, where changes need only affect today's teenagers, than in literacy, which reflects the past provision of education for generations of adults. Global progress is made categorically clear by OECD recently changing the definition of low education from being illiterate or having only a primary education: it now defines it as the lack of an advanced secondary education.

References

Eberhard, David M., Simons, G. F., and Fennig, C. D., eds., 2022. *Ethnologue: Languages of the World*. Dallas: SIL International, 25th edition.

Leung, Frederick K. S., 2017. 'Making Sense of Mathematics Achievement in East Asia: Does Culture *Really* Matter?' In Gregory Kaiser, ed., Proceedings of 13th International Congress on Mathematical Education, ICME-13 Monographs, https://link.springer.com/book/10.1007/978-3-319-62597-3.

Lindert, Peter H., 2021. *Making Social Spending Work*. Cambridge: Cambridge University Press.

Nye, Joseph S., 2004. *Soft Power: The Means to Success in World Politics*. New York: Public Affairs Press.

OECD (Organization for Economic Cooperation and Development), 2020. *Education at a Glance*. Paris: OECD Indicators.

Rose, Richard, 2008. 'Political Communication in a European Public Space', *Journal of Common Market Studies*, 46, 2, 451–75.

Sen, Amartya, 2005. 'Human Rights and Capabilities', *Journal of Human Development*, 6, 151–66.

UNESCO, 1988. *Compendium of Statistics on Literacy*. Paris: UNESCO.

United Nations, 1950. *United Nations Statistical Yearbook, 1949–50*. New York: United Nations.

United Nations, 2020. *Inclusion and Education*. New York: UNESCO Global Education Monitoring Report.

Woessmann, Ludger, 2016. 'The Importance of School Systems', *Journal of Economic Perspectives*, 30, 3, 3–32.

World Bank, 2018. *Learning to Realize Education's Promise*. Washington DC: World Bank World Development Review.

Zhao, Y., 2020. 'Two Decades of Havoc: A Synthesis of Criticism against PISA', *Journal of Educational Change*, 21, 245–66.

7
Work for Women

Work is a social construct; it reflects legal criteria and social mores as well as economic activities. Growing food, looking after children, and do-it-yourself repairs produce goods and services whether or not the person doing the work is paid money (see Chapter 3). In whatever form it takes, work can contribute to welfare not only by producing a service but also by giving a person a status in society, a sense of accomplishment, and money if they are paid for what they do. However, in the economic analysis of highly developed countries the term 'work' is normally restricted to participation in the labour force of the officially defined economy.

Women are the largest group of adults not included in official definitions of the labour force, because they are more likely than men to be non-waged workers in the home, in family shops, and in rural fields. This work is an economic activity because its products can in principle be sold or consumed in the household. Empirical studies of the use of time by men and women show that women often work more hours in a week than men without being paid for all their efforts (Gershuny and Sullivan, 2019).

Industrialization did little to mobilize women into the official labour force. It expanded heavy industries such as coal mining and railways that disproportionately employed men. Being a housewife was an unpaid occupation in itself and women could expect to spend a third to half their adult life in pregnancy or looking after their numerous children (Titmuss, 1958: 91). About a third of British women were in paid employment from the 1860s onwards, often working as domestic servants (Joshi, Layard, and Owen, 1985: table 1). In the United States an estimated 18 per cent of women were in the labour force in 1890 and 25 per cent by 1930 (Smith and Ward, 1985: table 1). In spite of the mobilization of women during the Second World War, only 30 per cent of American women and 40 per cent of British women were in the labour force in 1950. In Sweden, where female participation was highest in Europe, 50 per cent of women of working age were then in paid employment. In France, the *aides familiaux* (unpaid family workers, mostly women and youths) totalled more than 3 million in 1950 (Page, 1985).

Since 1945 opportunities for women to undertake paid employment have increased. The decline in family size has greatly shortened the period of time a woman spends caring for young children and a longer lifespan has increased the years a woman can be employed outside the home. In highly developed societies, the decline of agriculture has greatly contracted the role of rural women as unpaid workers in the domestic economy of a peasant household. In developing countries the urbanization of the population has brought women to labour markets where there are many more opportunities to be paid for working in street markets, public services, and private companies.

There has also been an increased cultural acceptance of women having paid employment. In 1945 only 18 per cent of Americans thought married women should work if their husband could earn sufficient money to support the household, while recent surveys have found more than four-fifths approve of women being employed (Ortiz-Ospina, Tzvetkova, and Roser, 2018). In Muslim countries, however, a Pew Research Centre survey (2012) found that more than three-quarters of respondents endorsed the view that when jobs are scarce men should be given preference. In highly developed countries no more than one-fifth favoured giving men preference in employment.

While many adults combine both formal employment and household work, this chapter shows there are nonetheless significant gender differences in both the official labour market and unpaid employment. Men are more likely to be formally employed than women. Unlike the figures of health and education, women are more likely to be employed in countries that are least developed, where labour-intensive forms of agriculture are widespread and a shortage of money creates the necessity to work or do without. Within developing countries, cultural values influence whether women should be and are in paid work. Women are more likely to work in the household than men, and women who combine unpaid household work with paid employment work significantly more hours than men. The result is a significant degree of gender inequality.

7.1 Employment and gender

International employment statistics conventionally define the labour force as that portion of a country's adult population that is either working in the official economy or unemployed but actively seeking work. The statistics exclude people who are working at home caring for children and older household members. Those not in paid employment constitute what Germans call the *Stille Reserve* (silent reserve), because they may be drawn into employment if there is a demand for more workers and the pay is attractive. If unemployment is high, then some people stop trying to find work and leave the labour force.

The definition of the population of working age as individuals between the ages of 15 and 64 is an artifice that does not fit many countries today. When there was no free or compulsory education, there were no laws forbidding child labour, and children could begin working in their household by the age of 10. Countries that today have laws regulating youth employment differ in the minimum age for legally employing youths; it ranges from 12 to 18. The age at which adults stop being employed is likewise not fixed. In many developing countries there is no state pension paying older people an income if they stop work. Within highly developed countries the age of retiring on a pension varies and often allows retirement before the age of 65. The value of pensions also tends to vary with the number of years for which contributions are made to pension funds. This especially affects women who do not contribute to a pension fund during the years when they work as unpaid carers of their family (Addati et al., 2018).

Participation in the labour force competes with other welfare goals. At age 15 many youths are legally required to be in education, and a significant fraction continue in voluntary study to the age of 18 or beyond (see Chapter 6). Women are more likely than men to undertake unpaid work caring for their children when they are young. In highly developed countries many women and men choose to retire with a pension below the age of 65. In short, participation in employment is a right not an obligation.

Employment is higher in less developed countries

Theories of economic development emphasize the importance of investing in sophisticated technologies to increase the productivity of a skilled labour force. Countries low in development lack the capital to invest in new technologies and lack lots of skilled labour; their chief resource is cheap and plentiful labour (cf. Lewis, 1954; Todaro and Smith, 2020:122 ff.). The contrast is very evident in agriculture. In Africa employment in agriculture averages 47 per cent of the labour force, in India 42 per cent, and in Asian developing countries 38 per cent. By contrast, in highly developed countries capital-intensive farming results in an average of only 4 per cent of the population being employed in agriculture.

At any one point in time, about half to two-thirds of a country's adults of notional working age are counted as participating in the labour force.

Cross-continental differences in employment do not follow the same pattern as differences in health and education. The percentage employed is highest on developing continents: 68 per cent in sub-Saharan Africa and China; 66 per cent in Latin America; and 64 per cent among developing countries of Asia. Yet participation is also lowest in some developing continents: 49 per cent in India and 51 per cent in the Middle East and North Africa region. Employment in highly developed countries, which is where there is the most capital to invest in labour-saving devices, is middling—60 per cent.

Throughout the world there has been a decline in participation in the labour force as the proportion of young people remaining longer in education increases. In China there has been a fall of 11 percentage points from 1991, when 79 per cent were employed, and India has had a 9 percentage point fall in employment. Contraction on other developing continents has been significant but less. In highly developed countries, where secondary school attendance has long been normal along with pension-financed retirement, there has been no significant change in the percentage of the population in employment.

Gender differences in the labour force

Measures of participation in the official economy treat men and women the same: both are described in gender-neutral terms as participants or non-participants in the labour force. However, structural features in the economy have differential effects on the employment of women and men (Giuliano, 2017). All over the world men are more likely to be employed in industry and women in service jobs such as teaching, health care, and retailing. Today there are far fewer jobs than in the past for men in heavy industries such as coal mining and steel (Ortiz-Ospina, Tzvetkova, and Roser, 2018).

The state's increasing commitment to social services has created many paid jobs that women have long done as unpaid workers in their household. Public institutions are major employers of teachers, nurses, and carers (OECD, 2019: 88 f.). In highly developed countries, women constitute an average of 60 per cent of the public sector labour force. In the four Nordic countries 70 per cent of public employees are women, and the figure is two-thirds in the United Kingdom. The proportion of women who are public employees falls to just over two-fifths in Japan and India. Turkey, a Muslim society, is distinctive in that almost three-quarters of public sector employees are male.

In every society men are expected to work; male participation in the labour force averages 72 per cent, and this figure is similar across continents. There is a difference of only 12 percentage points between the continent where it is

Percentage employed, ages 15–64

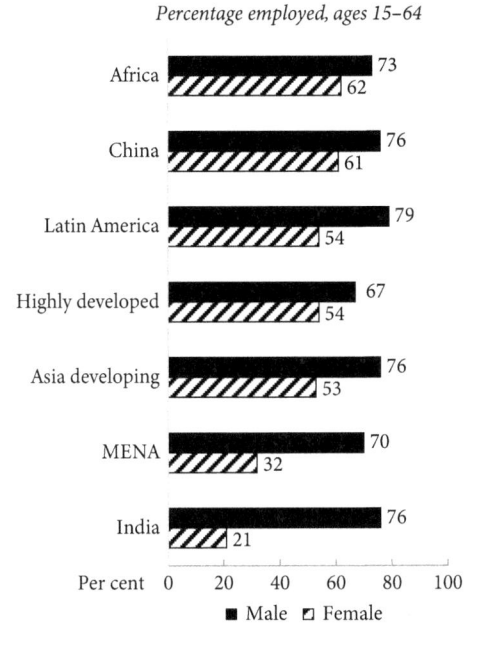

Region	Male	Female
Africa	73	62
China	76	61
Latin America	79	54
Highly developed	67	54
Asia developing	76	53
MENA	70	32
India	76	21

■ Male ◊ Female

Figure 7.1 Female and male participation in employment
Source: Global Welfare Database.

highest, Latin America, and lowest, highly developed countries (Figure 7.1). In Zimbabwe and Madagascar the proportion of employed men rises to 88 per cent and in Guatemala to 86 per cent. Male employment in highly developed countries is less high, 67 per cent, as opportunities for further education and early retirement have an effect. The highly developed country with the most employed men, New Zealand, has a lower proportion of men in employment than India.

Globally, an average of 54 per cent of women are nationally employed, one-third less than the average for men. There are differences of up to 41 percentage points between continents (Figure 7.1). Participation by women is highest in Africa, 62 per cent, reflecting the widespread persistence of rural practices in which all members of a household work. Limited access to education has meant that girls can be employed before they are 15 or not go to school at all. The participation of African women in employment is highest in Rwanda, 84 per cent.

The high rate of female participation in China, 61 per cent, reflects the Great Leap Forward strategy of Mao Zedong. In order to develop the national economy rapidly, the power of the Communist Party and a shortage of food were used to mobilize women as well as men into officially controlled employment.

While Beijing's power over its subjects is not matched in Asian developing countries, a low standard of living has likewise spurred an average of 53 per cent of women to be employed in these countries. However, there is a range of 60 percentage points between Nepal, where female employment is 82 per cent, and Muslim countries such as Pakistan and Afghanistan, where only 22 per cent of women are employed.

Culture and politics differentiate countries in the Middle East and North Africa. An average of 32 per cent of females are employed, but the proportion falls as low as 11 per cent in Iraq. In successor states of the Soviet Union, the aggressive combination of secularization and mobilization of women in the state economy under communism has left a legacy of high female labour force participation, reaching 63 per cent in Azerbaijan and Kazakhstan. Cultural values result in only 21 per cent of women in India being officially employed, reflecting Hindu traditions actively promoted by the ruling Bharatiya Janata Party (Datta, Endow, and Mehta, 2020).

In highly developed countries 54 per cent of women of working age are in paid employment (Figure 7.1) and there are limited differences between countries. Participation is highest in countries that attract young men and women as immigrants: 65 per cent in New Zealand and 61 per cent in Canada and Australia. It is also around three-fifths in Nordic states with small populations and labour forces. However, there are seven highly developed countries in which less than half of women are in the labour force; the figure is lowest in Greece, 44 per cent, and Italy, 41 per cent.

On every continent and in almost every country the percentage of men in employment is significantly greater than women, but gender differences tend to be a matter of degree not kind, except where cultural values discourage female employment. A majority of women as well as men participate in the labour force on five continents. In Africa, where employment is highest, the difference averages 11 percentage points, and high female employment limits the degree of gender difference in China to 15 per cent. In highly developed countries the gender gap averages only 13 per cent because male employment is relatively low. The gender bias is largest in India, where men are three and a half times more likely to be employed than women, and the Middle East and North Africa region, where men are more than twice as likely to be employed as women.

Accounting for cross-national differences

The importance of gender in employment is shown by regression analyses that account for more than twice the variation in female employment as in male

Table 7.1 Contrasting influences on female and male employment

	Female	Male
Agriculture, per cent	0.33***	0.14***
	(0.05)	(0.03)
Ex-communist country	3.95	−3.33
	(2.92)	(1.96)
Muslim country	−21.10***	−2.44
	(2.35)	(1.58)
Constant	49.50***	69.60***
Variance explained R2	48.2%	19.8%

**p<0.01 ***p < 0.001.
Source: Ordinary least squares regression analysis of Global Welfare Database. Standard errors in parentheses.

employment (cf. Table 7.1). This is consistent with the national level of female employment varying much more than the level of male employment.

It is lack of development, as measured by the percentage employed in labour-intensive agriculture, that has a significant positive effect on the employment of both men and women (Table 7.1). Where national income and household income are low, there is a demand for cheap labour in default of the capital to buy labour-saving equipment; there is also a plentiful supply of labour willing to work for a low wage. A high level of agricultural employment is particularly important for mobilizing women, who may rely on multigenerational households for childcare. The effect of agriculture on increasing participation in work is twice as high for women as for men.

When the Index of Development is substituted for agriculture employment in a regression equation, it is statistically significant but its influence is the opposite of its effect on health and education measures. A higher Index of Development significantly reduces the level of participation in the labour force by both men and women. However, the depressing effect of development on the percentage of adults employed is not so strong as the boost given to employment in agricultural societies. Moreover, replacing agriculture with the Index of Development in a regression reduces the variance accounted for in female employment by one-third.

Variable effect of Muslim cultures

There are thirty countries in the Global Welfare Database in which a majority of the population is nominally Muslim: half are in the MENA region, ten in sub-Saharan Africa, and the remainder scattered across Asian developing countries. Since there is no Islamic prohibition on men working, there is no significant difference between males being employed in predominantly Muslim and non-Muslim societies (Table 7.1). However, living in a society in which the majority of the population is Muslim has a big negative effect on female employment. It tends to reduce female employment by 21 percentage points by comparison with non-Muslim societies.

Generalizing about Muslim societies requires care, because there is a tension between the strict interpretation of Islamic proscriptions and the international norm that women have the right to work outside their household. The balance between these conflicting values is struck differently among Muslim societies. In the Middle East and North Africa region, average female employment is by far the lowest of any continent, 32 per cent. However, in the sub-Saharan Muslim societies of Africa an average of 52 per cent of women are employed. Republics of the former Soviet Union with a nominal Muslim majority were subject to intense pressure from Moscow to adopt secular norms. Female employment in the Soviet successor states ranges from 29 per cent in Tajikistan to 63 per cent in Azerbaijan and Kazakhstan.

Big variations in female employment between Muslim societies require refining cultural generalizations. A sociological hypothesis is: *the larger the non-Muslim minority in the country, the less the effect of Muslim culture.* This assumes that a substantial number of non-Muslim women in employment makes it a visible and accepted practice for women to be employed, thereby reducing the social pressure on Muslim women to restrict themselves to unpaid work in their household. The proportion of nominal Muslims in countries where they are a majority of the population ranges from 99 per cent in six countries to 53 per cent in Nigeria.

Another explanation is that Muslims, like members of other religious groups, differ in their doctrinal beliefs and in whether they identify strongly with their religious faith (Akyol, 2022). The identity hypothesis is: *the stronger the identification of individuals with a distinctive religious faith, the more likely they are to follow its fundamental religious precepts.* In a survey of Muslim majority countries, the Pew Research Centre (2012) asked nominally Muslim respondents whether they identified with a distinctive Muslim denomination such as Sunni or Shia, thought of themselves simply as Muslims, or had no religious identity. On average 65 per cent of respondents identified with a specific denomination, usually the Sunni branch of Islam, while 35 per cent had a weak or no religious identification. There are big differences in religious identity between Muslim societies. Nine-tenths identified with a distinctive Muslim denomination in seven countries, while in five

Table 7.2 Muslim differences influence female employment

	Female employment	Gender equality
Agriculture, per cent	0.43***	0.50***
	[0.11]	[0.12]
Ex-communist	13.54	22.61***
	[5.43]	[6.15]
Per cent Muslim	−0.35***	−0.46***
	[0.06]	[0.07]
Constant	52.84***	72.08***
Variance explained R^2	70.8%	75.2%

**p<0.01 ***p<0.001.
Source: Female employment: Global Welfare Database. Percentage of Muslims in thirty-two Muslim-majority countries: Wikipedia.

countries three-quarters or more had only a weak religious identification or none.

Regression analyses confirm both the sociological and religious belief hypotheses. The greater the dominance of Muslims in a society in percentage terms and the higher the percentage identifying with a distinctive Islamic faith, the lower the level of female employment and of gender equality. Table 7.2 presents the regressions for the sociological hypothesis because the percentage of Muslims in a society has the greater impact. It accounts for 70.8 per cent of the variation in female employment within Muslim societies and 75.2 per cent of the variation in gender equality. The proportion of the population working in agriculture also gives a significant but lesser boost to female employment and gender equality. The legacy of communist mass mobilization of women raises gender equality by 22 percentage points compared to Muslim societies not subject to the secular influence of communist indoctrination.

7.2 Accounting for gender inequality

Gender equality in the labour force has a natural target: a one-to-one ratio of women to men reflects 100 per cent gender equality. If men are more numerous in a country's labour force than women, as is almost invariably the case, the gender ratio can range from 16 per cent in Iraq to above 100 per cent in three African countries in which more women are employed than men. Because it is a ratio, gender equality can increase not only because of a rise in female participation in employment but also because of a decrease in the participation of men.

Gender inequality differs between and within continents

The mean level of gender equality is highest on continents that differ greatly in development (Figure 7.2). In sub-Saharan Africa, women are under economic pressure to work in order to augment the low cash incomes of men in their household; this creates a gender equality ratio of 85 per cent. However, there is a 60 percentage point difference in gender equality between three African countries where women are more likely to be employed than men and Mauritania, where men are more than twice as likely to be employed as women. In highly developed countries gender equality averages only four points below the African average. It is highest in Norway and Sweden, 90 per cent, and lowest in Italy, 69 per cent. In China there have been political as well as economic pressures on women to work; the gender equality ratio is 80 per cent.

Gender inequality varies greatly among Muslim countries. The ratio of female to male employment differs by as much as 89 percentage points between in the African state of Guinea and as low as 16 in Iraq. The mean gender equality ratio for Muslim societies is 56, compared to a gender equality ratio of 80 in non-Muslim countries. In the Muslim Middle East and North Africa region the gender equality ratio averages 46 per cent, while the variation between countries is extremely high. There is a 74 percentage point difference in gender equality between the post-Soviet state of Azerbaijan and strictly Islamic Iraq.

In the developing countries of Asia there is a 72 percentage point difference in gender equality; it reaches a high in Papua New Guinea, which has no state religion, and is lowest in Pakistan, where fundamental Islamic values tend to be observed (Figure 7.2). The importance of national culture rather than multinational religious norms for female employment is underscored by the 70 percentage point difference in gender equality between two nominally Hindu societies, Nepal and India.

A regression analysis of influences on gender equality confirms the importance of Muslim culture and of agriculture; both are statistically significant (Table 7.3). Moreover, the size of their effects is also similar. After controlling for all other influences, in predominantly Muslim societies gender equality is 24 percentage points lower than in non-Muslim societies. The percentage in

Figure 7.2 Gender inequality in employment

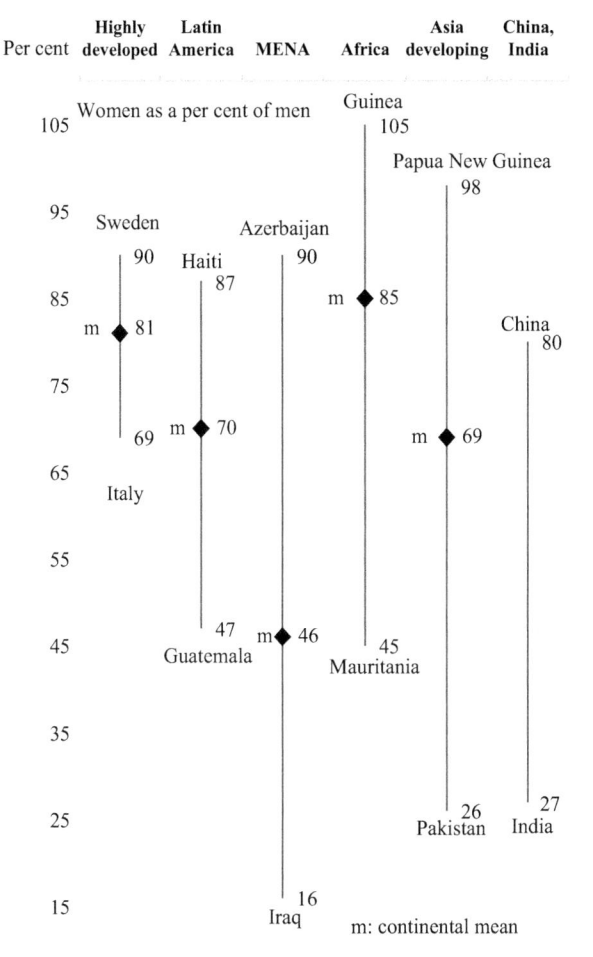

Per cent	Highly developed	Latin America	MENA	Africa	Asia developing	China, India
	Women as a per cent of men			Guinea 105		
105					Papua New Guinea 98	
95	Sweden 90		Azerbaijan 90			
85	m ◆ 81	Haiti 87	m ◆ 85			China 80
75						
65	69 Italy	m ◆ 70		m ◆ 69		
55						
45		47 Guatemala	m ◆ 46	45 Mauritania		
35						
25					26 Pakistan	27 India
15			16 Iraq			

m: continental mean

Figure 7.2 Gender inequality in employment
Source: Global Welfare Database.

Table 7.3 Influences on gender equality

Agriculture, per cent	0.29***
	(0.06)
Ex-communist country	8.52
	(3.95)
Muslim country	−26.59***
	(3.18)
Constant	71.82***
Variance explained R2	39.7%

**p<0.01 ***p<0.001
Source: Ordinary least squares regression analysis of Global Welfare Database. Standard errors in parentheses.

agriculture tends to increase gender equality substantially, but the effect is less than for female employment. Thus, the total amount of variance accounted for in the gender equality regression, 39.7 per cent, is less than the variation accounted for in female employment (cf. Table 7.1).

7.3 Rethinking what work is

Work is a necessary activity in every society. From the time of the pharaohs, political authorities have required subjects to contribute their labour to building everything from pyramids to canals and roads. The practice was formalized as *corvée* in feudal times. In the United States in the nineteenth century, local and state governments accepted farmers paying taxes by contributing labour rather than money (Sellers, 1991). Only recently have work activities been compartmentalized into separate categories: paid employment in the official economy; working untaxed in the shadow economy; and unpaid work in the household (Section 3.3; Lucassen, 2021).

On every continent today many households juggle a mixture of economies. People can participate in one economy or two, or combine activities in all three economies. In about two-thirds of households in the developing world, families have plots of land of up to 2 hectares on which they can grow food for their own consumption. As European peasants once did, families in developing countries can augment what they produce in their household by one member having a paid job or by borrowing money from friends and relatives if there is a need for medical treatment (cf. Rapsomanikas, 2015; Franklin, 1969).

Everyone works, but women and men work differently

Studies of how people use their time differ from labour force data. Official statistics classify as outside the labour force people who are neither in official employment or unemployed but are seeking work (ICLS, 2013: para. 15). This excludes up to half of a country's adult population, especially women. By contrast, time-use studies include the whole adult population and record how they spend their time over 168 hours each week. Thus, the time spent by a retired person caring for their partner is given equal weight with the time spent by a carer who is a paid employee in a nursing home.

Women are much more likely to work without pay than men (Figure 7.3). Time-use studies by the International Labour Organization (ILO) in fifty-eight

Minutes worked unpaid each day

Region	Male	Female
MENA	73	305
India	31	297
Latin America	102	285
Highly developed	141	262
Africa	68	239
China	94	237
Asia developing	60	235

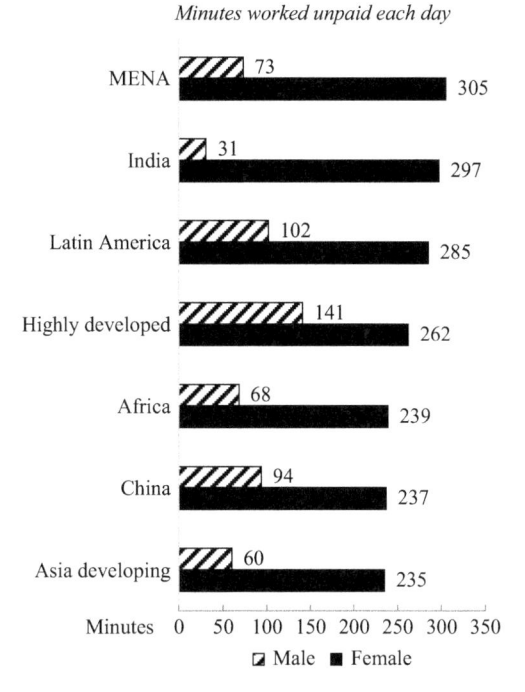

Figure 7.3 Women spend more time in unpaid work than men
Source: ILO, 2018: 368ff, surveys in 58 countries.

countries find that women on average spend almost four and a half hours a day doing unpaid household work (see Addati et al., 2018: 368 ff.). Moreover, there is limited difference across continents in the amount of unpaid work that women do. It is five hours a day in India and the MENA region and more than four hours a day in Latin America and highly developed countries. Men tend to spend two-thirds or less time in unpaid work than do women. India is an extreme case: women spend nine times as much of the day in unpaid work as do men, while men are almost four times as likely to be in paid employment than women. In the Middle East and North Africa women on average devote four times more hours daily to unpaid work than do men. The gender inequality in unpaid work is not so big in highly developed countries; it averages two hours a day.

The ILO study found that 59 per cent of women who were not seeking paid employment gave family responsibilities as a reason for doing so, compared to 15 per cent of men. By contrast, women living on their own were more likely to be employed than the female average. In addition, economic necessity results in women who are single parents of children being more likely to engage in paid work than the average woman (Ortiz-Ospina, Tzvetkova, and Roser, 2018).

The worldwide decline in fertility and the increased use of contraceptive methods have reduced the number of children that must be cared for by the average woman. This has made childcare an interruption in a woman's working career rather than a long-term obstacle to employment (Lundborg, Plug, and Rasmussen, 2017). Concurrently, the development of labour-saving equipment to do housework formerly undertaken by hand has given women more time to undertake paid employment outside their household (Greenwood, Seshadri, and Yorukoglu, 2005).

Even though the time that individuals in high-income countries spend in paid work is less than in developing countries, individuals still spend a lot of time in unpaid work—for example, preparing home-made meals. Whether children receive a public or private education or childcare, for most of the time they are looked after in their household rather than at school. The billions spent on do-it-yourself supplies show that people are doing a lot of unpaid work to maintain and improve their home too. Longer life expectancy increases the need of the elderly for care, whether it is provided within the family, by carers employed by business, by the state, or by a mixture of all three.

The chief influences on the unpaid work of women and men differ, but not in the same way as for paid employment. A regression analysis of the time men spend in unpaid work finds it is heavily influenced by a country's Index of Development. The more highly developed a country, the more time men spend in unpaid household work. This is likely to reflect the influence of the cultural norm of gender equality in highly developed countries, as well as men spending fewer hours in employment than in less developed countries. In addition, men spend significantly more time in unpaid work if they live in ex-communist societies. This reflects a legacy of people having to make do for themselves because shortages were endemic in non-market economies and there was a high mobilization of women in paid employment. These two significant influences together account for 66.5 per cent of the cross-national variation in unpaid work by men.

The tendency of women to do lots of unpaid work, whatever their country's level of development, results in the variance accounted for by unpaid women's work, 19.1 per cent, being less than one-third that for men. The only significant influence on the time that women spend on unpaid work is living in a Muslim society. Because of Islamic cultural norms restricting employment outside the household, women spend an average of 45 minutes more each day doing unpaid work than women in non-Muslim societies.

The combination of paid and unpaid work results in women on average spending three-quarters of an hour more each day working than men. The big gender difference is in the rewards of work. Men tend to have a higher cash income than women because they work more hours in paid employment, and in highly developed countries they qualify for work-related benefits such as a pension. By contrast, women who spend years as the primary carer for a family's children are more likely to earn the psychological reward that goes with being the central figure in family life and having more control over how they work in the absence of an employer controlling their working day.

7.4 Uneven globalization of gender equality

Institutions do not change cultural practices

The founding charter of the United Nations identified freedom from gender discrimination as a human right. Six decades later United Nations Secretary-General António Guterres has described the achievement of gender equality as 'the unfinished business of our time' (United Nations, 2022). To promote progress in gender equality, international organizations have promoted the adoption of national laws to reduce gender inequality in many fields. 'To provide the data necessary for transformative policy change' in gender equality, the Development Centre of the OECD (2019) has created a Social Institutions and Gender Index (SIGI) to monitor gender discrimination in 180 countries.

The SIGI shows major cross-cultural differences in the practice of gender equality on a 100-point scale in which 0 represents the complete absence of obstacles to gender equality and a high score a high level of discrimination. The countries with the best SIGI ratings tend to be highly developed countries. The average rating for highly developed countries is 17. Switzerland has a SIGI rating of 8, and in Denmark it is only 10 points short of complete equality. By contrast, the mean score for Muslim countries is 44, and there are nine countries with ratings that are closer to the worst rating of 100 than to the most positive rating of 0.

When the SIGI indicator is added to regression analyses reported above, it fails to show a significant effect on female employment and on gender equality. The failure of formal institutions to have a significant influence on female employment underscores the influence on female employment of a country's culture and intensive agriculture as the dominant influences on female employment.

Convergence and divergence

Empirical data questions the existence of a global consensus about female employment as assumed in statements of international organizations. Differences between countries and continents in the employment of women are extreme. Even though female employment is lower on average in Muslim societies, there is likewise no cultural consensus within this group. The fact that female employment is lowest in India, a predominantly Hindu society, also challenges treating dissensus as simply a reflection of fundamentalist Islamic values. While the UN and feminist groups promote an increase in the proportion of women participating in the labour force, dozens of UN member states are diverging from this target as their percentage of employed women decreases.

There were substantial differences in gender equality between and within continents in 1991. There was a gap of 50 percentage points between the world's two most populous countries, China and India, and 70 percentage points within the Middle East and North Africa region while in Burundi and Mozambique there were more women in work than men. In the three decades since 1991, female participation in the labour force has risen in 78 of 127 countries. Where this has been combined with a fall in male employment, as is the case in sixty-nine countries, movement in opposite directions creates convergence. Catching up in gender equality has occurred in twenty-three countries in which male employment has fallen more than that of females and in six countries in which female employment has risen more than male employment.

There has been a divergence of female and male employment in twenty-nine countries. This has occurred in five highly developed countries where one legacy of the communist command economy was a very high rate of female employment (Rose, 1994). Gender equality has also fallen in nine Muslim societies. In China the fall has been because female employment declined more than male employment. Gender inequality in India has been stable in the absolute sense, since employment has declined by the same amount, 9 percentage points, among both men and women. However, in relative terms this was a decline in the employment of one-quarter of employed women but barely one-tenth of Indian men.

The lack of a consensus about goals means that the globalization of female employment and gender equality has been uneven. African countries set the global standard for the percentage of women who participate in the labour force, and China comes second (Table 7.4). Instead of being the global leader in female employment, the average highly developed country ranks third

Table 7.4 Africa leads in women's employment

	HiDev	LatAm	MENA	Africa	AsiaDev	China	India
	As percentage of best performing group						
Men employed	85	100	89	93	97	96	97
Women employed	87	87	51	100	84	97	33
Gender equality	96	82	54	100	82	94	32

Source: Calculated from Global Welfare Database.

along with the average Latin American country. The average MENA country and India are distant from the global standard because of cultural values. Since restrictive cultural norms do not apply to male employment, the range in male employment between the top-ranking continent, Latin America, and the lowest-ranking group, highly developed countries, is only 15 percentage points.

Even though complete equality is not achieved, African countries come closer than any other continent in approaching this target; its gender equality ratio is 85. Highly developed countries and China are close to this standard (Table 7.4). India stands out because it rejects gender equality as a target. Female employment in India and its gender equality is only one-third that of the average African country. Even though there are nine Middle East and North African countries with a lower level of female employment than India, because of cultural divisions among Muslim countries, the MENA average for gender equality is significantly higher than that of India.

If maximizing the number of men and women in employment were the only welfare goal, then maintaining a labour-intensive peasant economy would be an effective means to this end. However, this would maintain a low level of development in which men and women worked more years and had less education and a shorter life expectancy. That is not the goal of the globalization of welfare.

References

Addati, L., Cattaneo, U., Esquivel, V., and Valarino, I., 2018. *Care Work and Care Jobs.* Geneva: International Labour Organization.

Akyol, Mustafa, 2022. *Reopening Muslim Minds.* London: Sift Press/Forum.

Datta, A., Endow, T., and Mehta, B. S., 2020. 'Education, Caste and Women's Work in India', *Indian Journal of Labour Economics,* 63, 387–406.

Franklin S. H., 1969. *The European Peasantry.* London: Methuen.

Gershuny, J., and Sullivan, O., 2019. *What We Really Do All Day.* London: Pelican.

Giuliano, Paola, 2017. Gender: A Historical Perspective. NBER and IZA Institute of Labor Economics. Discussion Paper No. 10931.

Greenwood, J., Seshadri, A., and Yorukoglu, M., 2005. 'Engines of Liberation', *Review of Economic Studies*, 72, 1, 109–33.

ICLS (International Conference of Labour Statisticians), 2013. 'Resolution concerning Statistics of Work, Employment and Labour Underutilization'. https://www.ilo.org/wcmsp5/groups/public/---dgreports/---stat/documents/normativeinstrument/wcms_230304.pdf.

ILO (International Labour Organization), 2018. *Care Work and Care Jobs*. Geneva: ILO.

Joshi, Heather, Layard, R., and Owen, S. J., 1985. 'Why Are Women Working in Britain?' *Journal of Labour Economics*, 3, 1/2, 147–76.

Lewis, W. Arthur, 1954. 'Economic Development with Unlimited Supplies of Labour', *The Manchester School*, 22, 139–91.

Lucassen, Jan, 2021. *The Story of Work: A New History of Humankind*. New Haven: Yale University Press.

Lundborg, P., Plug, E., and Rasmussen, A. W., 2017. 'Can Women Have Children and a Career?' *American Economic Review*, 107, 6, 1611–37.

OECD (Organization for Economic Cooperation and Development), 2019. *The Social Institutions and Gender Equality Index*. Paris: OECD Development Research Papers. Centre Working Paper 2 by Gaëlle Ferrant, Léa Fuiret and Eduardo Zambranos.

Ortiz-Ospina, E., Tzvetkova, S., and Roser, M., 2018. *Women's Employment*. https://ourworldindata.org/female-labor-supply#labor-force-participation.

Page, Edward, 1985. 'France: From L'État to Big Government'. In Richard Rose, ed., *Public Employment in Western Nations*. Cambridge: Cambridge University Press, 97–126.

Pew Research Centre, 2012. *The World's Muslims: Unity and Diversity*. Washington, DC: Pew Forum on Religion and Public Life.

Rapsomanikas, George, 2015. *The Economic Lives of Smallholder Farmers*. Rome: Food and Agricultural Organization of the United Nations.

Rose, Richard, 1994. *Comparing Welfare across Time and Space*. Vienna: European Centre for Social Welfare Policy and Research, *Eurosocial Report* 49.

Sellers, Charles, 1991. *The Market Revolution*. New York: Oxford University Press.

Smith, James, and Ward, Michael, 1985. 'Time-Series Growth in the Female Labour Force', *Journal of Labour Economics*, 3, 1, 559–90.

Titmuss, Richard, 1958. *Essays on 'The Welfare State'*. London: George Allen & Unwin.

Todaro, Michael P., and Smith, Stephen C., 2020. *Economic Development*. Hoboken, NJ: Pearson, 13th edition.

United Nations, 2022. *Gender Equality*. https://www.un.org/en/global-issues/gender-equality.

PART III
THE GLOBALIZATION OF COUNTRIES AND PEOPLE

8
Countries Going Global

Globalization has created a multicontinental group of countries that meet global standards of health, education, and/or employment. A large number of countries at a global standard come from the standard-setting continent. This is usually but not always a group of highly developed countries, but for female employment it is a set of African countries.

While a big majority of the world's countries have been making progress in welfare, they remain divided into two groups: the minority that have reached global standards at a given level and those that have not. It is misleading to say that the latter group has failed, since a large majority have been making progress. It is more appropriate to say that, in spite of making progress, a majority of countries have not yet reached a global standard of welfare. A major reason for this is that they were much further from the global standard in 1991.

The resources required to make progress towards a given goal differ between targets. The technical knowledge already exists to reduce a country's infant mortality to the limit of zero deaths, and this know-how can be transferred across national borders. There is no quick technological fix to decide when or whether a woman should participate in the official labour market between the age of 15 and 65. Moreover, it is harder for a country to catch up with an open-ended goal, for even if life expectancy is increasing in a developing country, it is likely to be increasing in standard-setting countries too. Because complete adult literacy requires the turnover of generations, patience is required to meet this goal.

Since the resources required to reach a global standard differ between health, education, and female employment, a country can be at a global standard in some forms of welfare and a low standard in another. This is the case in the United States, where the standard of education is much higher than the standard of health. In a complementary manner, a country can be very low on gender equality in employment while making rapid progress towards the global standard of almost no infant mortality; this is the case in India. There are dozens of ways in which a country can partially achieve global standards in its welfare mix.

Catching up with global standards is a lengthy process, for a majority of developing countries are at a significant distance from this goal. A country's health, education, or employment is not immediately altered by the enactment of a law or by a change of government. Annual rates of progress can be in tenths of a percentage point. The first step in catching up is to sustain progress from one year to the next. If a target is fixed, such as eliminating infant mortality, then it is only a matter of decades or generations before that goal is reached. If a goal is open-ended, such as increasing life expectancy, a country must progress at a faster rate than countries that are the standard-setters. Otherwise it will fall further behind, because applying the same percentage rate of progress to its lower status will produce less change than applying it to the higher base of the standard-setters.

This chapter charts critical steps in the globalization of welfare. The first section reports how many countries have been making progress on six different welfare measures in the past three decades. It also shows whether developing countries are progressing fast enough to catch up with global standards of welfare, either sooner or later. The second section reports the increase in the number of countries that are now at global standards compared to 1991. As the distance of countries from global standards is influenced by their resources, the third section summarizes the relative effect of a country's Index of Development, national culture, or communist legacy. In Section 8.4 consistent outliers are identified; that is, countries that achieve a higher or a lower standard of welfare than their resources would be expected to produce.

8.1 Many countries making progress

Progress occurs when a country's welfare changes in a positive direction, whatever the starting point and whatever the amount of change. Assessing change over three decades since 1991 shows the extent to which the globalization of welfare is occurring, notwithstanding major disruptions in the world economy. Evaluating progress across multiple measures takes into account differences in the characteristics and dynamics of particular forms of welfare.

A large majority of countries have been making progress across each of six different measures of health, education, and welfare (Figure 8.1). However, because of differences in the way in which global standards are set in each field, the number of countries making progress differs between goals. There is virtually universal progress both in measures of health and in the abolition of adult illiteracy. Progress in secondary school enrolment falls short of being complete because it requires money to build schools and train and pay teachers. In a sixth of countries these resources are not readily available. Because of value

Progress since 1991

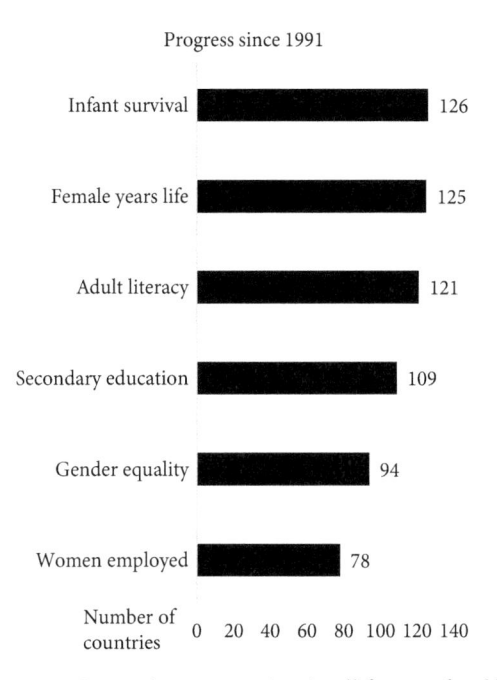

Category	Number of countries
Infant survival	126
Female years life	125
Adult literacy	121
Secondary education	109
Gender equality	94
Women employed	78

Figure 8.1 Countries progressing in all forms of welfare

Source: Global Welfare Database of 127 countries. 2019 is normally the final year, except for adult literacy (2018) and secondary education (2017).

conflicts about the direction of female employment, there is no common pattern; for every three countries where it increases, there are two in which it contracts.

The global improvement in health is a paradigm example of the advances achieved through the adoption of social technologies by the institutions of a country's welfare mix. Whatever a country's health three decades ago, there has been progress since in all but one country, the small African state of Lesotho. Progress has been greatest in absolute terms where life expectancy was initially lowest. Female life expectancy has increased by 12 years in India, 11 years in the average African and Asian developing country, and 10 years in China. This is double the years added to life in the average highly developed country. Progress has similarly been worldwide in the reduction of infant mortality; the chief cross-national difference has been the rate of progress. Because almost 98.8 per cent of infants in highly developed countries survived to age 5 in 1991, it progressed less than 1 percentage point in the next three decades. There was much more need and scope for progress in developing countries because infant deaths were much more numerous. Applying known social technologies has enabled virtually every developing country to make a significant contribution to the global reduction in infant mortality.

Techniques for teaching children to become literate have been known for centuries, but the resources needed to provide compulsory education have taken more than a century to go global. By 2019 compulsory primary education was the global practice, and progress towards achieving complete adult literacy was made in all but two developing countries reporting data. Once literacy is achieved through free primary education, most governments have made basic secondary education compulsory, and more youths are voluntarily remaining longer in school. However, increasing school enrolment requires a government having the resources to allocate to meet the increased cost of secondary education. It also requires the cooperation of youths to remain longer in school rather than starting work. Five-sixths of countries have shown progress in the percentage of youths now in secondary education.

Interpreting quantitative evidence about changes in female employment is problematic because there is no consensus about what constitutes progress. This is very evident in the division of countries between the seventy-eight where female employment has been increasing and the forty-nine where it has been contracting in the past three decades. Insofar as an increase in the proportion of adults earning an income in the official economy is deemed good for women and for the economy, then there is progress in three-fifths of countries. Insofar as it is considered desirable that more women are available to spend more years as unpaid carers in their household, there has been progress in two-fifths of countries in which female participation in the official labour force has been decreasing.

Because gender equality is a ratio between the percentage of women and of men in work, there is more than one way in which progress can lead to an increase in equality. Progress in equality will result as long as an increase in female employment is greater than that of men or any decrease is less than that of men. By these criteria there has been progress towards gender equality in ninety-four countries, in five-sixths of the cases because of a positive increase in female employment (Figure 8.1). Among countries where female employment is discouraged, five countries, including India, have increased gender inequality.

8.2 Some countries catching up

Making progress is a necessary but not sufficient condition for countries to catch up with global standards. They must also make progress at a faster rate than the standard-setters. Countries that are not at a global standard do have one asset: they do not have to spend the time and resources that leading countries have invested in finding ways to achieve high standards of welfare. Because they are followers, by going second they can more easily start making progress by adopting methods that have produced welfare for the leaders.

Technocratic theories of globalization treat progress in welfare as a challenge that can be met by the global diffusion of social technologies. Standard-setting countries have developed social technologies for reducing infant mortality, teaching literacy, and recruiting women into the labour force. The technologies are social because success depends not only on the technical knowledge of doctors, educators, and anti-discrimination lawyers but also on the resources and institutions of the welfare mix. Developing countries can progress by learning lessons from countries that have created these effective technologies (Rogers, 1995; Rose, 2005). As second movers, they do not have to spend many decades developing the means of improving welfare as did countries where innovation first occurred. Japan is the leading historical example of a country achieving high welfare by borrowing technologies from countries that initially set global standards (Westney, 1987). Today international aid agencies such as the World Bank give technical assistance and offer money for the transfer of social technologies that increase what the Bank calls a country's human capital. The hypothesis is: *if there are social technologies to increase welfare, second-mover countries can progress faster than standard-setters*.

Because welfare policies must serve the whole of a country's population, the health clinics, schools, and employment offices needed to implement welfare policies must be built wherever people live. That is usually a political as well as a geographical distance from national policymakers and foreign aid agencies. The tempo of progress depends on the financial and administrative resources that a government has to implement an improved welfare policy. Moreover, the time it takes to achieve effectiveness differs between policies. Secondary schools can be built in a few years, whereas replacing adult illiterates with literate cohorts takes generations.

Welfare progresses faster in second-mover countries

The six continents of developing countries have been progressing faster in health and education than the highly developed countries that set global standards (Table 8.1). This is true not only where there is little scope for further progress by standard-setters, as is the case with literacy and the survival of

Table 8.1 Developing countries progressing faster

	HiDev	LatAm	MENA	Africa	AsiaDev	China	India
(Total progress from 1991 to 2019)							
Life expectancy female (years)	5	7	8	11	11	10	12
Infant survival (%)	0.8	4	5	9	7	5	9
Adult literacy (%)	2	6	10	12	12	19	26
Secondary educ'n (%)	11	31	12	16	23	n.a.	n.a.
Women employed (%)	4	10	1	0.5	−0.4	−13	−10
Gender equality (%)	10	15	3	5	2	−6	−8

Source: Global Welfare database. Change is measured as the arithmetic difference between the continental mean in 1991 and 2019. Infant survival is the percentage change in live births per thousand.

newborn infants, but also for an open-ended goal, increasing life expectancy. Highly developed countries have added 5 years on average to female life expectancy in the past three decades, while most developing continents have added 10 or more years to life expectancy. As more than one-sixth of youths in highly developed countries were not enrolled in secondary education in 1991, there has been more scope for progress, leading to an 11 percentage point increase in youths in secondary education. Even though the cost of expanding secondary education is relatively higher in developing countries, they have expanded enrolment almost three times as fast in Latin America and at double the rate of progress in Asian developing countries.

The speed at which continents have been making progress varies among developing continents. Particularly striking is the fact that welfare has progressed at a double-digit rate in Africa and India on measures of health and education, even though they are low in resources for development. This suggests that a low level of development is not a major constraint on countries making rapid progress in health and education by adopting social technologies that highly developed countries have used to become global standard-setters. This interpretation is supported by very fast progress being shown by Asian developing countries and India, notwithstanding their relatively low development. Latin American countries have tended to grow at a slower rate than countries on other developing continents. This may be due to having already achieved second-mover advantages prior to 1991.

There is divergence between continents in changes in female employment (Table 8.1). It has grown on two continents, shown no significant change on three continents, and contracted substantially on two continents. As explained in Chapter 7, the lack of growth in developing continents reflects high levels of female employment three decades ago, when women worked for low wages to increase their low household income. With development women have had a choice of reducing their commitment to paid employment. India is the exception; notwithstanding it being a low-income country, pressures against women working outside the home have strengthened. Even if there is a national consensus on the desirability of increasing female employment, there is not a social technology that can be applied in practice, short of state direction of labour, which led to the mobilization of women in the Soviet Union and in the People's Republic of China in early stages of development.

The social technology hypothesis is supported with one qualification: there must be a political consensus about goals for a developing country to benefit as a second mover. Where there is a cultural conflict about goals, as is the case for female participation in the labour force, then technology transfer requires changes in cultural values.

Increased minority of countries at global standards today

In 1991 the number of countries at global standards of welfare was limited. Fewer than one-sixth were at the fixed standard for female life expectancy and enrolment in secondary education, and fewer than one-fifth for the survival of newborn infants (Figure 8.2). The largest group, countries at the global standard of gender equality, constituted just under one-third of the countries in the Global Welfare Database.

As long as global standards are fixed standards, it is in principle possible for every country to catch up. The fixed-target hypothesis is: *if a country is making progress towards a fixed welfare goal, then it will catch up with a global welfare standard in time.* The key term in this hypothesis is 'in time'. For example, in 1991 the mean for adult literacy was 96 per cent in highly developed countries, while 82 per cent of adults in Turkey were literate. As a second-mover country, Turkey reached the global standard by 2019. Turkey caught up by raising literacy at a rate half again higher than the average developing country. By contrast, Nigeria would not be expected to reach the 1991 global standard of literacy until the twenty-second century, because its annual rate of progress has been barely half that of Turkey and it was 41 percentage points distant from the global standard in 1991.

The worldwide diffusion of social technologies to improve health has doubled the number of countries at the global standard of health in three decades

154 WELFARE GOES GLOBAL

Number of countries at fixed global standard

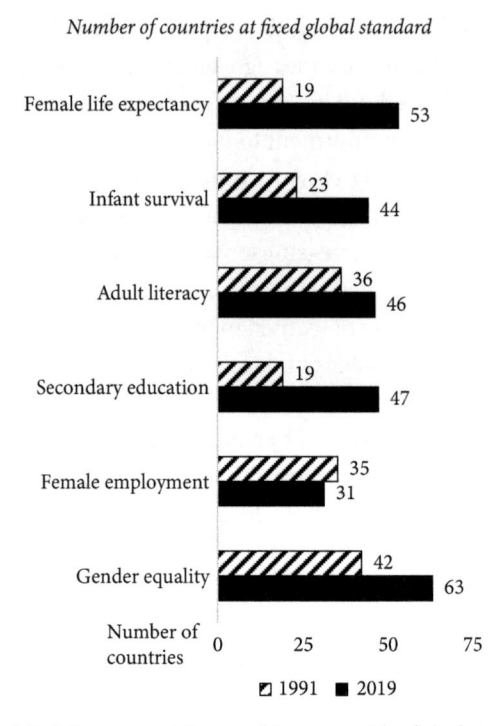

Indicator	1991	2019
Female life expectancy	19	53
Infant survival	23	44
Adult literacy	36	46
Secondary education	19	47
Female employment	35	31
Gender equality	42	63

Figure 8.2 More countries catching up with global standards

Source: Global Welfare Database of 127 countries. 2019 is normally the final year, except for adult literacy (2018) and secondary education (2017). Global standards as of 1991.

(Figure 8.2). In 1991 only eighteen highly developed countries plus one developing country, Costa Rica, met the global standard for female life expectancy. Three decades later, all highly developed countries have reached the fixed standard, along with nineteen developing countries from three continents and China. Three decades ago developing countries were substantially distant from global standards for reducing infant mortality (see Figure 5.3), and only two-thirds of highly developed countries were at that standard. By 2019 all highly developed countries had reached the global standard, but even though most developing countries were making progress at a faster rate than the highly developed group, only ten had caught up with the global standard because their starting points were so distant.

The number of countries at global standards in secondary school enrolment has more than doubled in the past three decades, while the number at global standards of literacy has increased by only one-quarter. This is because youths can be compelled to attend secondary schools, but a substantial increase in adult literacy requires a generation to realize because it depends on generational turnover. Developing countries averaged 65 per cent of their adult population being literate in 1991, 31 percentage points below the global standard, whereas they were 52 points distant in secondary education. Notwithstanding being more distant, twenty-two developing countries caught up with the secondary standard by 2019 compared to nine catching up with the literacy standard. Enacting legislation to raise compulsory school attendance makes for faster progress than the steady but slow process of generational turnover.

Multiple and conflicting standards for evaluating female employment have produced contrasting patterns of catching up. There has been an increase of twenty-one countries at the global standard for gender equality alongside a decrease of four countries in the number at global standard for female employment. The reduction in the number of countries with a large proportion of employed women reflects more young females remaining at school above the age of 15, and rising national incomes have given women the choice of retiring from the labour market before they reach the age of 65. The ILO standard fails to take into account the lifetime experience of individuals. If women participate in the labour force for 30 years of their adult life and work as unpaid carers in their household for 20 years, the ILO counts them as non-participants in the labour force for two-fifths of their working life.

Since gender equality is a ratio between female and male participation, progress can be realized by male employment falling more than female employment since 1991. Male participation in the labour force fell in 115 countries in the past three decades while female participation has risen in 78 countries or fallen less than men in dozens of countries. The most change in gender equality has occurred in highly developed countries; those at the global standard have risen from seven to twenty-two countries. Notwithstanding the widespread decline in female employment in Africa, the number of countries there has risen to twenty-nine at the global standard for gender equality.

Most countries partially globalized

Three decades is not a long enough time for a majority of countries to reach global standards on all forms of welfare. The number of countries able to catch up varies between measures: thirty-four countries have caught up with the global standard for female life expectancy and twenty-eight in secondary school enrolment, while the proportion catching up falls to ten for adult literacy and falls by four countries for female employment. Even though big majorities are making progress, their distance from global standards means that it can take half a century or longer for a country to catch up with a fixed standard (see Chapter 10). This consequence is recognized by the United Nations' practice of setting goals for shorter periods of time, such as twenty years ahead, while success depends on progress rather than catching up.

Of the 127 countries in the Global Welfare Database, more than three-quarters are partially globalized; that is, they are at the global standard on at least one measure but not on all six measures of health, education, and female employment (Figure 8.3). The median country has caught up on two welfare measures, and forty have caught up on at least two-thirds of the six welfare measures (Figure 8.3).

Among highly developed countries, only New Zealand and Switzerland are at global standards on all six measures of welfare. Nineteen are at global

Number of countries

Number of times countries at global standard	Countries
0	29
1	20
2	33
3	5
4	19
5	19
6	2

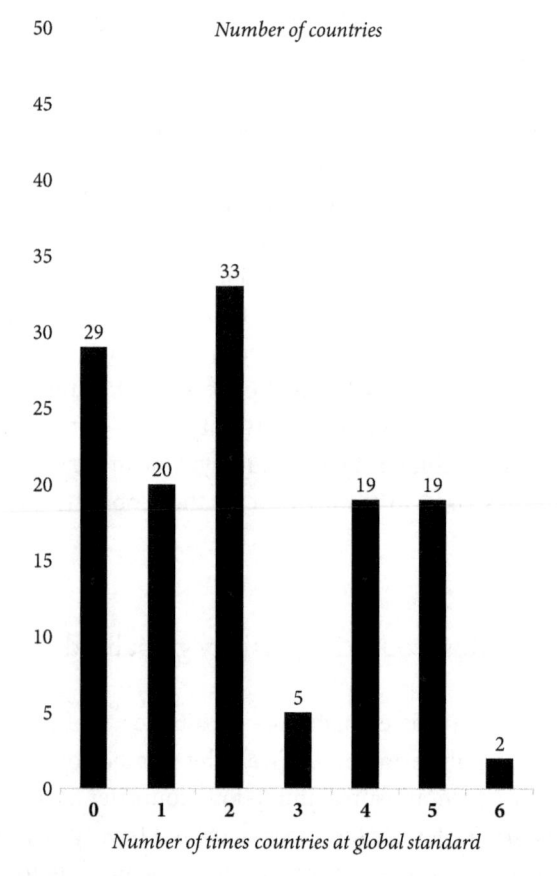

Figure 8.3 Times countries at global standards
Source: Global Welfare Database.

standards for all but one measure, usually having a lower level of female participation in the labour force than the global standard set by African women. The countries at global standards on four counts are those with a communist legacy or, like Japan and Korea (Rose and Shiratori, 1986), those having had the advantage of being second movers because they were relatively late to develop.

China is at global standards for four measures of welfare but falls short on secondary school enrolment, and, due to its higher level of development, it has a lower level of female employment than standard-setting Africa. Two Middle East countries, Azerbaijan and Kazakhstan, are high on four indicators because of their emphasis on female employment due to their communist legacy. Argentina and Uruguay are high on four welfare measures because they are among the most developed of developing countries.

Notwithstanding relatively low levels of health and education, twenty-two African countries are at global standards on two measures of development because of their high level of female employment and gender equality. In addition, eight African countries meet one but not both employment standards. Even after taking the significance of female employment into account, ten African countries do not reach global standards on even one measure of welfare. Development in India is likewise below global standards on all six welfare indicators.

Latin American countries and those in the MENA region differ greatly in their degree of globalization; on both continents countries are distributed among five different categories of partial globalization. While a majority of countries are partially globalized, one-third of MENA countries and two-fifths in Latin America are below global standards on all measures of welfare. Asian developing countries are similarly heterogeneous. Five countries are not at the global standard on any welfare measure, while Sri Lanka and Vietnam are at global standards on three measures.

8.3 Accounting for national differences

Even though all countries are making progress in raising their national welfare standards, a majority have yet to reach global standards on each measure of health, education, and female employment. This raises the question: why? Chapter 4 offers four explanations. Cross-national variation in welfare is influenced by a country's level of development, its historical legacies, its culture, and public expenditure on social policies. In addition, distinctive national characteristics may cause some countries to deviate from the global pattern.

Six regressions reported in Chapters 5, 6, and 7 have tested the empirical support for the four hypothesized influences. The columns in Table 8.2 show whether a potential influence has a statistically significant effect on a particular welfare measure. If so, the size of the effect is given in years of life, in infant deaths per thousand, or as a percentage of its change in the measure. The results illustrate the importance of testing generic hypotheses with different forms of welfare, since the effect of development, the legacy of communism, and a Muslim population differ significantly between six measures of welfare. These differences are also reflected in the final column, which shows how much of the total variation in each welfare indicator is altogether accounted for.

A country's Index of Development has a substantial effect on health and education (Table 8.2). Women can expect to live at least six more years in countries that combine a high level of both urbanization and gross domestic product per capita with a government that respects the freedom of its citizens and delivers public services with little corruption. The Index of Development has a substantial effect on infant mortality too; there are an estimated thirty-nine fewer deaths per thousand in highly developed countries. Adult literacy is 21 percentage points higher than the global average in countries high in development. The effect of the Index on enrolment in secondary education is even greater—an increase of 40 percentage points in those enrolled in secondary education.

Even though development increases the importance of working in the official economy, the Index of Development has only a slight effect on officially recorded levels of female employment. Moreover, its impact is negative: a country high in development tends to have up to 7 per cent fewer women in

Table 8.2 Influences differ with forms of welfare

	Index Develop	Ex-Comm	Muslim	Variance R^2
	(Change in dependent variable)			
Life expectancy female (yrs)	13	4	n.s.	63.5%
Infant deaths (per thousand)	−39	−22	n.s.	51.7%
Adult literacy (%)	21	18	n.s.	50.4%
Secondary educ. (%)	40	24	n.s.	69.0%
Employed females (%)	−7	n.s.	−21	32.2%
Gender equality (%)	n.s.	n.s.	−25	29.7%

Source: Ordinary least squares regressions in Chapters 5, 6, and 7; n.s. = not significant. The effect of the Index of Development is standardized for comparability with the two categoric variables by multiplying the b coefficient of the Index by twice its standard deviation of 2.68.

employment, and the Index has no significant influence on gender equality. By contrast, in countries low in development, necessity spurs more women to engage in low-paid work in agriculture and the informal economy. A high level of agricultural employment, an indicator of many people living close to the bare subsistence level, is a significant positive influence on employment (see Table 7.1).

Development increases the amount of money that government can spend on welfare policies, and politicians often talk as if public expenditure is all-important in determining welfare. This assumption cannot be tested for female employment, since anti-discrimination legislation, not public spending, is the chief resource a government has to promote gender equality. When the potential influence of public expenditure on health as a percentage of gross domestic product is tested, it fails to achieve statistical influence. Likewise, public expenditure on education as a percentage of GDP has no significant influence on educational attainment. The Index of Development, which includes gross domestic product per capita, is a better measure of economic influence on welfare, because it takes into account money spent in the market and by households as well as government spending (see Section 4.2).

8.4 Outlier countries

The theory of globalization assumes that a country's level of welfare ought to vary with the resources in its Index of Development, its historical legacy, and its culture. Regression analyses in the preceding chapters have offered substantial support for the theory because there is usually a good match between regression estimates of what a country's welfare is predicted to be and what it actually is. Nonetheless, because of statistical margins of error, there is normally a small difference between a country's estimated and actual level of welfare.

In addition to identifying many countries where welfare is in keeping with national resources, the regression analyses identify countries that are outliers—that is, their actual standard of welfare differs significantly from what would be expected on the basis of their resources. If an outlier country does much better than predicted, this may be due to its governors exercising their powers to make better use of resources than is normal, or it may be due to an influence that is not included in the regression. Underachieving countries illustrate negative agency; that is, the institutions of the welfare mix do not make as much use of their resources as is done by other countries like them.

The match between the actual and estimated level of female life expectancy is illustrated in Figure 8.4. The diagonal line traces the number of years an average woman is expected to live given her country's resources (cf. Section 5.1). The closer a dot comes to the diagonal line, the closer a country is to having a perfect fit between its expected and actual achievement. The mean difference between actual and predicted female life expectancy is 3.9 years. Two countries have a perfect fit, Malawi and Madagascar; their predicted and actual life expectancy is the same. China is a positive outlier, because its actual life expectancy is 10.4 years higher than an estimate based on its national resources. By contrast, Nigeria is a negative outlier, because female life expectancy is 16.4 years below its estimated level.

Most countries tend to do a bit better than predicted on some measures of health, education, and female employment, and are below their estimate on other measures. These random fluctuations reflect the error margin inherent in statistical estimates. To avoid positive and negative fluctuations cancelling each other out when added together, a country's welfare fit is calculated by summing variations from a perfect fit in six regressions without regard to whether the difference is positive or negative.

The welfare fit of the great majority of countries is normal: the mean difference from a perfect fit is 7.9 per cent. Highly developed countries have the best welfare fit; the mean difference between the predicted and actual welfare of countries in this group is 5.1 per cent. Japan comes closest to having a perfect welfare fit, differing on average by only 2.4 percentage points; both the United

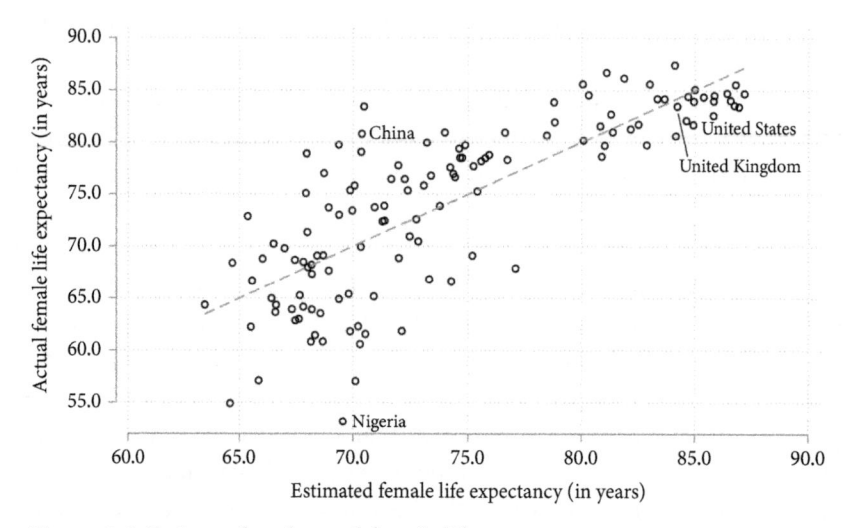

Figure 8.4 Estimated and actual female life expectancy

Source: Calculated from multiple regression reported in Table 5.1

Kingdom and the United States are closer to a perfect fit than the average highly developed country. Latin American countries also have a better than average fit between their predicted and actual welfare. The welfare fit tends to be less good on average in African and Asian developing countries, because having fewer resources makes it harder for these countries to advance their welfare as efficiently as highly developed countries. This is particularly so in the MENA region, where the average difference between actual and predicted welfare is 10.7 per cent.

The status of an outlier is a matter of degree. Given the large amount of variance accounted for in the regressions, differences in the welfare fit are not large. Nonetheless, all 127 countries can be ranked according to the degree to which they come close to or fall short of achieving a perfect fit between their predicted and actual welfare. Table 8.3 lists the biggest over- and underachievers. The profile of outliers confirms the importance of highly developed countries setting the standard for the globalization of welfare. Of the thirty-four highly developed countries, only one is an outlier. Similarly, of the twenty countries of Latin America, where many are well above the mean global level of development, only one is an outlier.

The countries that have a much higher mean welfare than expected are spread across three continents plus China. Since the welfare fit is a measure of the use a country makes of its resources rather than the size of its resources, the Index of Development of these overachievers varies greatly between 56 for Malaysia and 8 for Cambodia. The dozen countries that are the biggest underachievers, having a much lower level of welfare than predicted, come from four different continents plus India. The underachievers are not uniformly lacking in resources: their Index of Development varies between 54 in Romania and 7 in Afghanistan.

Culture rather than level of development is the chief cause of a country being an outlier. Although Muslim countries are less than one-quarter of all the countries in the Global Welfare Database, they are more than two-fifths of the countries that are the chief outliers. Moreover, instead of being clustered around one extreme, they are divided between overachievers and underachievers. Muslim countries are half of the dozen countries that are the biggest overachievers and one-third of those that are underachievers. The significance of Muslim societies among outliers is especially surprising because the regression equations took into account their culture when estimating their welfare achievement.

The nominal description of Muslim societies does not take into account very substantial differences between these societies (see Table 7.2). The six Muslim countries that are overachievers are societies in which there has historically

162 WELFARE GOES GLOBAL

Table 8.3 Biggest outliers in welfare achievement

Country	Muslim	Continent	Welfare fit
More welfare than predicted			
Kazakhstan	yes	MENA	13.6
Azerbaijan	yes	MENA	13.0
Indonesia	yes	AsiaDev	11.4
Malaysia	yes	AsiaDev	10.3
Uzbekistan	yes	MENA	9.8
Thailand	no	AsiaDev	9.0
China	no	China	8.9
Laos	no	AsiaDev	8.8
Peru	no	LatAm	8.7
Turkey	yes	MENA	7.8
Cambodia	no	AsiaDev	7.7
Vietnam	no	AsiaDev	7.7
Less welfare than predicted			
Benin	no	Africa	−7.6
Mali	yes	Africa	−7.8
Guatemala	no	LatAm	−8.1
Romania	no	HiDev	−8.2
Mauritania	yes	Africa	−9.6
Afghanistan	yes	AsiaDev	−10.1
Liberia	no	Africa	−10.3
Pakistan	yes	AsiaDev	−12.1
Guinea-Bissau	no	Africa	−12.3
Central African Republic	no	Africa	−14.7
Côte d'Ivoire	no	Africa	−15.1
India	no	India	−15.8

Source: Calculated from regressions reported in Table 8.2.

been a substantial marginalization of fundamentalist Islamic beliefs because of political pressures. In societies that are underachievers in realizing welfare, there is an alignment between the political ideology of the ruling powers and proponents of fundamentalist Islamic doctrines. Cultural beliefs that cause countries to be outliers are not confined to Muslim societies. India, a predominantly Hindu society, is a more extreme underachiever than Pakistan, a Muslim society.

Welfare is going global by processes that differ in their scale, tempo, and extent of success. Every country is making progress on at least one measure, even if it had not yet reached the global standard on any measure of welfare and the median country is now making progress on five of the six welfare measures.

Moreover, countries that are not at global standards can benefit in making progress by applying proven social technologies. Some have caught up with fixed standards and many more are in the process of doing so because they are progressing faster than the standard-setters. However, because the population of the world is very unevenly distributed, evidence of welfare among the world's countries is not evidence of the welfare of the world's population.

References

Rogers, Everett M., 1995. *Diffusion of Innovation*. New York: Free Press, 4th edition.
Rose, Richard, 2005. *Learning from Comparative Public Policy: A Practical Guide*. London and New York: Routledge.
Rose, Richard, and Shiratori, Rei, eds., 1986. *The Welfare State East and West*. New York: Oxford University Press.
Westney, Eleanor, 1987. *Innovation and Imitation: The Transfer of Western Organizational Patterns to Meiji Japan*. Cambridge, MA: Harvard University Press.

9
People Going Global

In public policy the globalization of welfare is usually analysed in terms of countries because of the state's contribution to the welfare mix. International organizations focus on government policies because their members are states and the global statistics they report are collected and supplied by national governments. Of the seventeen Sustainable Development Goals of the United Nations, more than three-quarters concern policies for which governments are responsible, such as the economy; just four target the conditions of individuals. In the extreme case of the International Monetary Fund, its policies are not directed towards people but towards central banks and ministries of finance that manage a country's money. However, comparing welfare in sovereign states such as Norway and Nigeria takes no account of the fact that Nigeria has a population forty times greater than Norway.

Focusing on the world's population gives priority to the wellbeing of individuals rather than their nationality. For welfare to go global, it must reach a majority of the world's population, and the world's population is very skewed. Two countries, China and India, each have a larger population than any continent. Although the collective population of the highly developed countries that set many global standards is more than 1.2 billion people, its impact on global welfare is limited, because it has less than one-sixth of the world's population. Scandinavian countries are often held up as having welfare policies that other countries ought to emulate, but collectively they affect only three-tenths of 1 per cent of the world's population. However exemplary highly developed countries may be, they cannot match the impact that the world's most populous countries have on welfare going global.

The impact of population on the globalization of welfare is increased by the continuous growth in the world's population (United Nations, 2022). Between 1991 and 2019 the world's population increased by more than two-fifths from 5.1 billion to 7.7 billion. Growth has also been marked by a shift in the relative population of continents. In 1991 highly developed countries had more than double the population of Africa. Today, their population is only one-fifth more than Africa, as the latter's population has doubled while that of highly developed countries has increased by only one-eighth.

Welfare Goes Global. Richard Rose, Oxford University Press. © Richard Rose (2024).
DOI: 10.1093/oso/9780198908463.003.0010

The population of every country is divided between people who are and are not at the global standard of a given measure of welfare (World Bank, 2018). A minority at the global standard in a populous developing country can be much bigger than a majority at that standard in a country with a smaller population. Even though only 35 per cent of youthful Pakistanis are enrolled in secondary education, the total number enrolled is greater than in Britain, where more than 90 per cent of youths are enrolled, because Pakistan's population is more than three times that of Britain. The mammoth population of India means that it invariably accounts for hundreds of millions of people who are at the global standard of welfare and hundreds of millions more people who are not.

Section 9.1 shows the unequal distribution of the world's population between countries; it also documents how the size of a country's population is unrelated to its development. The following section reports the extent to which the world's population has reached global standards on six major measures of welfare. It is followed by a section that identifies the extent to which the increase in the number of people at global standards is due to population growth rather than progress in the percentage at global standards. The concluding section pinpoints the countries where the most people have yet to reach global standards of welfare.

9.1 World population skewed

Demography is more important than sovereignty in determining the world's welfare. National sovereignty treats each of the member states of the United Nations as equal, and each country's government contributes to its population's welfare mix. Global demography emphasizes inequality: a few countries have a population that is hundreds of millions more than that of the world's median country.

More than half the world's population lives in seven countries dispersed across six continents; only one of these countries is highly developed (see Table 9.1). China and India are mega-countries. Each accounts for more than one-sixth of the world's population and is four to six times larger than other countries with massive populations. The world's third most populous country, the United States, has only 4 per cent of the global population. Yet it is four times more populous than the second country in this group, Germany, and thirty times more populous than the median highly developed country. The four largest countries in the geographically sprawling Asian region—China, India, Indonesia, and Pakistan—collectively have more than two-fifths of the

Table 9.1 World's most populous countries

Country	Population (millions)	Continent
1 China	1,422	China
2 India	1,383	India
3 United States	334	Highly developed
4 Indonesia	270	Asia developing
5 Pakistan	223	Asia developing
6 Brazil	212	Latin America
7 Nigeria	203	Africa
Total population	4,047	
% world population	52.1%	

Source: Global Welfare Database.

world's population. By contrast, the largest country in the Middle East and North Africa region, Egypt, has barely 1 per cent of the world's population. With less than 1 per cent of the world's population, the United Kingdom ranks twenty-first in size, just below Iran and Thailand.

The world's population is unequally distributed between continents. Asian developing countries and sub-Saharan Africa each have a population of more than one billion people. Although the land area of the Latin America and of the Middle East and North Africa continents is extensive, the total population of each is little more than half a billion people. Global population is unequally distributed within continents too. Three Latin American countries—Brazil, Mexico, and Colombia—collectively account for 64 per cent of the continent's population. In the developing Asia group, Indonesia, Pakistan, and Bangladesh constitute 57 per cent of the population. Three countries—Egypt, Turkey, and Iran—have 51 per cent of the population of the Middle East and North Africa region. Population is less concentrated among highly developed countries; the United States, the Russian Federation, and Germany together account for just over two-fifths of this group's population. Nigeria, Ethiopia, and the Democratic Republic of the Congo together have 38 per cent of the total population of sub-Saharan Africa.

The distinctive position of the United States among highly developed countries owes a great deal to its combination of a high gross domestic product per capita and a growing population of 334 million. A country with an even higher GDP per capita, such as Norway, does not have the same global impact because its population is less than 2 per cent that of the United States. China is exceptional not only in having a massive population but also in being ten times more populous than its leading Asian economic competitor, Japan.

The smaller half of the world's population consists of 209 states and internationally recognized territories that differ greatly in population. Seven countries, including Russia, Mexico, and Japan, have populations between 102 million and 164 million people. The country at the median point of the world's population has six million people, less than one-tenth of 1 per cent of global population. The hundred plus countries below the global median for population include twelve that are member states of the European Union. The Global Welfare Database excludes fifty-eight countries with populations of less than one million people, since they can contribute little to global welfare. This group includes small oil-rich kingdoms in the Middle East, poor countries in Africa, and the UN's smallest member state, the Republic of Nauru with 11,000 people.

Taking account of national differences in population produces a radically different map of the world's welfare. For example, about three-fifths of the adult population of Haiti and of Pakistan are literate. However, because Pakistan has twenty times the population of Haiti, it accounts for 88 million of the world's illiterate population compared to Haiti's 4.4 million illiterates. Population-weighted calculations likewise alter the significance of evaluations within continents. Italy has much more impact on European welfare than the average Scandinavian country because its population is twelve times bigger.

In theory a country with a large population could have a higher standard of welfare because, even if its per capita resources are low, its total resources are big enough to support large-scale investments in safe water, teacher-training colleges, and universities. Even though the per capita GDP of India is low, its national GDP is one of the world's largest because of its massive population. An alternative hypothesis is that a country with a smaller national population could have a higher level of individual welfare because its resources are shared among fewer people, and its population is likely to be more willing to share because it is more socially cohesive. Small states are also less likely to devote a significant share of their income to military expenditure, as is done by the most populous states.

The correlations between national population and measures of health, education, and female employment are extremely low, and none is statistically significant. There are countries with a population below the global median where the level of welfare is low, particularly in Latin America and Africa, as well as Scandinavian countries with small populations and high levels of welfare. China's achievement of welfare shows that a large population is not an obstacle to achieving a substantial level of welfare with limited resources per capita, while the low level of welfare in India shows a large national economy and population are not always assets for achieving individual welfare.

9.2 Welfare of the world's population

The globalization of welfare is greatly dependent on a small number of very populous developing countries making progress. For example, a 1 per cent increase in a measure of welfare in India or China will affect more than 200 times as many people as a 1 per cent increase in a country with the world's median population.

In previous chapters the percentage of people at global standards of welfare was calculated in relation to groups differing greatly in size. For example, the literacy measure refers to all adults, while that for participation in secondary education today refers only to teenagers. Yet the welfare of groups of different size has a pervasive effect on the quality of life of the whole of a society. Everyone is affected directly or indirectly if they live in a society in which more people are in good health and educated and treated equally in employment rather than in a society in which many people die young, many are illiterate, and men and women are treated very unequally.

To estimate the welfare of the world's population it is necessary to standardize estimates of the number of people affected by different welfare measures. This is done by relating the percentage of a country's population with and without a given welfare measure to its total population. For example, the literacy rate in Pakistan today is 57 per cent and its population is 223 million people; this adds 127 million people to the world's literate population and 96 million to the world's illiterates. Summing the results of national calculations produces global estimates of the billions of the world's population who are literate and the billions who are not. Since the initial percentage estimates are based on countries with 95 per cent of the world's population, they are adjusted upwards by 5 percentage points to produce estimates of the total global population. The results are rounded off to take into account the variable quality of the national population statistics on which estimates are based.

Differing majorities at global standards of welfare

While most countries are not at global standards, the majority of the world's population is at global standards on four measures of health, education, and employment (Figure 9.1; cf. Figure 8.2). The number at global standards varies substantially between 7.5 billion people benefiting from a very high level of infant survival to 4.8 billion people living in societies with a relatively high level of gender equality in employment. Even though less than half the world's

170   WELFARE GOES GLOBAL

Percentage of world's population

Infant survival	97%
Literacy	83%
Secondary education	64%
Gender equality	63%
Female employment	47%
Life expectancy	47%

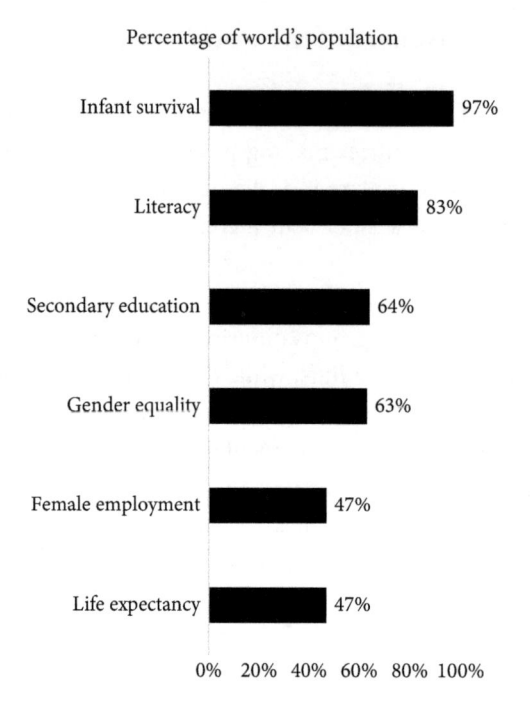

Figure 9.1 Population at global welfare standards
Source: Global Welfare Database.

population is at global standards of female employment and life expectancy, these minorities nonetheless consist of more than 3.5 billion people.

A vital measure of welfare, infant survival to the age of 5, is near the limit of the world's population. More than 7.5 billion people now live in households free from the experience of infant mortality. Moreover, the survival of newborn infants beyond childhood positively affects more than nine-tenths of the population of every continent. While the increase in infant survival since 1991 is only 5 percentage points, this nonetheless represents millions more infants living rather than dying. India, with its massive population and large scope for making progress, contributed the most to the decrease in infant mortality.

When the global standard for female life expectancy was set at the mean for highly developed countries in 1991, only 2 per cent of the world's population met this standard. Sixteen of the world's highly developed countries did not, along with virtually the whole of the population of developing countries. There was a gap of up to twenty-four years in female life expectancy between the average highly developed country and the average African country. Since then the number of countries at this standard of life expectancy has more than doubled (cf. OECD, 2020). When China reached this standard, it brought the total in countries at the global standard of life expectancy close to a majority of the world's population.

Since 1991 the number of literate adults has increased by about 2.8 billion people; India and China account for more than one billion of this increase. The big increase in literacy is also affected by generational change, as younger cohorts who have benefited from free compulsory education replace older generations who did not (see Table 6.4). China accounts for 22 per cent of the world's literate population today, and highly developed countries for another fifth. India accounts not only for more than one billion of the world's literates but also for one-third of the world's illiterates.

International institutions today endorse the state offering a modicum of free compulsory secondary education after completion of primary education (United Nations, 2020). In the past three decades there has been a worldwide increase of 32 percentage points in the proportion of youths extending their education past primary school. This has resulted in almost two-thirds of youths of secondary school age being enrolled in such schools today. Highly developed countries account for one-fourth of this total, China for one-fifth, and India for more than one-sixth of the five billion plus people in households affected by progress in education. Among those in households not reached by secondary education, more than one-quarter live in India and another quarter in sub-Saharan Africa.

Although fewer women are employed than men, the effect is sufficient to reach more than 3.6 billion people. While labour force participation has fallen in China as more women stay at school longer or can afford to retire, three-fifths are still active in the labour force. Therefore, China contributes more than one-fifth of the global total of employed women. Sub-Saharan Africa and highly developed countries each account for more than one-sixth of globally employed women, but for very different reasons. Economic necessity results in a high proportion of African women working for low wages, while domestic changes in highly developed countries have led more women to participate in paid employment rather than concentrate on unpaid work in their home.

Gender equality affects a billion more people than female employment because it is a ratio between women and men in employment. A total of 4.7 billion people live in societies where gender equality is at the global standard set by African countries—85 per cent. Population differences between countries affect their impact on welfare going global. A minority of people in India, where inequality is the norm, account for forty times more of the global total of gender equality than is contributed by Sweden, where gender equality is three times higher.

Most 'have' people live in 'have-not' countries

Conventionally, there is an assumption that people who live in highly developed countries have a high standard of welfare, while people living in developing countries do not. As preceding chapters have shown, the percentage of people at the global standard of health and education is consistently greater in highly developed countries than in developing countries. However, when the global standard for evaluating the welfare of countries is close to 100 per cent, this can have a perverse effect. Even though 93 per cent of Brazilian adults are literate, the whole of the country's population can be described as below the global standard of almost 99 per cent adult literacy.

The skewness in global population means that, even if a populous country is not at the global standard of welfare, it can have a very disproportionate impact on both the global total of people who are at the global standard and those who are not (Figure 9.2). On all six welfare measures the United States has a substantially higher percentage of its population at the global standard of welfare than India. However, because India has more than four times the population of the United States, on most welfare measures hundreds of millions more Indians are at the global standard than Americans. The difference

Percentage of people at global-standard welfare

	Highly developed	Developing
Female life expectancy	36	64
Infant survival	17	83
Literacy	20	80
Secondary education	25	75
Female employment	20	80
Gender equality	21	79

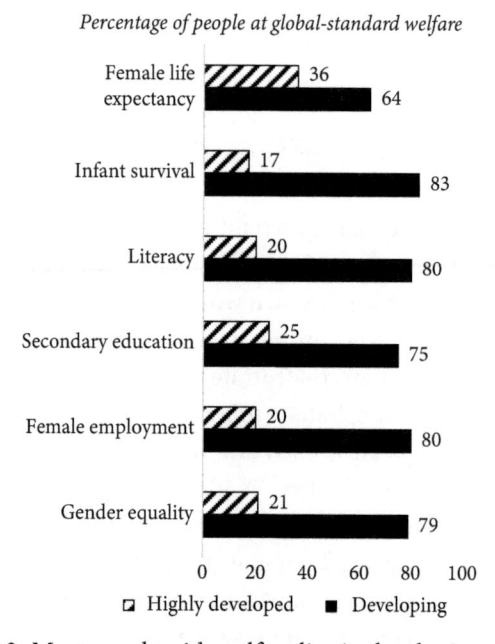

Figure 9.2 Most people with welfare live in developing countries
Source: Global Welfare Database.

is close to one billion Indians for infant survival and more than 675 million for adult literacy. Even though Indian cultural values about the employment of women are the opposite of American values, there are almost 100 million more women employed in India than in the United States.

Shifting the focus from countries to people at the global standard of welfare produces a big difference in the perception of welfare 'haves' and 'have-nots'. Even though the majority of countries are below global standards, the majority of the world's population is at global standards of health and education, including majorities of the total population of developing countries. This is because developing countries collectively have 85 per cent of the world's population. At a maximum, highly developed countries can contribute only 15 per cent of the world's population to the globalization of welfare. As long as two-fifths of the population of developing countries are at global standards, this is enough to bring half the world's total population up to a global standard.

9.3 How population growth impacts global welfare

The world's population has grown by more than 2.3 billion people since 1991, but growth has been very unequally divided between continents. Growth has been greatest in Africa, an increase of 542 million people; in Asian developing countries population has increased by 418 million people. An increase of 494 million has raised the population of India to almost 1.4 billion people, while the legacy of China's one-child policy is a relatively lower growth in population of 251 million. Growth in highly developed countries has been lowest, 145 million. This reduces the continent that sets most global standards of welfare from more than one-fifth to less than one-sixth of the world's population.

Population growth is not a cause of welfare, but it does have consequences, because it levies a surcharge on progress. It challenges a society to run faster to keep welfare up to a given percentage of a growing population. To do this, the state must provide more schools, the market must create more jobs for women and men, and state and market institutions must provide more health services. The extent to which population growth creates additional resources for welfare depends on whether the age group most affected is of working age or too young or too old to work.

The need to keep a growing population at a given standard of welfare has the first claim on progress, since it adds to the need for developing countries to run faster if they are to catch up with global standards. In Brazil, where 86 per cent were literate in 1991, the country's population increased by 60 million people in the following three decades. While the number of literates increased by 65 million, nine-tenths of this increase was needed to keep the literate percentage from falling due to increased population.

More people and more welfare globally

The increase in billions of people at global standards of welfare is a function of both population growth and faster rates of progress. For example, 74 per cent of the world's population of 5.1 billion were literate in 1991; by 2019 the world's population had risen to more than 7.7 billion. Educating the same percentage of this increased population added nearly 2 billion people to global literacy. Thus, three-quarters of the increase in the world's literate population was accounted for by population growth.

There are big differences in the influence that population change has on different forms of welfare (Figure 9.3). Where globalization was already widespread, there is little scope for increasing the percentage with welfare. Since the average rate of infant survival was 92 per cent three decades ago,

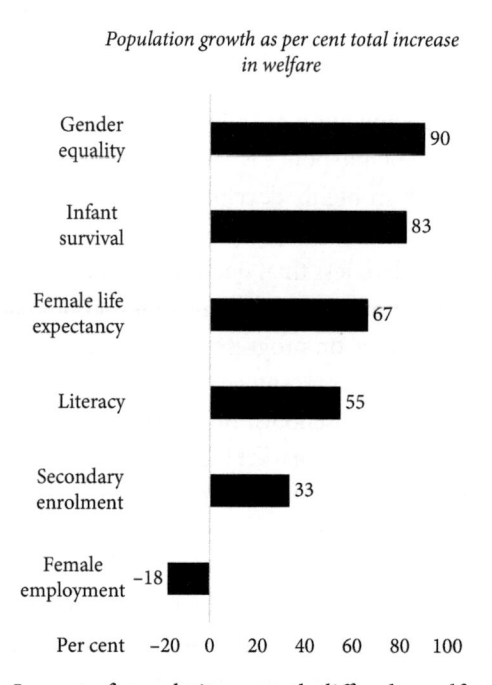

Population growth as per cent total increase in welfare

Measure	Per cent
Gender equality	90
Infant survival	83
Female life expectancy	67
Literacy	55
Secondary enrolment	33
Female employment	−18

Figure 9.3 Impact of population growth differs by welfare measure
Source: Global Welfare Database.

this means that only one-sixth of the increase in live births since then is due to a reduction in infant mortality. More babies being born is the principal cause of the increase.

Population change affects life expectancy through the turnover of generations, since each new generation consists of youths with better health and longer life expectancy than the generation dying off. The age groups most vulnerable to death in highly developed countries in 1991 were born at the time of the First World War. The groups most vulnerable to death in developing countries were born during the world depression before the Second World War. Generational turnover has similarly made population growth account for most of the increase in literacy. By contrast, two-thirds of the big rise in secondary school enrolment reflects positive actions increasing the percentage of youths in secondary schools. More governments in developing countries are making secondary education compulsory for the youngest teenagers, and more teenagers voluntarily remain at school to obtain the skills and knowledge provided by advanced secondary education.

The effect of population growth on female employment has shifted between phases in the life cycle. Younger women have chosen to spend more time in education and, when in work, to retire earlier. Concurrently, middle-aged women have had more years to participate in the labour force with the fall in family size reducing the number of years women allocate to working without a wage in their household. The aggregate effect has been that, while the absolute number of employed females has increased since 1991, those employed as a percentage of a much enlarged global population has fallen (Figure 9.1). Because men have similarly reduced the years they spend in the labour force, this has done little to alter the gender equality ratio. The result is that nine-tenths of the increase in gender equality is due to population change.

9.4 Where most people without welfare live

People living below global standards of welfare are found on every continent, but not in proportion to the population. Côte d'Ivoire is a country that has a below-average Index of Development, and it is among the leading underachieving countries in the use it makes of its resources to advance welfare. However, it has little impact on global welfare because it has only one-third of 1 per cent of the world's population (Table 8.3).

India, because of its massive population and limited resources and because it is a leading underachiever in their use (Table 8.3), accounts on average for

Table 9.2 Global distribution of people without welfare

		HiDev	LatAm	MENA	Africa	AsiaDev	China	India
		% world's population
		17	8	7	14	16	19	19
(bn) without		% below global standard
0.2	Infant survival	3	5	6	38	20	6	24
3.9	Long life	0	5	9	27	24	0	35
1.1	Literacy	1	4	8	32	19	4	32
2.2	Secondary educ'n	4	5	5	21	18	22	24
3.9	Female employment	15	7	10	10	16	14	28
2.7	Gender equality	9	7	13	6	18	11	37

Source: Global Welfare Database. Global standard for 2019 except adult literacy (2018) and secondary education (2017).

30 per cent of the world's population below global standards of welfare. It has more than a third of the world's population affected by gender inequality and substandard life expectancy and almost one-third of the world's adult illiterates (Table 9.2). The size of these groups lacking welfare is half again larger than India's share of the world's population. Nonetheless, because of its population size, India is consistently second only to China in the hundreds of millions living at high global standards of welfare.

Collectively, the forty countries of Africa make the second-largest contribution to the total number of people below global welfare standards. The continent accounts for an average of 22 per cent of those below standard, more than half again its share of the world's population. However, this average obscures the contrast between low achievement in health and education and high achievement in female employment. Because of economic need, African countries contribute fewer people than highly developed countries to the global total of people not at global standards of female employment and gender equality. By contrast, African countries account for the largest number of cases of infant mortality and have as many adult illiterates as India, even though Africa's population is only three-quarters that of India.

Within Africa Nigeria accounts for more than twenty times the population of the continent's average country and for a disproportionate share of people living below the average African country's standard of welfare. Female life expectancy in Nigeria is 11 years below the continental average, and so is its level of adult literacy. The inability of the federal government to report statistics for secondary school enrolment is an indicator of its limited capacity to deliver welfare policies in the face of ethnic conflict and civil strife. Since only a slim majority of Nigeria's population is nominally Muslim, its level of female employment is above average for Muslim societies, but 14 percentage points below the African mean.

Asian developing countries collectively rank third in the number of people who are below global standards of welfare because they have large populations, one-sixth of the world's total. Although Indonesia and Pakistan can be grouped together as very populous Asian developing countries, their welfare achievements differ. In addition to ranking fourth in global population, Indonesia is fourth in the people it adds to the global population with high standards of welfare. Although Indonesia is nominally a Muslim country, its culture does not endorse strict Islamic precepts; female employment and gender equality are in keeping with global standards. By contrast Pakistan's culture is that of a strict Islamic society: it ranks third-highest globally in the number of women who are not employed, and it is also low in gender equality. In addition, Pakistan has the fewest number of literates of any very populous country and less than half the number of pupils in secondary education compared to other countries with large populations.

Countries in the Middle East and North Africa region have a very limited impact on the global population without health and education because their collective population is only 7 per cent of the world's total and the proportion lacking global standards is in proportion (Table 9.2). Although all MENA societies have some form of Islamic culture, values affecting female employment differ. Turkish women are twice as likely as those in Iran to participate in the labour force. This significantly reduces the region's impact on the global total of women without employment.

Latin American countries have little impact on the global total of people with substandard welfare, since their collective population is half a billion less than most continents. Moreover, countries there make good use of their resources for welfare, which are high by comparison with developing countries on other continents. The mean Index of Development of Latin American countries is almost twice that of African and Asian developing countries. They do particularly well in health and literacy, and the absence of a significant Muslim population means there is no cultural pressure on women to stay out of the labour market. Thus, Latin America contributes less than its 8 per cent share of global population to the total number of people doing without health, education, and employment. The most populous country on the continent, Brazil, has a population similar to that of Pakistan and Nigeria but an Index of Development double either of these countries. Even though welfare in Brazil is not up to that of highly developed countries, a significant fraction of its very large population does reach global standards of health, education, and female employment.

China has a big impact on the global distribution of welfare; the complement of its being an overachiever in welfare is that it contributes less than its share of world population to the total doing without welfare. On average China accounts for just under 10 per cent of the global population without welfare at global standards; this is half its share of the global population. Moreover, even though their populations are very similar in size, China contributes on average only one-third as many people as India to the global population with sub-standard welfare.

Since highly developed countries set global standards, the group contributes the fewest number of people to the world's population with substandard health and education. The relatively high number of women who are not in employment reflects women having alternative ways of allocating their time in the fifty years between ages 15 and 65. The few countries in this group that are below standard on welfare are typically low-population Mediterranean countries such as Portugal and Greece and countries such as Bulgaria and Romania, where catching up with global standards is still handicapped by a communist legacy.

The policy implication is clear: bringing hundreds of millions or billions more people up to global welfare standards requires continued progress among a very small number of very big countries in Asia, such as India and Pakistan, and a large number of small African countries plus Nigeria. As long as there is no global consensus, bringing more people up to global standards of female employment and gender equality is possible up to the point at which the cultural definition of progress is rejected by populous states such as India with a different cultural goal. Progress towards complete literacy and the reduction of infant mortality can be secured through the continuing application of widely known social technologies. Resources for development can be increased not only through economic growth but also by reducing levels of corruption and increasing democratic governance. These institutional reforms would simultaneously impose costs on governors while bringing benefits to their citizens.

References

OECD 2020. *Health at a Glance: Europe 2020*. Paris: OECD Social Indicators.
United Nations, 2020. *Inclusion and Education*. New York: UNESCO Global Education Monitoring Report.

United Nations, 2022. *World Population Prospects 2022: Highlights*. New York: United Nations Department of Economic and Social Affairs, Population Division.

World Bank, 2018. *Poverty and Shared Prosperity 2018: Piecing Together the Poverty Puzzle*. Washington DC: World Bank.

10
Unfinished Business

The extent to which welfare has gone global depends on the time perspective, because globalization is a gradual process continuing for many decades. In the past three decades there has been substantial catching up, as seemingly small annual rates of progress have compounded to bring billions of people up to global standards of health, education, and employment. However, as of today billions of people are not living at global standards of welfare. The scale of this unfinished business poses the question: How long will it take before billions short of welfare reach global standards?

To describe the lack of welfare as unfinished business assumes that the population of every country can reach the same high standard of welfare that global leaders have already achieved. In principle this is possible if the goal is a fixed target, and if there is a social technology for achieving it and sufficient resources in countries' welfare mix. In countries that now have free compulsory education for all, progress toward a fixed target of complete adult literacy is locked in as cohorts of literate youths replace generations of older illiterates. Open-ended welfare targets such as life expectancy are more difficult to achieve, since countries that set today's global standard can keep raising it higher by continuing to make progress. The only way to make an open-ended goal attainable by a majority of the world's population is to fix the goal at the highest standard in a given year.

Long-term progress towards globalization puts in perspective shock events that can stop or even reverse progress. For example, the global recession of 2008 caused a key component of the Index of Development, gross domestic product, to contract in 2009 rather than grow. Pessimists extrapolated the effect into the future, with an implied contraction in global welfare. However, the shock demonstrated the resilience of national societies. The following year national economies returned to economic growth at a rate more than double that of 2007, and short-term negative effects soon dissipated (cf. Hellwig, Kweon, and Vowles, 2020).

The immediate effect of the coronavirus pandemic that began in 2020 has been a significant increase in total global deaths, with the increase

Welfare Goes Global. Richard Rose, Oxford University Press. © Richard Rose (2024).
DOI: 10.1093/oso/9780198908463.003.0011

often attributed to COVID-19 (Our World in Data, 2023). However, the World Health Organization (2021) cautions that these figures are approximations subject to cross-national differences in practices and methods for recording deaths. The long-term effects of the COVID pandemic on progress in global health, education, and female employment are speculative, since sufficient evidence will not become available until the 2030s.

There are many precedents of resilience from the effect of past pandemics, and short-term contractions in welfare are common on every continent. Between 1991 and 2019 female life expectancy contracted or failed to increase for one or more years in 115 countries, including every highly developed country. In the average country life expectancy failed to progress in five years. In the United Kingdom life expectancy fell on six occasions and in the United States three times. In two former communist countries life expectancy fell in nine years.

Insofar as many conditions of individuals tend to be set in youth, the adult population is significantly insulated from the loss of welfare due to shocks that have a short-term negative effect on the welfare mix. Literate adults do not suddenly become illiterate if today's youths lose a year or two of in-person schooling because of the coronavirus pandemic. Contractions in economic resources of a few per cent do not shut hospitals, and a doubling in unemployment can still leave upwards of 90 per cent of the labour force in work. Although Japan experienced a lost decade of economic growth in the 1990s, at the same time Japanese life expectancy continued to progress at its normal rate. The collapse of an authoritarian regime and the break-up of a state can have a positive impact, as millions of East Europeans have found in the decades since the fall of the Berlin Wall in 1989.

The time required for scores of countries and billions of people to reach today's global standards is explained in Section 10.1. The following section shows the extent to which the majority of the world's population is likely to be at global standards of health, education, and employment by 2050. Once a fixed welfare goal is achieved, this does not mean an end to progress. Instead, as the third section shows, it leads to the definition of new health, education, and employment goals. Transnational problems such as climate change can also challenge individual welfare. They are wicked problems because national governments cannot control them on their own, and international organizations lack the political authority and resources to deal with wicked problems effectively.

10.1 Catching up sooner or later

Catching up with global standards challenges the institutions of developing countries to maintain progress in future at a rate that will reduce or eliminate their current distance from global standards. The distance each developing country is from the global standard for each of six measures of welfare is known. So too is the compound rate of progress for each measure from 1991 to 2019. However, whether that rate will persist, slow down, or even reverse is a known unknown. Furthermore, the extent to which population growth will require a faster rate of progress is also a known unknown. These unknowns present challenges that forecasters face too.

Distance from global welfare standards

The size of the challenge a country faces to catch up depends upon how distant it is from a fixed welfare goal, set at the highest level of welfare of any continent in 2019. This year avoids long-term analysis being affected by the coronavirus pandemic that erupted in 2020. Since welfare goals differ in how they are measured, a standard metric is needed of a country's distance from global standards. Distance is calculated by dividing the current level of welfare in a country or continent by the 2019 global standard. For example, female life expectancy in Africa averages 64 years and in China 79 years; both are below the global standard of 83 years set by highly developed countries. China falls 5 per cent short of the global standard, while the average African country is 23 per cent distant.

The less a country's distance from a global standard, the sooner its chance of catching up with global leaders in future. The world's two most populous countries, China and India, differ greatly in their distance from global standards (Table 10.1). China is now at the global standard for infant survival at birth and within 6 percentage points of the global standard on four measures of welfare. By contrast, India's distinctive cultural norm for female employment rejects the global definition of progress, resulting in India being 67 percentage points distant from the global standard for female employment and 68 points for gender equality. India is also 34 percentage points distant from the global standard for secondary education and 25 percentage points distant from that for adult literacy. Thus, the globalization of welfare will be accelerated by progress in China, which on average is already within 7 percentage points of global standards.

Table 10.1 Distance from global welfare standards

	HiDev	LatAm	MENA	China	AsiaDev	Africa	India
(Continental mean in relation to best performing continent)
Infant survival	100	99	98	100	97	94	97
Female life expectancy	100	93	91	97	88	77	87
Adult literacy	100	92	90	98	81	65	75
Secondary education	100	78	80	71	64	38	66
Women employed	87	87	51	97	84	100	33
Gender equality	96	82	54	94	82	100	32

Source: Global Welfare Database.

The process of globalization will be slowed down by India, which averages 35 percentage points distant from global standards—and female employment is decreasing from a very low standard.

African countries have a substantial impact on global prospects for catching up because they are collectively becoming the most populous continent. The average African country is the standard-setter for female employment and gender equality. However, on the four measures of health and education the average sub-Saharan country is the furthest from the global standard, thereby slowing down the rate of the globalization of welfare.

The mean distance from global standards of Middle East and North African countries is similar to that of Africa, but for the opposite reason: it is closer to global standards for education and health but distant on female employment on cultural grounds. Asian developing countries tend to be consistent in their significant distance from global standards, an average of 17 per cent. Latin American countries are consistently closer to global standards of welfare, on average being 12 percentage points distant. However, the impact on the global population is limited because the total population of Latin America is half that of most developing continents.

Even though the mean achievement of highly developed countries sets global standards for health and education, upwards of half the group's countries, including Russia and Portugal, were below the highly developed mean for measures of health and education. Moreover, the average highly developed country is 4 per cent below the average African country on measures of gender equality in employment and 13 percentage points distant from the African level of female participation in the labour force.

However, many developing countries are still at such a distance from global standards that they will have to sustain future progress for many decades before they can catch up. The adage 'Never say never in politics' leaves open how long it will take before progress will lead to billions of people now without welfare catching up with global standards on one or more welfare measure (see Table 9.3).

Catching up requires countries to persist in progress

Progress in health, education, and employment has persisted globally during the past three decades, notwithstanding a major global economic recession, a global health pandemic, and a variety of localized natural and avoidable disasters. In the next three decades the capacity of the institutions of the welfare mix to improve welfare will benefit from countries having a healthier and more educated labour force, the continuing diffusion of social technologies to less developed countries, and a consequent growth in gross domestic product. Given this, it is more realistic to assume welfare progress will continue in the next three decades rather than become static or radically reverse direction. The estimates that follow assume persistence—that each country's annually compounded rate of welfare will continue in the next three decades as in the past three (see Figures 8.1 and 8.2). This central assumption leaves open the possibility that progress in future could be at a higher or lower rate than in the past.

Since the future is an indefinite span of time, both near- and long-term forecasts of globalization are presented. The near future is defined as the year 2030, just over a decade from 2019, the year in which global standards have been fixed. This gives scope for countries already near the global mean to catch up with global standards; for example, East European societies will then have had four decades since the fall of the Berlin Wall to raise their standards. It also gives scope for China to complete its progress into the ranks of countries high in welfare. The distant future is set at 2050, a similar length of time to that used to calculate annual rates of progress. This gives countries now distant from global standards substantial time to catch up or show that it will be up to half a century or more before they are likely to catch up.

Three decades ago infant survival in many developing countries was already close to the global standard of 99.6 per cent of newborn infants surviving to age 5. The average developing country was less than 4 percentage points below the global standard. So small a gap, combined with the continuing spread of social technologies to reduce infant mortality, makes it possible for globalization to advance at a rapid rate. China should reach the global standard by 2030, and 99 per cent of the world's infants should survive to age 5. By 2050 continuing progress should result in 121 of 127 countries reaching the global standard for the survival of newborn infants (Figure 10.1).

Life expectancy in developing countries averaged 18 per cent distant from highly developed countries in 1991. Although developing countries progressed faster than standard-setters in the next three decades, they were still an average of 12 per cent behind the global standard set in 2019, which was based on mortality statistics extending back to the Second World War and before, when individual resources for health and medical knowledge were much less than today. Hence, only twenty-three countries were then at the global standard for female life expectancy. Since then life expectancy has been lengthening as calculations are increasingly based on the lower mortality of people born after living standards had begun rising significantly from one decade to the next (cf. Kontis et al., 2017).

The immediate effect of the coronavirus pandemic on life expectancy has been uneven. From 2019 to 2020 life expectancy fell in ninety-five countries, while continuing to rise in thirty-two countries. In the following year there was a fall from the 2020 level in ninety-one countries and a rise in thirty-six countries (Aburto, Schöley, and Kashyap, 2022). Given past

Indicator	Number of countries
Infant survival	121
Female life expectancy	107
Secondary education	94
Adult literacy	91
Gender equality	87
Female employment	52

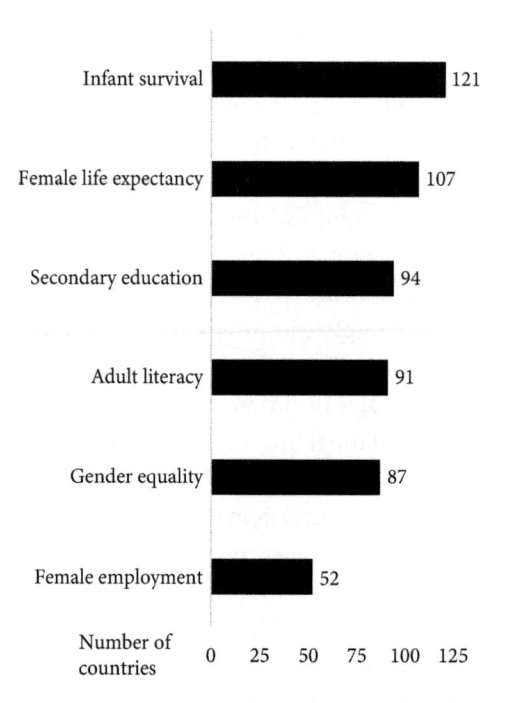

Figure 10.1 Countries at global standard of welfare, 2050
Source: Calculated from Global Welfare Database; see text.

resilience, 107 countries are forecast to be at the 2019 global standard of female life expectancy by 2050 (Figure 10.1). China could reach this standard later in the 2020s, the United States in 2033, and India by 2039.

The enrolment of youths in secondary schools in developing countries has long been very distant from global standards: it was barely half the rate of highly developed countries in 1991 and averaged a third lower than in highly developed countries in 2019. Because it does not depend on the turnover of generations, it can expand rapidly provided that there is money. By 2050 three-quarters of countries are expected to be at the global standard for secondary school enrolment (Figure 10.1). Looking three decades ahead gives time for the turnover of generations to have a substantial effect on national literacy. By 2030 the process of generational turnover should add twenty-one more countries, including three highly developed countries, to the group in which at least 98.8 per cent of the adult population is literate, including the world's two most populous countries, China and India. Africa will be the only continent in which a majority of countries have yet to achieve complete adult literacy by 2050.

Forecasting the direction of change in female employment is problematic; it depends on whether cultural values that have opposed female employment in predominantly Muslim countries will remain as strong in the next three decades as in the past. If that happens, this will restrict the number of countries at the global standard for female employment to fifty-two (Figure 10.1). However, if traditional values were to decline with the demographic turnover of the population, this could add another dozen or more countries to the global total of those at the global standard for female participation in the labour force.

Because gender equality in employment is a ratio, a decline in male employment can raise the ratio as long as it is greater than a decline in female employment. If female employment is increasing, this would accelerate a country catching up with the global standard for gender equality, which was 85 per cent in sub-Saharan Africa in 2019. Without any change in cultural values in predominantly Muslim societies, gender equality is forecast to be at global standards in an additional nine countries by 2030 and in two-thirds of all countries by 2050 (Figure 10.1).

Running fast to keep up with population growth

Whatever its level of welfare, the first charge on every country is ensuring that the welfare needs of a growing population are met. By the time this book is published, global population will have risen above eight billion people, and by 2050 the world's population is forecast to increase by another two billion people (United Nations, 2022). However, population change is not uniform across nations. More than one-quarter of the world's countries are forecast to see their population contract in the next three decades.

Population growth affects claims for welfare by changing the age composition of society. Where it is due to high birth rates and progress in the survival of newborn infants, as is the case in Africa, the average age of the population becomes younger, and more and more youths must be educated. Longer life expectancy is a challenge to the welfare mix to meet the health needs of an older population and of elderly people who need care within their household, from paid carers and/or health services. Increased longevity has already made state-funded health care and pensions the two biggest claims on public budgets in highly developed countries (OECD, 2020a; Tsuji, 2020).

An increase in population will not only increase demands for health, education, and employment but also provide more resources to meet demands (cf. Eurostat, 2022). Insofar as the increase is due to high birth rates and low infant mortality, in due course it will increase the number of educated and healthy adults in the labour force and gross domestic product. In turn this will contribute to a higher Index of Development.

Population growth is forecast to be greatest where welfare is lowest (Table 10.2). By 2050 the population of Africa is estimated to increase by more than a billion people, and Nigeria, low in welfare by African standards, is likely to tie with the United States as the world's third most populous country. India will replace China as the world's most populous country, as India's population increases by 301 million. The population of the Middle East and North Africa region is forecast to grow by two-fifths, but its global impact is much less because the region has fewer people than the African and Asian continents.

The population of today's highly developed countries is expected to grow very little or even contract by 2050, thereby reducing their share of the world's growing population to 13.6 per cent. The population increase in Latin America, the most developed of the developing continents, will decline to 7.5 per cent of an increased global population. Although the Chinese government has now revoked its one-child family policy, the country still faces the consequences. Its total population is forecast to decline by 115 million people by 2050. Together, the most developed groups in 2050—highly developed countries, Latin America, and China—will have their share of the world's population fall to 35 per cent of the global total. Reciprocally, continents where welfare tends to be more distant from global standards will have almost two-thirds of the world's population.

Table 10.2 Population growth to 2050 by continent

Continent	2019	2030	2050	Change 2019–50
			Millions	
Africa	1,099	1,442	2,149	1,050
India	1,453	1,591	1,754	301
Asia Dev	1,205	1,362	1,583	378
China	1,494	1,486	1,379	−115
Hi Dev	1,312	1,327	1,313	1
MENA	574	659	802	228
Lat Am	629	678	730	101
Total	7,765	8,546	9,709	1,944

Source: Global Welfare Database and United Nations, 2022.

In three decades all countries are forecast to have reached at least one global standard of welfare, and twenty-six countries are expected to do so on all six measures of health, education, and female employment. Only four sub-Saharan countries and Pakistan are expected not to meet at least two global standards. Differing patterns of catching up will result in China and India each being at global standards on a majority of measures of welfare.

Forecasts of the future of welfare are subject to a degree of error but not to an error in kind. A country's rate of progress could decline because of a slowdown in the national economy, democratic backsliding, or an increase in corruption in the delivery of social services. While this would reduce its progress, it would only cause a delay when a country reaches a fixed global standard. The impact on globalization would depend on the population of the country where this occurred. Since the median country in the Global Welfare Database has less than one-tenth of 1 per cent of the world's population, this would limit the impact of most societies' actions. There is also the possibility of political, social, and economic changes accelerating progress—for example, the weakening of cultural values that inhibit female employment. Only a global disaster would have sufficient scope to reduce or reverse the continuing globalization of welfare.

10.2 Most but not all people at global standards by 2050

The total globalization of welfare for the great majority of the world's population is most likely for infant survival at birth and literacy. As long as the current progress continues, almost 100 per cent of live births will survive to the age of 5. Of the small number of cases of infant mortality, a portion may be due to unavoidable causes such as congenital disorders. As a consequence of the turnover of generations, adult literacy will be achieved by 95 per cent of the world's population by 2050. The largest number of adult illiterates is likely to be found in Nigeria and Pakistan, a consequence of many adults having been born when primary education was not universally available.

Institutions of the welfare mix will increase the proportion of youths enrolled at a global standard of secondary education in 2050 to cover more than four-fifths of the world's population (Table 10.3). Development will give more countries the resources to build secondary schools and make enrolment compulsory, and the benefits of secondary education will increase the proportion of youths voluntarily remaining in education. Among the 19 per cent likely not to be at global standards in 2050, the most populous countries are likely to include India and Pakistan. In addition, national statistics for secondary education are missing for such very populous countries as Nigeria, the Democratic Republic of the Congo, and Vietnam. This suggests that their national education systems are unevenly distributed and unlikely to reach global standards in the foreseeable future.

Almost seven billion people are estimated to be living in countries at the global standard of female life expectancy by 2050, and China, India, and the United States are likely to reach this goal well before then. In spite of this achievement, there will still be 2.7 billion people in countries with a life expectancy that is below the standard fixed in 2019. This category includes seven countries that by 2050 will have a combined population of more than 1.7 billion people: Nigeria, Pakistan, Indonesia, the Democratic Republic of the Congo, Egypt, the Philippines, and Mexico.

Table 10.3 World population at and below global standards, 2050

	At standard		Below standard	
	Millions	Per cent	Millions	Per cent
Infant survival	9,705	100	5	0
Adult literacy	9,225	95	485	5
Secondary enrolment	7,851	81	1,859	19
Female life expectancy	6,998	72	2,711	28
Gender equality	6,501	67	3,208	33
Female employment	4,544	47	5,165	53

Source: Distributions in Global Welfare Database projected on 2050 global population estimates in United Nations, 2022.

The number of people affected by countries falling short of global standards for female employment depends on how the standard is defined. In 2050 a narrow majority of the world's population, 53 per cent, will be living where female employment is not expected to be at the global standard set in 2019, 62 per cent of women aged 15 to 65. On the other hand, due in part to falls in male employment, two-thirds of the world's population will be in countries where the gender equality ratio will be at the global standard (Table 10.3).

The continuing globalization of welfare reflects the steady and substantial progress of welfare in very populous developing countries such as China and Brazil. It also reflects the United States, which was below global standards on five of six measures of welfare in 2019, catching up. Notwithstanding continuing worldwide progress, in 2050 there are likely to remain more than one billion people living below global standards on five welfare measures. This does not mean that countries that are progressing slowly and are at a considerable distance from global standards can never reach fixed goals. Nonetheless, in 2050 hundreds of millions or billions of people will lack a high level of welfare because of their country's slow progress.

10.3 Redefining welfare goals

Success in achieving welfare goals is not the end of welfare as a concern of people and of public policy; it opens up a space in the political agenda to focus on fresh goals. This is particularly the case in highly developed countries that have reached or are approaching the limit of fixed goals. For example, many highly developed countries have stopped publishing data on adult literacy because they are so close to the limit that any changes found are likely to be caused by random fluctuations in measurement rather than reflecting progress or backsliding.

Individuals can redefine welfare goals too. More women in highly developed countries are seeking employment, while more young women in developing countries are giving employment a lesser priority than education. The development of new indicators of welfare can involve the articulation of competing goals—for example, whether further education should give priority to technical skills relevant to an individual's employment or to ideas that may enhance their quality of life.

As people live longer, a new *health* standard has been developed that is especially relevant to older people—the quality of life. It is defined as the number of years in which people are free of restrictions on their normal activities due to physical and mental disabilities. In the highly developed countries of Europe, Eurostat (2022) calculates that men have a satisfactory quality of life for 78 per cent of their total lifespan and women for 82 per cent of their longer lifespan. Health economists have used quality of life measures to impute a cash value to the years in which an individual lives with a reduced quality of life and set this benefit against the cost of medical measures prolonging life (Augustovski et al., 2018).

The survival of almost all newborn infants to age 5 implies that women should have more live births as a consequence of the reduction in infant mortality, especially in developing countries. However, this is not the case. There has been a global fall in fertility rates from 3.2 live births per woman in 1990 to 2.5 births in 2019 (United Nations, 2020). While the fertility rate in Africa is still high enough to maintain global population growth, in Europe and North America there has been a reduction to 1.7 births per woman, a rate that in the long term will result in their population contracting.

The decrease in live births reflects the bottom-up development of a new health goal: women having the capacity to choose when and whether to have children, and if so how many. This requires women to have knowledge of modern methods of contraception, which can be gained through informal personal contacts, the sale of contraceptives in the marketplace, and the promotion of contraceptive knowledge by public health services. Knowledge of modern methods of contraception has spread with literacy. An estimated 49 per cent of the world's population aged 15 to 49 now use some form of contraception, and rates of progress indicate more widespread use in future (United Nations, 2022: 3).

Concurrently, there has been a global increase in women having the right to terminate an unwanted pregnancy through the legalization of abortion. The legalization of abortion has occurred in the world's most populous countries, China and India, as well as in a large majority of highly developed countries (United Nations, 2017). The conditions for doing so vary greatly. Abortion is legal almost everywhere to save the mother's life, in two-thirds of countries it is legal to protect a woman's mental health, and in one-third of countries a woman can request an abortion on personal, economic, or social grounds. In these countries the termination of pregnancies by choice is now substantially higher than the national rate of infant mortality*.

The globalization of primary *education* has focused attention on the welfare of youths before and after primary school. In most highly developed

---

* https://ourworldindata.orgigrapher/abortion-rates.

countries there are policies to promote preschool child welfare. One-quarter of children under the age of 3 participate in public sector and market-financed programmes with multiple welfare goals (OECD, 2020b: 166 f.). The absence of statistics for the great majority of developing countries is an unobtrusive sign that there is little state provision of preschool education; it is exclusively the responsibility of a child's household.

The globalization of compulsory secondary education and voluntary further education has given institutional expression to different ways in which education can contribute to individual welfare. It can do so by teaching skills relevant to getting a job, by exposing youths to diverse ideas and cultures, and by enhancing lifelong wellbeing (see Chapter 6). While these multiple goals are not contradictory, they are competitive. Ministries of education face choices about funding vocational training or liberal arts institutions, and youths face choices about what type of institution to attend, what course to study, and when to leave formal education and enter the labour market.

The behaviour of men and women challenges the statistical definition of employment as participation in the labour force from ages 15 to 64. For men, employment covers a long uninterrupted period of work. Women can alternate between or combine two careers as a homemaker giving primary care to children and as a paid employee. International survey evidence shows that more women than men would prefer not to be employed at some point in their life (Addati et al., 2018). In highly developed societies gender equality in paid employment is increasingly an issue in private enterprises as well as the subject of government legislation, while equality in unpaid work is determined within households.

While gender inequality in employment is widely discussed, gender inequality in life expectancy receives little attention. A Google search in September 2023 found 130 million references to the gender gap in employment compared to less than 8 million references to the gender gap in life expectancy. While there has been progress in the life expectancy of both men and women for a century, the life expectancy of women has remained higher everywhere (see Figure 5.2). The difference tends to be greater in more developed countries. In 2019 the gap in life expectancy between women and men was six years in highly developed countries and Latin America. The gap is less where the life expectancy of women as well as men is substantially lower, especially Africa and India. Over three decades the gender difference in life expectancy has increased marginally in most continents; only in highly developed countries has the difference been significantly reduced, by an average of 1.7 years.

By 2050 life expectancy is predicted to increase by a global average of 12 years for both men and women. However, if progress in the world's two most populous countries continues at present rates, the existing inequality in life expectancy will widen by 1.8 years in India, China, and a majority of developing countries. Concurrently, gender inequality in life expectancy is forecast to rise in thirty-one of thirty-four highly developed countries. Globally, the result of these trends will be an increase in gender inequality in life expectancy in countries with a combined total of more than 6.7 billion people.

10.4 Global challenges to global welfare

Many problems that affect individual welfare are collective in nature: they affect the whole of the population of a society. Even though deaths from a national epidemic claim the lives of a small percentage of a country's population, there is a collective problem since everyone in a society is at risk of a fatal infection. Individuals and households cannot protect themselves from a national epidemic, and activities in the market place can spread a contagious disease. A national government responsible for public health has the authority and institutions to take collective action to deal with this threat to welfare. When a problem crosses national and continental boundaries, it creates a global challenge to welfare. The coronavirus infection originating in China went global in 2020. This has created a challenge to governments on every continent to respond to the pandemic's threat of infection and death.

The collective nature of the coronavirus pandemic has mobilized responses from all kinds of national institutions in the welfare mix (see, for example, Lynch, Bernhard, and O'Neill, 2022). National governments have imposed restrictions on gatherings of people and travel, and there has been a high level of compliance. Global pharmaceutical companies have created vaccines giving protection from coronavirus. Most vaccinations have occurred in highly developed countries with the resources to meet the costs and the health institutions to vaccinate the whole of the adult population. While the medical technology to inoculate people against coronavirus is known globally, collective action by international institutions such as the World Health Organization have concentrated on monitoring and recommending actions by national governments that administer vaccinations. An estimated 68 per cent of the world's population have been treated, but the distribution between countries has been very uneven. Only one-quarter of people in low-income countries have been vaccinated at least once (Our World in Data, 2023).

The protection of the environment has concerned governments since urbanization created a need for collective action to prevent epidemics by providing clean water and sanitation. In the past half-century scientific studies of climate change have found substantial evidence of global warming. Political action groups and green political parties have advocated government action to reduce global warming. A number of national governments have responded by enacting laws to reduce their country's contribution to global warming, however small it may be. Unlike pandemics, which directly affect the health of a limited minority of the population, climate change is a potential threat to the whole of the world's population.

The causes of climate change are not confined within national boundaries, but there is no international institution with the power to enforce collective measures to reduce the threat of climate change. The United Nations has sought to fill this void. At the 1992 Earth Summit in Rio de Janeiro 154 nations endorsed the United Nations Framework Convention on Climate Change to combat 'dangerous human interference with the climate system'. The 26th UN Climate Change Conference in 2021 adopted explicit targets to reduce the consumption of fossil fuels and methane gas emissions. It proposed that developed countries should meet the targets in the 2030s and that developing countries should do so in the 2040s, 'or as soon as possible thereafter'. The 27th UN Climate Change Conference in 2022 endorsed the creation of a network institution to advise on minimizing damage to the climate, but it could not reach agreement on a policy for fossil fuels threatening the environment.

Collective problems are wicked problems when they are global public goods; that is, when a national government cannot resolve a national problem on its own (cf. Shanmugaratnam, 2022). This is because their causes are the outcome of a global welfare mix; that is, the interaction across national boundaries of individual choices, impersonal market forces, and national government policies. Such interdependence can have multiple, unintended, and often unwanted consequences. For example, governments build roads that encourage the use of cars; motor manufacturers build cars to sell for a profit; and individuals buy and drive cars for work and leisure. This increases convenience and mobility for individuals but also local, national, and international environmental pollution.

Identifying the causes of wicked problems offers no assurance that a national government has the means or the political will to resolve a wicked problem. Even when national governments have the resources and political will to take action, problems cannot be resolved simply by passing laws. Ministers of health address the consequences of coronavirus by treating those who are ill, but they cannot fine the virus or put it in jail. The effect on the environment of actions to reduce pollution by the great majority of national governments is very small, because they account for a limited portion of the world's pollution, while adopting policies to combat climate change can impose a substantial cost on their national economies.

The United Nations lacks the authority of a global constitution, the financial resources of national governments, and democratic legitimacy (Dellmuth et al., 2022). The implementation of its policy pronouncements is at the discretion of national governments. Developed countries with little more than 1 per cent of the world's population have adopted long-term measures to reduce their contribution to climate change. However, the most populous countries—China, India, and the United States—have not committed their countries to fully meeting internationally defined targets for climate change.

The globalization of individual welfare continues. Developments in communication have diffused knowledge of what individuals can do to improve their welfare; economic growth has given institutions of the welfare mix more resources; and national governments are taking more responsibility for the welfare of their population. In the past three decades people in countries at every level of development have become healthier and more educated, and in many countries women have gained more opportunity to participate in employment. Even though most countries have not caught up with multiple welfare standards, a majority of the world's population has done so on important measures of health, education, and employment. The dynamics of progress in the past three decades indicates that the globalization of welfare will continue in future.

References

Aburto, J. M., Schöley, J., and Kashyap, R., 2022. 'Quantifying Impacts of the COVID-19 Pandemic through Life-Expectancy Losses', *International Journal of Epidemiology*, 51, 1, 63–74.

Addati, Laura, Cattaneo, Umberto, Esquivel, Valeria, and Valarino, Isabel, 2018. *Care Work and Care Jobs*. Geneva: International Labour Organization.

Augustovski, F., et al., 2018. 'Measuring the Benefits of Healthcare: DALYs and QALYs', *International Journal of Health Policy Management*, 7, 2, 120–36.

Dellmuth, Lisa, et al., 2022. 'The Elite–Citizen Gap in International Organization Legitimacy', *American Political Science Review*, 116, 1, 283–300.

Eurostat, 2022. *Healthy Life Years Statistics*. Brussels: European Commission, https://ec.europa.eu/eurostat/statistics-explained/index.php?title=Healthy_life_years_statistics.

Hellwig, Timothy, Kweon, Yesola, and Vowles, Jack, 2020. *Democracy under Siege? Parties, Voters and Elections after the Great Recession.* Oxford: Oxford University Press.

Kontis, Vasilis, et al., 2017. 'Future Life Expectancy in 35 Industrialised Countries'. *The Lancet,* 389 (1 April 2017), 1323–35.

Lynch, J., Bernhard, M., and O'Neill, D., 2022. 'Pandemic Politics', *Perspectives on Politics*, 20, 2, 389–94, doi:10.1017/S1537592722000676.

OECD, 2020a. Social Expenditures Makes Up 20 Percent of OECD GDP'. https://www.oecd.org/els/soc/OECD2020-Social-Expenditure-SOCX-Update.pdf.

OECD, 2020b. *Education at a Glance 2020.* Paris: OECD Indicators.

Our World in Data, 2023. 'Coronavirus Pandemic (Covid 19)'. https://ourworldindata.org/coronavirus (accessed 8 January 2023).

Shanmugaratnam, Tharman, 2022. 'Confronting a Perfect Storm', *Finance and Development*, 59, 2, 4–9.

Tsuji, I., 2020. 'Epidemiologic Research on Healthy Life Expectancy and Proposal for Its Extension', *Journal of the Japan Medical Association*, 148, 9 (2019), 1781–4; 3, 3 (2020), 149–53.

United Nations, 2017. *Abortion Laws and Policies: A Global Assessment.* New York: United Nations Department of Economic and Social Affairs, Population Division.

United Nations, 2020. *World Fertility and Family Planning.* New York: United Nations Department of Economic and Social Affairs, Population Division.

United Nations, 2022. *World Population Prospects 2022: Highlights.* New York: United Nations Department of Economic and Social Affairs, Population Division.

World Health Organization, 2021. 'The True Death Toll of Covid-19'. https://www.who.int/data/stories/the-true-death-toll-of-covid-19-estimating-global-excess-mortality (accessed 8 January 2023).

APPENDIX

The Global Welfare Database

We live in an era in which quantitative data is superabundant. The United Nations and the World Bank annually collect hundreds of social, political, and economic indicators from more than 200 national governments and territories. These efforts are complemented by intergovernmental institutions, such as the Organization for Economic Cooperation and Development, which collect additional measures monitoring changes in countries setting global standards. International non-governmental organizations such as Transparency International produce measures on topics such as corruption that governments prefer to ignore.

International organizations are not promoters of data but aggregators of data. National governments are the primary source of data about the welfare of their population. The World Bank's Statistical Capacity Index shows that the ability of governments varies substantially.* On a scale that runs from 0 to 100, the average developing country has a rating of 67. Among the countries in the Global Welfare Database the Capacity Index is as low as 34 in Iraq and Turkmenistan.

The Global Welfare Database consists of dozens of indicators that give quantitative weight to the model of welfare set out in Figure 1.1. It includes 127 countries that have 95 per cent of the world's population. It excludes countries with less than one million people, thereby avoiding giving equal weight to mini-countries and those with many millions of people. Eight countries were excluded because of a lack of key measures included in the Index of Development critical for testing hypotheses: Cuba, Eritrea, North Korea, Somalia, South Sudan, Syria, Venezuela, and Yemen. The database excludes twelve states that have not controlled the whole of their notional territory because of strife: Albania, Armenia, Belarus, Bosnia and Herzegovina, Cyprus, Georgia, Kosovo, Lebanon, Libya, Moldova, Serbia, and Ukraine. It also excludes nine countries with very large expatriate populations whose welfare was formed in different national contexts. These countries are led by Qatar, with an 87 per cent expatriate population, followed by the United Arab Emirates, Oman, Kuwait, Bahrain, Israel, Singapore, Hong Kong, and Saudi Arabia.

There are complete annual series from 1991 to 2019 for the two key measures of health and female employment. A number of highly developed countries no longer collect literacy data because it is virtually complete. Statistics on net secondary school enrolment of youths are unavailable for six and outdated for eight countries, and the mathematics examination of the Programme for International Student Assessment (PISA) is only available for sixty countries for a limited period of time. If data is missing for 1991, the baseline year for measuring progress, a later year is used if it is no later than 2000. If it is missing for the latest year, 2019, then a recent year from 2013 onwards is treated as the latest year. Since welfare indicators correlate by as much as 0.99 between successive years, these estimates have a high degree of validity.

Table A.1 gives for each of 127 countries the statistics for six key measures of welfare analysed in preceding countries, and for the Index of Development. The complete Global Welfare Database, plus additional continental and country trend data, are available online by clicking on the following link: www.oup.co.uk/companion/WelfareGoesGlobal

---

* https://datatopics.worldbank.org/statisticalcapacity/scidashboard.aspx.

Table A.1 Key measures of welfare by country and continent

	Health LifeExpFemale years	Inf. Mort. per '000	Education Literacy %	Secondary %	Female %	Employment Gender equality %	Index Develop 0–100
			Highly developed countries				
Australia	85.1	4	98.8	92	60.8	85	91
Austria	84.2	4	98.8	87	55.2	83	84
Belgium	84.0	3	98.8	95	49.0	83	94
Bulgaria	78.6	7	98.8	89	50.4	79	57
Canada	84.4	5	98.8	100	61.1	87	89
Croatia	81.6	5	98.8	92	45.4	78	56
Czech Republic	82.1	3	98.8	91	52.8	77	72
Denmark	83.4	4	98.8	91	57.9	87	99
Estonia	82.6	2	98.8	94	57.5	82	78
Finland	84.5	2	98.8	96	55.7	88	95
France	85.6	5	98.8	95	50.7	85	82
Germany	84.0	4	98.8	85	55.6	83	90
Greece	83.9	4	97.9	93	44.5	74	65
Hungary	79.7	4	99.1	89	48.5	73	57
Ireland	84.0	3	98.8	99	56.3	82	98
Italy	85.6	3	99.2	95	41.0	69	70
Japan	87.4	3	98.8	99	53.6	75	87
Korea, Rep. of	86.7	3	98.8	98	53.8	74	75
Latvia	79.7	4	99.9	94	55.8	82	65
Lithuania	80.6	4	98.8	98	57.3	85	71
Netherlands	83.6	4	98.8	93	59.0	85	98
New Zealand	84.4	5	98.8	97	64.9	87	93
Norway	84.7	2	98.8	96	60.6	90	100
Poland	81.7	4	98.8	94	48.6	74	64

Portugal	84.5	4	96.1	95	54.7	85	71
Romania	80.2	7	98.8	83	45.6	70	54
Russian Federation	78.8	6	99.7	91	54.6	78	36
Slovak Republic	81.0	6	98.8	85	52.3	78	59
Slovenia	84.2	2	99.7	96	53.3	85	68
Spain	86.2	3	98.4	97	52.2	82	78
Sweden	84.7	3	98.8	99	61.2	90	97
Switzerland	85.6	4	98.8	85	62.9	86	98
United Kingdom	83.5	4	98.8	97	58.1	85	88
United States	81.7	7	98.8	92	56.8	83	89
Mean	(83.3)	(4)	(98.8)	(93)	(54.3)	(81)	(78)
Latin America							
Argentina	80.7	9	99.0	91	51.3	71	63
Bolivia	70.5	26	92.5	76	63.7	79	40
Brazil	78.5	14	93.2	82	55.1	74	52
Chile	82.7	7	96.4	89	51.8	71	75
Colombia	79.7	14	95.1	77	56.2	70	49
Costa Rica	82.0	9	97.9	82	51.9	67	65
Dominican Republic	77.0	28	93.8	70	54.3	68	47
Ecuador	80.0	14	92.8	85	55.2	68	41
El Salvador	76.8	13	89.0	60	45.4	60	42
Guatemala	75.8	25	80.8	44	40.5	47	28
Haiti	67.3	63	61.7	–	63.7	87	21
Honduras	75.4	17	87.2	44	52.3	61	27
Jamaica	73.9	14	88.1	73	60.3	82	44

Continued

Table A.1 Continued

	Health		Education		Employment		Index
	LifeExpFemale years	Inf. Mort. per '000	Literacy %	Secondary %	Female %	Gender equality %	Develop 0–100
Mexico	77.6	14	95.4	81	45.6	58	46
Nicaragua	77.0	17	82.6	48	49.7	59	22
Panama	81.0	15	95.4	64	54.9	69	56
Paraguay	76.4	19	94.0	66	60.0	71	38
Peru	78.5	13	94.4	86	70.6	83	48
Trinidad & Tobago	77.7	18	–	–	50.1	71	50
Uruguay	81.3	7	98.7	88	55.5	76	79
Mean	(77.5)	(18)	(90.9)	(73)	(54.4)	(70)	(47)

Middle East & North Africa

Algeria	77.8	23	81.4	–	17.0	25	36
Azerbaijan	75.8	20	99.8	89	63.3	90	23
Egypt, Arab Rep. of	73.7	20	71.2	82	18.5	26	23
Iran, Islamic Rep. of	79.1	14	85.5	81	17.6	24	29
Iraq	73.4	26	85.6	45	11.5	16	27
Jordan	78.5	16	98.2	62	14.6	23	47
Kazakhstan	75.3	11	99.8	100	62.8	83	34
Kyrgyz Republic	75.4	18	99.6	83	44.1	59	20
Morocco	76.4	21	73.8	63	21.6	31	34
Sudan	68.4	58	60.7	31	29.4	43	5
Tajikistan	73.0	34	99.8	83	29.2	58	7
Tunisia	79.4	17	79.0	–	24.9	36	46
Turkey	81.0	10	96.2	87	34.3	47	45
Turkmenistan	72.5	42	99.7	–	44.4	62	15
Uzbekistan	73.9	17	100.0	91	48.8	65	16
Mean	(75.6)	(23)	(88.7)	(75)	(32.1)	(46)	(27)

Africa

Angola	64.9	75	66.0	11	76.1	97	27
Benin	61.9	90	42.4	47	68.8	94	38
Botswana	67.9	42	86.8	–	65.3	86	58
Burkina Faso	61.8	88	39.3	29	58.5	78	27
Burundi	64.3	57	68.4	28	80.5	103	0
Cameroon	63.0	75	77.1	46	71.3	88	19
Central African Rep.	57.1	110	37.4	13	64.5	81	10
Chad	54.9	114	22.3	19	64.0	83	5
Congo, Dem. Rep.	62.2	85	77.0	–	61.0	92	10
Congo, Rep. of	64.2	48	80.3	–	67.6	95	20
Côte d'Ivoire	60.6	79	43.9	38	44.6	71	30
Equatorial Guinea	63.5	82	–	–	54.8	82	23
Eswatini	64.4	49	88.4	42	48.6	86	14
Ethiopia	68.8	51	51.8	31	73.3	86	12
Gabon	68.9	43	84.7	–	43.3	70	38
Gambia	65.2	52	50.8	–	51.1	75	32
Ghana	66.8	46	79.0	55	63.9	89	43
Guinea	60.8	99	39.6	32	62.7	105	20
Guinea-Bissau	62.9	79	45.6	9	65.9	84	17
Kenya	65.3	43	81.5	47	72.0	94	19
Lesotho	57.1	86	76.6	41	60.4	80	27
Liberia	62.3	85	48.3	16	72.0	90	29
Madagascar	68.2	51	76.7	29	83.2	94	21
Malawi	68.0	42	62.1	34	72.5	90	19
Mali	60.8	94	35.5	29	57.8	71	22

Continued

Table A.1 Continued

	Health		Education			Employment	Index
	LifeExpFemale years	Inf. Mort. per '000	Literacy %	Secondary %	Female %	Gender equality %	Develop 0–100
Mauritania	67.7	73	53.5	28	28.1	45	23
Mauritius	78.2	16	91.3	85	45.0	63	52
Mozambique	63.9	74	60.7	19	77.4	98	20
Namibia	66.6	42	91.5	52	55.8	88	46
Niger	63.9	80	35.0	20	60.8	73	16
Nigeria	53.2	117	62.0	–	48.5	77	26
Rwanda	68.5	34	73.2	32	83.9	101	19
Senegal	71.0	45	51.9	38	35.1	61	38
Sierra Leone	61.6	109	43.2	38	57.5	99	29
South Africa	69.1	35	87.0	72	49.6	79	50
Tanzania	69.1	50	77.9	25	79.7	91	23
Togo	61.4	67	63.7	41	56.3	92	21
Uganda	65.0	46	76.5	22	66.9	91	14
Zambia	65.4	62	86.7	43	70.4	89	28
Zimbabwe	63.7	55	88.7	49	78.1	88	13
Mean	(64.3)	(67)	(64.2)	(35)	(62.4)	(85)	(25)

Asian developing countries

Afghanistan	66.7	60	35.5	48	21.8	29	7
Bangladesh	75.1	31	73.9	64	36.4	45	19
Cambodia	72.9	27	80.5	38	76.9	88	8
Indonesia	72.6	24	95.7	78	53.8	65	40
Laos PDR	70.2	46	84.7	60	76.5	96	14
Malaysia	78.3	9	94.9	74	51.3	66	56
Mongolia	76.6	16	98.4	–	55.3	78	48

Myanmar	69.8	45	75.6	60	46.2	61	16
Nepal	71.4	31	67.9	58	81.5	97	20
Pakistan	69.1	67	57.0	35	21.7	26	21
Papua New Guinea	68.7	45	–	32	46.4	98	18
Philippines	73.7	27	98.2	66	47.0	64	33
Sri Lanka	79.7	7	91.7	89	33.5	46	26
Thailand	83.4	9	93.8	77	58.8	78	31
East Timor	69.9	44	68.1	61	61.9	85	29
Vietnam	78.9	20	–	–	72.7	89	20
Mean	(73.6)	(32)	(79.7)	(60)	(52.6)	(69)	(25)
China	80.8	8	96.8	67	60.6	80	30
India	72.4	34	74.4	62	20.8	27	35
Global mean	(74.2)	(32)	(83.0)	(66)	(53.8)	(75)	(43)

Notes: Life expectancy: Female life expectancy at birth. *Source:* United Nations, Department of Economic and Social Affairs, Population Division, 2022. Data Portal, custom data acquired via website. United Nations: New York. Available from https://population.un.org/DataPortal/ (accessed 2 September 2022).

Infant mortality: Under-5 mortality rate per 1,000 live births. *Source:* World Bank, 2021. Mortality rate, under-5 (per 1,000 live births), https://data.worldbank.org/indicator/SH.DYN.MORT (accessed 1 April 2021).

Literacy: Literacy rate of people aged 15 and above. *Source:* World Bank, 2021. Literacy rate, adult total (% of people ages 15 and above), https://data.worldbank.org/indicator/SE.ADT.LITR.ZS (accessed 26 November 2021). In highly developed countries with missing data the entry is mean literacy of highly developed countries supplying data.

Secondary: Net secondary school enrolment. *Source:* World Bank, 2021. School enrolment, secondary (% net) (accessed 1 April 2021), https://data.worldbank.org/indicator/SE.SEC.NENR.

Female: Female labour force participation rate. *Source:* World Bank, 2021. Labour force participation rate, female (% of female population aged 15+) (modelled ILO estimate) (accessed 1 April 2021), https://data.worldbank.org/indicator/SL.TLF.CACT.FE.ZS.

Gender equality: Ratio of female to male labour force participation rate. *Source:* World Bank, 2021. Ratio of female to male labour force participation rate (%) (modelled ILO estimate) (accessed 1 April 2021), https://data.worldbank.org/indicator/SL.TLF.CACT.FM.ZS.

Development Index: Global Welfare Database; see Chapter 4.

Index

For the benefit of digital users, indexed terms that span two pages (e.g., 52–53) may, on occasion, appear on only one of those pages.

Africa, Sub-Saharan, 27–29, 184, 188
Agricultural employment, 132–133, 135
Asian developing countries, 27–29
Asian learning, mathematics, 119–120
Automobiles, cause of death, 100–103
Avoidable deaths, 97–103

Beveridge, Lord, 34
Birth rates, 192
Bismarck, Otto von, 42

Catching up, 22–25, 150–157, 183–185
Camdessus, Michel, 51
Catholic Church, 43
China, 30, 36–37, 117–40, 131–132, 159–163, 169–173, 183–184, 188
Climate change, 195–196
Collective action problems, 194–196
Communist system, welfare, 74, 81, 92–97, 102–103, 111–112, 115, 132–133, 158
Comparison, 13, 21, 23
Corruption, 27, 74
Cost-benefit analysis, 54
Covid, 18–19, 90–91, 181–182, 186–187, 194
Development, 69–79, 151–153, 172–173
  Influence of Index of Development, 79–83, 92–94, 96–97, 99–100, 102–103, 111–112, 114–115, 129–130, 140, 158, 161

Economy, household, 33, 62–64
Economy, official, 51–64
Economy, shadow, 60–62
Economy, unofficial, 59–64
Education, 39, 107–125
  Primary education, 109, 122
  Secondary education, 113–116, 171, 187, 193

  Tertiary education, 115–116
Employment, female, 17, 127–143, 171, 187, 193
English as a Foreign Language (EFEL), 120–122

Freedom, 43, 70

Germany, 93
Gender differences in welfare, 97–100, 111, 112, 128–141, 171, 187, 193
Generational turnover, 123–125, 181
Gini index, 82
Global Welfare Database, 19–22
Globalisation of welfare, 69, 73, 91, 103–106, 113–116, 122–125, 141–143, 148, 185–187, 189–191
Gross domestic product (GDP), 28, 49, 65

Haiti, 168
Happiness, 19
Health, 36 (*see also* life expectancy, infant mortality, smoking, road safety)
Highly developed countries, 14, 27, 29–30, 184, 188
Hindu society, 161–162
Household welfare, 35, 138–141

Income, 18–19, 39, 44–45
India, 30, 44, C7 P18, 159–163, 169–173, 175–176, 183–184
Infant mortality, 89–94, 170, 185–186
International Labour Organisation, 138–139
ISCED, 108

Latin America, 29
Learning, 117–122

Life expectancy, 88–94, 149, 170–171, 182, 186, 194
Life styles, 97– 102–103
Literacy, 65, 109–112, 171, 181
Lucas, Robert, 49

Market for welfare, 33–34, 36
Marshall, Alfred, 51–52
Middle East and North Africa (MENA) region, 29
Models of welfare, 15–18, 35–37, 82–83
Muslim societies, 81, 92–94, 96–97, 100, 102–103, 112, 119, 133–135, 158, 161–162, 187

Nigeria, 51, 153, 176–177
Nkrumah, Kwame, 81–82

Outlier countries, 159, 162–163

Pakistan, 168, 189
PISA (Programme for International Student Assessment), 117–120
Population, 30, 123–125, 165–178, 187–189
Poverty, 59
Progress, 19–22, 88, 94–96, 101–102, 107–111, 124, 148–150, 153–155, 185–187
Public expenditure, 34, 36–37, 40, 53, 81, 96–97, 102–103, 112, 158
Purchasing Power Parity (PPP), 58–59

Quality of life, 191–192

Reagan, Ronald, 15
Resources, 44–46, 71–76, 147
Road safety, 101

Sen, Amartya, 15
Smoking, 97–100
Social indicators, 26, 49–51, 64–67
Social technology, 149, 151, 154–155
Soviet Union, 42
Statistical capacity, 26, 57–58

Technocrats, 43, 151
Thatcher, Margaret, 15
Time horizons, 20–22, 181
Time use, 62–64, 138–141
Trade unions, 39

United Kingdom, 13, 121, 127, 160–161
United Nations, 196
United States, 13, 37–38, 64–65, 116, 127, 160–161, 167, 191
Unpaid work, 62–64, 138–141
Urban population, 73–74

Welfare, definition, 18, 22–23, 191–194
Welfare economics, 53–54
Welfare mix, 33–46, 87
Welfare standards defined, 21–22, 183
Welfare state, 35–42
Welfare targets, 24–25
Wicked problems, 195
Work, 17, 130–132